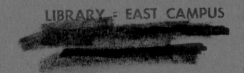

Money of the World

Money of the World
by Richard G. Doty

A Ridge Press Book / Grosset & Dunlap / New York
A Filmways Company

**The author wishes to thank the
staff of the American Numismatic Society
for their generous cooperation and
assistance in making this book possible.**

Editor-in-chief: Jerry Mason
Editor: Adolph Suehsdorf
Art Director: Albert Squillace
Associate Editor: Ronne Peltzman
Associate Editor: Joan Fisher
Art Associate: Liney Li
Art Production: Doris Mullane
Picture Editor: Marion Geisinger

Photo Credits
Jacket and chapter openers: Arie de Zanger
All other photography: Joseph D. Garcia

All coins and bills courtesy the American
Numismatic Society except the following:
pages 155 (bill), 164, 181 (4-dollar bill),
courtesy the Eric P. Newman Numismatic
Education Society.

Acknowledgments
p. 10-11: props, Greek Island Ltd.
p. 50-51: jade, Collector's Cabinet;
jade perfume bottle, Funchies, Bunkers,
Gaks and Gleeks.
p. 70-71: stereoscopic slides,
collection of Marion Geisinger.
p. 102-103: mosaic by Cosante Crovatto.

Library of Congress Catalog Card Number: 78-58609
ISBN: 0-448-16450-7
Printed and bound in The Netherlands

For my parents and M.D'A.

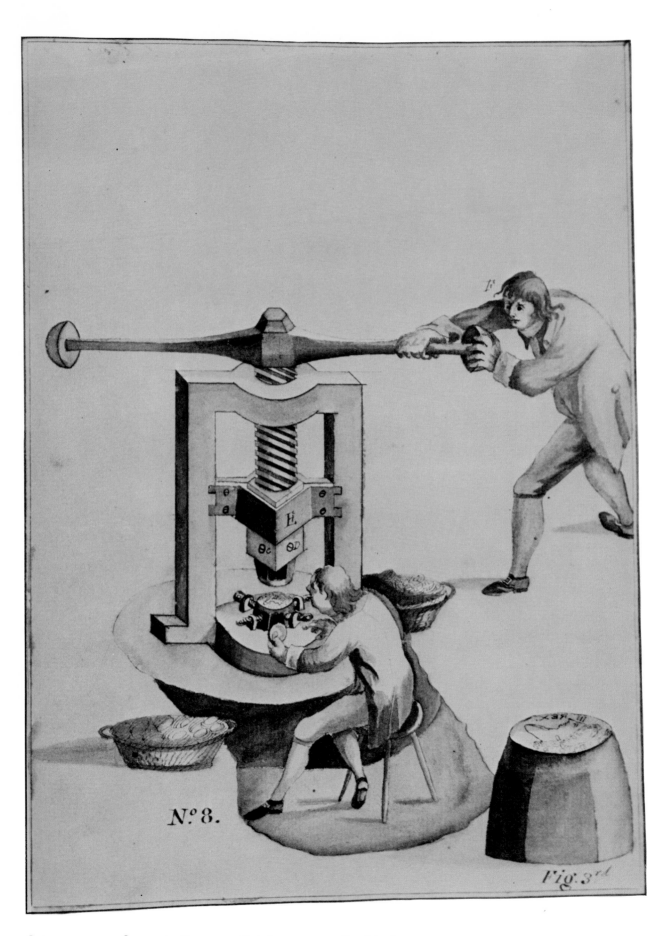

A screw press from *An Essay on Coining,* **a one-of-a-kind hand-drawn book by Samuel Thompson, 1783.**

Contents

10 **The Pioneers - Lydia and the Greeks**

30 **The Great Eastern Empires**

50 **The Oriental Coinage Experiment**

70 **Rome**

102 **Coinage during the Age of Faith**

130 **The Age of Awakening in Europe**

154 **The Expansion of European Coinage**

174 **The Age of Revolution**

202 **Modern Money and the Modern State**

230 **Epilogue: Money's Future**

235 **Bibliography**

236 **Index**

Introduction

Coins have been with us for several thousand years, and they will almost certainly be around for the foreseeable future. Throughout the many centuries of their existence, coins have been intimately connected to the larger story of human history, joined so closely, in fact, that much of the story of man's development—the rise and fall of great empires, the flowerings and eclipses of artistic inspiration—may be traced and chronicled through coins. For no other product of the human mind, over so many centuries, can this claim be made.

This book is the story of the relationship between human beings and their coinage. Like most relationships, it has had its ups and downs, periods of greater and lesser intensity, and, like any other relationship, no one can exactly foretell the future of this one.

Before detailing this history of a relationship, several basic questions must be answered. What exactly is a coin? Is the word "coin" synonymous with "money?" If it is not, where does the difference lie? Finally, as other types of money have come and gone, why have coins remained—or, to continue our analogy, why has this particular relationship endured, while others have disappeared?

A coin is a small, ordinarily round object used in exchange. It tends to be relatively thin in proportion to its diameter. It contains inscriptions as to who made it, what its exchange value is, and, frequently, when it was manufactured, or struck. It usually includes a pictographic representation of some sort as well (a ruler's portrait, the national arms—the list is endless).

It may be made from a variety of metals. In ancient and early modern times, gold, silver, and copper or bronze predomi-nated; nowadays, a series of base-metal alloys serves for most coins.

An additional point must be made. Coins are *official* products of political entities. This has been true since the beginning, and it is one of the characteristics distinguishing coins from other forms of money. A moment's reflection will give us the reason for the long-term official nature of coinage: this medium of exchange was originally invented as a means of facilitating economic transactions, and one of the basic problems in the precoin era was a lack of universal agreement over the value of a particular object, including a piece of precious metal. Was it real, or merely gold-plated? How pure was it? In the case of gold and silver, this uncertainty over fineness and value meant that the metal had to be weighed every time a transaction took place. Eventually, some forgotten genius hit on the idea of having a universally recognized, disinterested authority do the weighing in advance, and then marking each piece to show that it had done so. This would save merchants a good deal of trouble and acrimony in their dealings.

So it was done, and coinage emerged. Since that time it has been governments who have been responsible for coinage. In modern times, they have even indicated the exact value of the coin on the coin itself. The people have the final say in the matter, however: if they believe that a government's money is worth less than it should be, they will only accept it at a discount. This is known as inflation, and the problem has been with us for almost as long as coinage itself. Putting it another way, money has worth only as long as the people who must use it believe it has worth.

This brings us to the second point. While all coins are money, not all money is composed of coinage. At present, we are using coinage and paper currency, items that everyone would consider money. But we are also using checks, credit cards, and several less important mediums of exchange. These, too, are money.

Early peoples used other things for money. The ancient Aztecs employed thin copper pieces shaped like agricultural utensils, while their northern neighbors used wampum, strung beads made from shells. In Mongolia, pressed bricks of tea served as money, as did cowrie shells in Africa and China. And cattle, textiles, even human beings have been employed as money from time to time.

For an item to find use as a medium of exchange, or as money, it is only necessary that it be widely regarded as having value to the prospective recipient ("If I accept this item in trade, can I be certain of getting as much as I paid for it when I trade it to someone else?"). Coins fit neatly into this trading concept, as we have seen, due to their widely recognized value. They have had other advantages, however, which have led to their becoming the most common form of money in modern times.

A major factor in coinage's replacement of other forms of money was the relatively high value for its small size and weight. It was easy to carry from place to place, to collect, and to safeguard. This was not the case with many other forms of money, cattle being the most obvious example. Cattle tended to wander off, they had to be fed and maintained, and their value decreased as they grew older. Coins were there whenever you wanted them, and if they were made of good gold or silver, a merchant knew they could instantly be converted into other commodities. Parenthetically, this process of looking for an easy-to-use form of money didn't stop with coins. Paper money was more convenient than coinage, and the credit card has gained popularity because it pre-

sents even fewer problems than does paper.

At any rate, coins were worth more and were easier to use than most forms of money available to ancient peoples. Coinage therefore began to drive more traditional monetary items out of circulation. This did not happen everywhere all at once, of course. As we shall see, the universal use of coinage did not become fixed until modern times. But coinage spread rapidly enough, and for ancient Greeks and Romans, "coins" and "money" meant essentially the same thing. And they have ever since.

It is impossible to overestimate the significance of coinage on human history. Coins have facilitated the transaction of business for over two millennia—indeed, modern economic systems, capitalism, socialism, communism, would be impossible without this form of money. Coinage has provided the wherewithal to wage wars, and, if wisely employed, the means of repairing war's damage. It has been instrumental in creating a leisure class, and, as a byproduct of that, coinage has been the patron of the arts, instrumental in the creation of beautiful things, in the liberation of the human mind.

For the historian, coins have another role to play. They can tell us who we were, what we did, what we thought, what we held beautiful over the centuries. Ancient coinage has long had this function for the archeologist and the student of the classical past, but it is now becoming evident that more recent coinage—and paper money—can serve the same purposes. A Roman coin of the fourth century A.D. can bespeak the near-deification of an emperor; a 1923 German bank note for ten million marks can bear eloquent witness to the collapse of an entire economy, spreading the germs of cynicism and despair that would produce an Adolf Hitler. Old or new, beautiful or ugly, each coin, each piece of paper money, has a tale to tell.

Preceding pages. Athens, tetradrachm, 480–470 B.C.
Below. Clockwise from top: Lydia, electrum one-
third stater, 610–561 B.C.; Lydia, gold stater, 561–
546 B.C.; Aegina, silver stater, 6th century B.C.;
Lydia, gold stater, 561–546 B.C.

The Pioneers-Lydia and the Greeks

As we have noted, coinage is a reflection of human history. This fact is evident in the time and place of its invention. It must be emphasized that there is nothing miraculous about the birth of coinage. It did not spring forth from a vacuum. Rather, it was the result of a need for a convenient medium of exchange. And this in turn was an indication that humankind had evolved and advanced beyond the barbaric state.

By the first millennium B.C. more and more peoples had risen above the level of subsistence farming, of total economic autonomy. More and more of them were performing specialized tasks and were dependent on the labors of others for most of their needs. The population increased in cities and towns, and more people directly or indirectly made their livings through trade. It was only at this point that a need for a more convenient medium of exchange was created, and it was only at this point that coinage emerged.

This is not to say that coinage is an inevitable phase in human development, for it is not. By the early sixteenth century, Tenochtitlán, capital of the Aztec empire in Mexico, was larger than most cities in Europe, but it never produced a coinage. However, it is true that, in a general way, mankind was developing urban trading cultures some centuries before Christ, and that coinage shortly appeared in two of these, the Lydian and the Chinese. Significantly, neither seems to have borrowed from the other, which again points out the logical nature of the invention of coinage.

Which came first? Who were the true pioneers? The Chinese seem to have originated a type of coinage by around 1000 B.C., which would put their discovery about four centuries earlier than that of the Lydians. But we would not recognize their products as coins. While it is true that they often carried marks of value and were manufactured at government behest, they were cast in molds, ordinarily in the form of cowrie shells, knives, and agricultural implements, items of earlier importance in barter.

On the other hand, the earliest Lydian coins were recognizable as *coins*—they were round, they carried designs, and they were struck. So we might say that while the Chinese pioneered in the *intent* of coinage, the western peoples pioneered in its *form*, while devising its intent independently. Add to this the fact that all later European (and American) coinage directly descends from the Lydian experiment, and you have the reasons why most scholars assign the invention of coinage to this people.

Lydia was a small but wealthy state in Asia Minor. One of its bases for prosperity was the copious quantity of electrum, a natural alloy of gold and silver, found in the sands along the shores of the Pactolus River. The Lydians had other things to trade as well, and they were soon doing a thriving business up and down the Mediterranean. For such a people, the attractions of coinage are obvious, and eventually, perhaps between 620 and 600 B.C., someone had the idea of making lumps of electrum of the same size and purity, then stamping them with a seal to show that the government had given them its official blessing as a trade medium. And the first true coins emerged.

The idea was almost immediately adopted by adjacent Greek colonies in Ionia (today western Turkey). They, too, were traders, and the new concept would make life easier in the marketplace.

These first coins were primitive affairs. Some Ionian issues merely had parallel striations on one side, and an indented punch mark on the other. Other issues had depictions of animals. At this early point, their minters were not worried about creating beautiful designs but rather about coming up with something that would facilitate trade. And crude or not, the first coins did just that.

But this early coinage soon ran into difficulties. Electrum can vary tremendously in the relative proportions of gold to silver, and people were soon complaining that the coins contained too much silver, too little gold. In short, they began losing faith in the new invention. If the Lydian state first devised coinage, it was also responsible for a solution to this early threat to the new invention. Lydia's last king, Croesus (561–546 B.C.), came up with a coinage consisting of gold and silver *staters*, twenty of the silver pieces equaling one of the gold. As long as gold and silver contents remained stable, the coins would circulate at this fixed ratio. This was the world's first bimetallic currency, and this concept of coinage in more than one metal, each with a fixed value in relationship to the other, would be the rule until modern times. Croesus' gold and silver staters enjoyed wide circulation. Animal types were chosen for the designs, the foreparts of a lion and a bull facing each other. Lydia fell to the Persian Empire in 545 B.C., but its concept of coinage—and a bimetallic one at that—had already spread to other parts of the ancient world.

So the Lydian invention endured, and the Lydian method of making coins (explained below) was also retained, for it was simple and could easily be modified and improved as occasion demanded. In fact, the basic methods of coining devised by this ancient people would be employed for slightly more than two thousand years. It was not until the sixteenth century A.D. that a new way of minting money would be found, a fact that emphasizes the lack of many technological advances during those twenty centuries of man's experience.

Lydian coins (and those of the Greeks, Romans, and medieval peoples) were hammered, or struck by hand. Their manufacture occupied three distinct stages.

First of all, a die was prepared. The design or pattern that was to adorn the coins was cut into a hard piece of metal, ordinarily bronze or iron. In the case of the Lydians and ancient Greeks, the resulting die was five to eight inches (13–20 cm) long. It looked something like a chisel, with the design engraved on the wide end. The other end might actually come to a point, and it would be fixed in an anvil when the striking process took place.

After the die was prepared, a coin blank, or planchet, had to be manufactured. In the ancient world, this often involved a casting process. The Lydians and early Greeks cast their planchets in a globular form. This explains the relative thickness and rounded edges of these early coinages. After the lumps were weighed for content and uniformity, they were probably heated. This would make them softer, an essential condition for the last step, the striking of the coins.

This final step was the simplest to execute. The coin die was firmly fixed in an anvil, and the softened planchet was placed on top of it. A punch was positioned on the top side of the coin blank, and this punch was struck once or repeatedly with a sledge hammer, forcing the metal into the die beneath. This punch explains the crude marks on the "reverses" of very ancient coins. Eventually, a second coinage design was engraved on the upper punch, where it came into contact with the coin blank. It would now be possible to talk of coins with obverse and reverse types, and, with this last development, the technology of coinage had essentially reached the form it would retain until modern times. Using these primitive methods, ancient peoples, particularly the Greeks, would strike some of the most beautiful coins ever designed, which revealed their cultural, artistic, and political status at the time.

Below. Top l to r: Cyzicus, electrum stater, early 5th century B.C.; Thebes, silver stater, late 6th to early 5th century B.C.; bottom: Methmna, didrachm, c. 500–480 B.C.

Opposite. Top to bottom, l to r: Eretria,
didrachm, 5th century B.C.; Lycia, silver stater, c. 480–
460 B.C.; Syracuse, tetradrachm, c. 400 B.C.; Athens,
tetradrachms (both), 135–134 B.C.
Above. Clockwise from top l: Athens, tetradrachm,
480–470 B.C.; Syracuse, decadrachm, c. 400 B.C.;
Emisa, large bronzes (both), 211–217 A.D.

Opposite. Clockwise from top: Athens, decadrachm, 467 B.C.; silver-plated tetradrachm, 390s B.C.; gold stater, 407–406 B.C.; emergency tetradrachm, 483–480 B.C.

Greek coinage faithfully reflects the rise, flowering, and decay of Greek civilization as a whole. For example, the high point of Greek numismatic artistry occurred during the fifth century B.C., and this coincides fairly well with the period of the greatest spread of classical Hellenic political influence, military prowess (the Greek defeat of the Persian Empire early in the century), prosperity, and developments in other areas of the arts and literature. This link in cultural achievements was by no means accidental, and we shall see it repeated time and again throughout history. The care that fifth-century Greeks devoted to their coins shows their great pride in being Greek, a fruitful state of mind for achievements in other areas.

While generalizations on the rise and decline of Greek coinage are difficult (if only because what appears beautiful to one scholar may seem mediocre to another), it is possible to establish several categories into which most Greek coins will fit. These categories largely coincide with more-or-less established periods in Greek history, when specific political, artistic, and economic developments were taking place.

We may call the time span from about 600 to 480 B.C. the archaic period of Greek coinage. While the spread of coinage was rapid, a reflection of Greek economic expansion and colonization of the Mediterranean Basin, the coins themselves remained fairly crude. Many tended to be small and bean-shaped, for the coining process had yet to be perfected. Animal types or inanimate objects dominated design. The human head was rarely portrayed, but in the few instances when it was, it was modeled in a curious fashion—in profile, but with the eye drawn as if seen from the front.

Improvements in coining and artistic technique distinguish the later years of this archaic period. The bean-shaped lumps became rounder with time. Designs, while still crude by later standards, became somewhat more elaborate, somewhat more refined in their execution. Toward the end of this period, the upper punch began seeing service as a design element: not only was it instrumental in the striking of a coin, but it now became obvious that it could be used to put a distinctive design on the other side of a coin, as already discussed. First attempts on this new technique were modest, as the squarish indentation made by the punch was often merely made more regular or subdivided. However, these early attempts pointed the way to future development.

The fifth century B.C. was the great age of Greek coinage—as indeed it was in virtually every other area of Greek development, both political and esthetic. In those days, there was no one Greece, but rather several hundred thousand *Greeks*, dwelling in scattered political communities from one end of the Mediterranean to the other. Each political entity (or *polis*, pl. *polei*) was independent of all the others, and as a reflection of its sovereignty, each tended to strike its own coins. It has been estimated that over 1,400 polei or other bodies issued coins at one time or another, and most of them did so during the fifth century B.C. This is one reason for the rapid improvement of coinage technique and artistry during the period: the independent city-states could copy from and improve upon each other's ideas.

Coinage progressed rapidly. In 500 B.C., style and execution were still crude by most modern standards. By 400 B.C. some of the most beautiful coins in history had been produced. Having completely mastered their craft, Greek engravers could do anything with it they wished. In the exuberance of their mastery, some now began signing their creations. Significantly, they were the only engravers to do so until the Renaissance. But

L to r: Syracuse, decadrachm,
405–400 B.C.; Massalia, drachm,
late 4th century B.C.;
Pantikapaion, gold stater,
c. 350 B.C.; Corinth, silver
staters, mid 5th century B.C.

then, the ancient Greeks were probably more individualistic than any other people before modern times.

By now the upper punch was fully exploited as a part of coinage technique. The square indentation made by the reverse punch was elaborated, made to contain a design, an inscription, or both, and enlarged, eventually occupying the whole of the coin's surface. The Athenians seem to have been among the first to carry the use of the reverse punch to this logical conclusion, with one of the best-known ancient coins, the Athenian *tetradrachm*. This large silver coin portrayed an owl, the sacred bird of the city's patroness, Athena. The earliest examples date from around 510 B.C. Other parts of the Greek world also adopted the new technique, and artistic expression was given an essential impetus. Very simply, there was now more space for design available to the engraver. He was working with two dies, not one.

As technique improved, so did art. The human face and form were now increasingly portrayed with great accuracy and often with incredible beauty. Portraits of living people were not part of the artistic repertoire at this time, but fifth-century Greeks made up for it by idealized, almost ethereal renditions of gods and goddesses, demigods, and heroes. This portraiture, done both in the traditional profile and toward the end of the century with the head turned almost full-faced, was probably the best ever achieved. The end of the period saw what some regard as the crowning glories of Greek, and world wide, numismatics—large *decadrachms* (silver pieces of ten *drachms*), from Syracuse, which we will soon discuss.

The third period of Greek coinage represents an era of decline, at first barely perceptible, later much more obvious. Issues of the fourth century B.C. are perhaps not quite as artistic as most of their fifth-century

predecessors, and coins of the third century represent a visible decline from those of the fourth. And so on—the decline was progressive. Human beings—kings and queens, are frequently portrayed on third-century issues, largely replacing the representations of divinities on the obverse. Reverse types gradually become somewhat standardized, and the coinage as a whole becomes less interesting.

This decline in Greek numismatic art is a reflection of parallel developments elsewhere, as in the political field, where the disastrous Peloponnesian War weakened the Greeks, making them easily conquerable prey for the expansionist kingdom of Macedon, which dominated much of the Greek mainland after 338 B.C. The numismatic decline was reflected in other areas of the arts, too: in drama, sculpture, and architecture.

By 146 B.C., Greece proper had lost all vestiges of independence. Now, too, the artistic life had gone out of Greek coinage.

Greek city-states would continue to coin money for several centuries more (a privilege extended by Rome, which had become the dominant power in the Mediterranean), but these last issues are scarcely recognizable as Greek coins. Crudely rendered, usually with a portrait of the current Roman emperor, these late Greek coins mark the end point in the long decline from the height of glory of the fifth century.

One of the prime attractions of Greek coinage is that it tells us a great deal about Greek life and thought. Even were it not for the rich legacy of Greek art, architecture, literature, and historical writings left to us by this ancient people, we would still know a good deal about them from their coinage—more specifically, from what they chose to put on that coinage.

We would know something of their political history, with its attendant triumphs and defeats, of how Greeks saw the individual in relation to the state. The link between politics and coins may be illustrated in several ways. For example, the political fortunes of Athens brought about several distinct changes in the basic Athenian coin, the tetradrachm. As we have seen, the Athena-owl type dates from shortly before 500 B.C., and, while still somewhat archaic in appearance, the early examples of this coinage were at least well struck and reasonably round. There is a second series of Athenian tetradrachms, much cruder in appearance than the first. They are badly struck, with parts of the design frequently absent, and the planchets are irregularly shaped. It was once argued that these coins must be older than the round, carefully stuck ones, simply because they were so crude. We now know differently. Rather than being of earlier manufacture, the crude issue of Athenian tetradrachms is actually later than some of the other emissions. Its almost barbaric appearance is a direct reflection of the political realities of early fifth-century Greece.

From 492 to 479 B.C., an intermittent conflict took place between the Greek city-states (led by the Athenians) and the gigantic Persian Empire. The Greeks won, but not before the hard-fought battles of Marathon (490), Salamis (480), and Plataea (479) had taken place. There were times when the Athenians seemed to be fighting virtually alone against the vastly superior Persian forces. Athens needed a large amount of money to meet her war expenses, and she needed it quickly. Here is the explanation for the crude Athenian tetradrachms: scholars now believe that they were struck 483–480 B.C. to help build the fleet which would defeat the Persians at Salamis.

Confronted with an exigent need for large amounts of silver tetradrachms, the mint in Athens seems to have relaxed its engraving and coining standards for the dura-tion of the emergency. A large number of only semiskilled workmen were taken on, and the Athenian mint struck many of these crude but serviceable coins to pay war expenses. After the war was won and the Persians departed, stricter mintage standards were reimposed, and the coinage returned to normal.

Political events found a different expression on Athens' coinage after the conclusion of the Persian War. To commemorate her victories over Persia, Athens struck a series of very large silver decadrachms. In basic design elements, these coins resembled the ordinary Athenian tetradrachm. The obverse bore a portrait of Athena, the reverse, her sacred owl. But the reverse of the decadrachm was radically different in the manner of the owl's portrayal. It now faced the viewer directly, with wings outstretched. Above the owl to the left, the Athenians added a sprig of olive leaves, symbol of a victorious peace. This beautiful decadrachm is one of the first commemorative coins, celebrating an important victory for Greek civilization and for the Western culture which arose from it.

Athenian coinage also reflected the stresses of political and military defeat. From 431 to 404 B.C., Athens was embroiled in the Peloponnesian War, which resulted in her defeat and precipitous decline from the position of dominance she had once enjoyed. Athens had not struck gold before this time—the tetradrachm and its subdivisions, made from the abundant, Athenian-controlled silver deposits at Laurium, had served her needs well enough. But the seemingly endless war imposed demands on the Athenian fiscal machine that could not be met using traditional means. This was particularly true after the mines of Laurium fell into enemy hands, cutting Athens off from her source of silver.

Athens attempted to solve this problem by melting down the golden statues of Nike, goddess of victory, which had been dedicated to her on the Acropolis. With this gold, she struck a series of emergency coinage in 407—406 B.C. At the same time, she attempted to spread her slender silver reserves as far as possible by striking tetradrachms from bronze and then silver-plating them, in in the hopes that the populace would accept them at par with earlier issues of good silver.

These currency expedients did not alter the course of war, and Athens was conquered in 404 B.C. It would take eleven years for the Athenian economy to recover to the degree that a resumption of ordinary silver coinage could take place.

Historical events find expression on the coins of many other Greek states. In Sicily, the wealthy Greek city of Syracuse struck a magnificent series of large silver decadrachms that featured a figure of Nike in a *quadriga* (a chariot drawn by four horses) on the obverse and the head of the nymph Arethusa on the reverse. Below the obverse figure we see armor, part of the spoils of war. The beginning of this coinage is thought by some scholars to commemorate the defeat of the Athenian expedition to Sicily in 413 B.C. There are other references to historical events on Greek coinage, but this one is probably the most beautiful.

The Syracusan decadrachm bespeaks a tremendous amount of local pride. Pride in one's locality and pride in being Greek are reflected on most Greek coins. This is even true after the loss of Greek independence: the series of bronzes struck by the former city-states under Roman rule almost always employed a local type for the reverse design—a famous temple, a celebrated work of art, and so on. A brief examination of the nature of Greek self-identity is important because of its persistent expression on coinage. It was somewhat more complex than it appears at first glance.

This self-identify was of a dual nature. A fifth-century Athenian was proud of the fact that he was a citizen of Athens rather than, say, of Sparta. (Spartans were considered crude, militaristic, and lacking in artistic sensibility.) On the other hand, even Spartans were Greeks, sharing a common language and culture with other Greeks, and this put them several notches above anybody else, such as the Persians. The Greeks tended to apply the word "barbarian" to anyone who wasn't Greek, and the very word was derived from a derisory attempt to mimic foreign languages, which the Greeks found stumbling and unintelligible.

So there was a two-tiered system of ethnic exclusivity at work here. It was considerably better to be a member of your own polis than any other, but it was much better to be a member of *any* Greek community than none at all. We cannot speak of Greek nationality, of the nationalism of the Greek people at this time, for these are modern concepts. The Greeks felt different from other peoples because of the uniqueness of their language and culture rather than because of political boundaries. Indeed, how could it have been otherwise, when there were polei spread from Marseilles to the Crimean Peninsula, all of whom felt equally Greek?

The local element in Greek ethnicity had a great influence on political and related developments in the area. Its effects were both positive and negative. On the positive side, there was much friendly competition between neighboring towns, which produced fruitful developments in the arts and other areas. On the negative side, it was perilously difficult to get Greeks together in united action against a common danger for any length of time. The Greek defeat by Philip of Macedon at Chaeronea in 338 B.C. was in part a result of excessive localism among Greek city-states.

Added to localism was a second strain. The average Greek was a rampant individualist. To a degree, this set him apart from other ancient peoples, such as the Romans. While the latter were greatly concerned with their civilizing mission, of making good Roman citizens out of the polyglot peoples of their empire, the Greeks were not especially preoccupied with any kind of civilizing mission. Moreover, while the more collectively minded Roman was content to be ruled by a republican form of government chaired by a Senate, the Greek wanted to be a part of the government himself.

This spirit of individualism had several curious effects on Greek coinage. As mentioned earlier, the Greeks were the first to allow a die engraver to sign his name, and they were very nearly the last to do so until modern times. This practice was rare in the Greek period, to be sure, but its existence at all is an indication of Greek concern for the individual. In some ways, the absence of depictions of living persons on Greek coins during the best period may also be an indication of this spirit. To a classical Greek, the raising of one person to so great a prominence over others that his likeness appeared on coinage may have seemed an affront to individuality, even a potential threat to individual rights. In any case, the logical place to use a human portrait would have been a monarchy, and most of Greece was firmly committed to alternate political systems down to the fourth century B.C. When living portraiture comes to Greek coinage, it will be influenced by outside sources.

With this set of political, national, and individual preconceptions, what exactly did ancient Greeks choose to put on their coins? In one way or another, most of their choices revolved around their polis. While people who were living during this period were not portrayed, literally hundreds of deities were. We have already seen some, such as Athena and Arethusa. But the list was virtually endless. Divine or mortal founders and patrons of polei were represented, in a splendid, idealized manner. Frequently, this sort of depiction would be combined with the foundation legend of a settlement. Tarentum, one of the most prosperous Greek settlements in southern Italy, used a local tale as the central design for most of its silver staters.

According to legend, Taras, the founder of the first settlement here, was saved from shipwreck by his father Poseidon, god of the sea. Poseidon sent a dolphin to rescue Taras and carry him safely to land. The Tarentine stater is often found with Taras on the reverse and a horse and rider on the obverse. This latter type reflects local pride in the area's fleet horses, which won many racing competitions of the day. The choice of subject matter on the Tarentine stater illustrates a basic fact about Greek coinage design: whatever the motif, it was often chosen to illustrate the uniqueness of that particular city. So local gods and heroes were portrayed, as were real or imaginary, animals, plants, and many other objects.

Some of the most striking representations appearing on Greek coins are of animals. They may be mythical, such as the man-headed bull on the early fifth-century B.C. coinage of Gela, a town in Sicily; or they may be representations of real animals, as seen on coins from Agrigentum, another prosperous Sicilian town. Agrigentum's coinage depicted eagles, crabs, and hares, and her fifth-century coinage contains what may be the most artistic renderings of those creatures in the history of Western art.

Plants, too, made their appearance on Greek coins, often in the form of agricultural products. Metapontum, a Greek settlement on the Tarentine gulf in Italy, depicted an ear of barley on both sides of its curious

coinage of the sixth and fifth centuries B.C. This type of coin, with identical images, one raised and the other incuse, was a feature common to several Greek towns in Italy during this period. Metapontum's choice of design may refer to the goddess Demeter, who was widely worshiped in this region, but it more certainly refers to the area's abundance of grain, one of the sources of the city's prosperity. The incuse relief combination was later abandoned in favor of more conventional coinage design, but the barley ear continued to be a constant reverse type, a god or goddess pictured on the obverse.

Rhodes, a Greek settlement on the eastern Mediterranean island of the same name, used a rose as its reverse type, and on the obverse was a facing portrait of Helios, the sun god to whom the island was sacred. The depiction of a rose was not accidental, but a deliberate pun—the Greek word for rose is *rhodon*, and Rhodes derived its name from this flower.

One of the most attractive depictions of a plant motif comes from Maronea, a town in northern Greece. Maronea was famous for its wine, and fifth- and fourth-century silver coins often have an incuse square (a holdover from the first days of coinage) which frames a grapevine with bunches of grapes, surrounded by a square inscription with the name of the official who issued the coin. The obverse features a prancing horse.

In addition to deities, animals, and plants, Greek towns portrayed inanimate objects of local significance. These were frequently things with religious meaning, such as a tripod on the coinage of Croton, another Greek state in southern Italy. Local legend was that Croton was founded according to the instructions of the oracle of Apollo at Delphi, and a tripod was one of Apollo's emblems. So it was used as a type on Croton's first coins, which appeared in the sixth cen-

tury B.C. Other inanimate objects chosen include shields on issues from Thebes, clubs and bows—the list of these and other subjects for design inspiration on Greek coinage is virtually endless. All had a common characteristic: if they had not possessed some local significance, it is unlikely that they would have been employed.

We have seen some of the objects placed on their coins, and it is clear that the choice of motifs was determined by factors other than the simple need to fill a particular amount of space. Behind this choice of subject matter lay a number of factors—local pride, historical and political events, and so forth. What can the ways in which these things are portrayed tell us about the ancient Greeks as a people?

The style of execution employed by Greeks on their coins is indicative of a deepseated concern for the Ideal—the image of perfection, the best example of anything of which man's mind was able to conceive. This emphasis on the Ideal runs like a thread through Greek philosophy, and it finds its most famous expression in the writings of Plato (427–347 B.C.). The influence of the concept was not confined to philosophy; on the contrary, it penetrated most aspects of Greek life, including the arts. And since coinage (at least in Greek days) was one of the minor arts, *apeth* (the Greek word for this train of ideas) found its way on to money as well. On coins, as in statuary, there was a great concern for the rendition of a person, animal, or object in such a way as to emphasize its inherent beauty. Great attention was paid to expression and musculature, as well as to minor details, such as the arrangement of the hair, the drapery of a costume. In all of this, the Greek was not attempting to accurately portray a real human being (which is something which sets off Greek portraiture from that of imperial Rome). Rather, he wished to

27

Below. Clockwise from top l: Maronea, tetradrachm, 5th century B.C.; Catana, tetradrachm, c. 420 B.C.; Elis, stater, c. 364 B.C.; Herakleia, silver stater, c. 350 B.C.

execute a perfect rendition of a human being, transmuted to a god or hero for the purposes of coinage. So it is that, while the Greeks probably gave the world the finest examples of human portraiture on coins, none of their creations was intended to portray a real human being. Several people in the Hellenistic period (and later the Romans) were more adept at depicting individuals as they really appeared, not how they *ought* to appear.

So the Greeks adorned their coinage with a series of beautiful, idealized, but essentially aloof deities. This fit in well with their general religious concepts. For the Greeks, gods, goddesses, and heroes resided on Mount Olympus, and they did not ordinarily directly intervene in human affairs. One suspects that the ancient Greeks preferred their relationship to the gods that way, in part perhaps because they believed that people were able to manage their own affairs. This is not to say that the Greeks denied that the gods could—and sometimes did—become involved in human affairs. The exploits of Zeus alone are sufficient proof of that. But the Greeks did feel that, basically, the gods had their own concerns and that mortals had theirs. Compared to several other ancient peoples, the Greeks were not religious fanatics, in part because the gods they envisaged did not require fanaticism as an element of worship. The religious devices on Greek coins were put there to satisfy the Greeks themselves, not to propitiate the gods.

The essentially secular nature of Greek life is further attested to by the fact that while gods, goddesses, and religious objects find frequent depiction on Greek coinage, so does a host of other things. In this respect, their coinage is inconsistent, at least in comparison with some later ones, such as those of the Byzantine Empire and medieval western European states. There, a rendition of a single religious symbol, the Christian cross, would dominate design for hundreds of years. This ties in well with the importance of religion in general during the Middle Ages, a time when humankind was not nearly as self-assured as it had been in the days of ancient Greece.

The presence of various elements on Greek coinage can tell us much about the Greeks themselves. So can the mode of presentation of those elements. At the same time, the absence of certain motifs can also afford us clues as to the nature of the ancient Greeks. Coinage can inform us that they were not especially militaristic, at least in comparison with their conquerors, the Romans. As we shall see, Roman coinage abounds in military depictions: Mars (god of war), soldiers leading captives, soldiers standing over prone captives, soldiers guarding camp-gates, military spoils, etc. This military element is usually absent on Greek coinage. To be sure, the Boetians regularly depicted a shield on their coinage, and we have seen one or two other examples of a military element in the course of this chapter, but such an element was never so deep or so consistent as it was with the Romans. This does not mean that military preoccupations were lacking in Greek civilization—indeed, the city-states squabbled constantly during the high point of Greek culture. But it does mean that war occupied less of a central place among Greeks than it did among Romans. One possible reason why this was the case was that, unlike their successors, the Greeks were not striving to change and civilize the world, at least, not ordinarily.

But a time came when a highly organized, very militaristic state in northern Greece, Macedon, attempted to do just that. The story of Macedonian expansion and the changes it wrought leads us into a consideration of a different sort of coinage, that of the great eastern empires.

2

D A H

Ochus

Nis

Hyrcania

HYRCANIA

Syringa

PAR

Zadracarta

TAPURI

HYRCANIA

Mardorum

Sa

Mons

Hecatompylos

Rhage

IA

Desertum

Salino-

-nitros

Ale

Aspadana

Preceding pages. Egypt, octadrachm, 246–221 B.C.
Below. Macedon, silver octadrachm, c. 480–454 B.C.

The Great Eastern Empires

By the fourth century B.C., weakened by wars and internal dissentions, the Hellenic world was in a state of decline. But this Greek decline coincided with the rise of a strong, Greek-speaking state to the north, Macedon. In 338 B.C., this emergent nation would become dominant among the Greeks. In the ensuing years, it would spread elements of Greek culture through Egypt, the Near and Middle East, and lands all the way to India. A new era would be born. Future historians would call it the Hellenistic (Greek-like) period, to distinguish it from the earlier Hellenic. This is to signify that the new era was a blend, a mixture of new Greek elements with a much older base of Oriental ones. This, of course, left its mark on coinage.

The rise of Macedon began in the early fifth century B.C., and the kingdom's first coinage dates from around 480 B.C. These first Macedonian coins were crude compared with contemporary Greek issues, and they were fairly indicative of the cultural state of the country at that time.

Macedonian coinage does not become abundant until the reigns of Philip II (359–336 B.C.) and his son Alexander III (336–323 B.C.). This is logical, for it was not until Philip's reign that the kingdom began its spectacular career of conquest, during which time much larger quantities of coins would be needed. This expansion also gave the Macedonian state a larger supply of precious metals from which to strike coins—the introduction of Philip II's gold stater was due in part to his acquisition of the rich Pangaeum mines in 356 B.C.

The key events in the rise of Macedon occupied much of Philip's reign and all of Alexander's. Philip conquered most of Greece, his career culminating in the battle of Chaeronea in 338 B.C. With the city-states successfully cowed, Philip reorganized them into the League of Corinth (of which he was the head),

and prepared to invade Persian territory in Asia Minor.

He did not live to do so. In 336 B.C., Philip was assassinated, and his son became king as Alexander III. History knows him as Alexander the Great, and with good reason. In a brief reign of thirteen years, Alexander conquered most of the known world. He struck north first, subduing the tribes in the upper Balkans. Then, after suppressing opposition in Greece itself, he left for Asia with thirty-five thousand men, to carry out the invasions his father had planned.

There were financial reasons for doing so. His father's campaigns had cost an immense amount of money and the army that Alexander had inherited was too large to support with the slender resources of the Macedonian state. In part, Alexander's invasion of the east was designed to find sufficient booty to pay the costs of war. His military activities were thus based on a curious mixture of local chauvinism, a desire to spread Greek ideals, and piracy.

Whatever the basic motivations, Alexander's campaigns were highly successful. In 334 B.C. he invaded Asia Minor, where local Greeks rallied to his support. He defeated the Persians at Issus the following year, capturing the family of the Persian king, Darius III. He then turned his attentions to Egypt, easily defeating the last ruler of the native dynasty. There he was proclaimed the new pharoah and was saluted as the son of the god Ammon. This deification of a ruler was one of the most striking characteristics of the age of great empires.

In 331 B.C., Alexander once more went to war against the Persians. At Gaugamela, a climactic battle took place, resulting in a Persian rout. Alexander pursued Darius and the remnants of his army into the heart of Persia. Taking Babylon, Susa, and Persepolis, Alexander was now in possession of vast stores of treasure. At last the campaign was beginning to turn a profit.

Darius was killed in 330 B.C., but it required three more grueling campaigns before Alexander became master of eastern Persia. He then pushed his army still further to the east, conquering Bactria and eventually, in 326 B.C., reaching the Hyphasis River, in the heart of modern India. But his troops would go no farther, and, after exploring the shores of the Persian gulf, Alexander turned homeward. He spent the last two years of his life reorganizing his exhausted armies, preparing for future conquests. These were denied him. He fell sick with a fever, possibly malaria, and died in June, 323 B.C. He named no successor, and, by the time of his death, his huge domains were already beginning to split apart. His passing accelerated the split, and his generals and their successors eventually carved three large states out of his former empire: Macedon, which included most of Greece; Egypt, which embraced part of North Africa; and Syria, which originally took in most of the eastern conquests but which was whittled down by successive losses until its eventual fall to Rome in the first century B.C. In addition, several smaller countries, such as Pergamum and Bithynia, came into being.

The new polities resulting from the expansion of Macedon were hybrid creations. That is to say, a thin veneer of Greek language, culture, and religion was superimposed on a much thicker layer of native ways of life. It must be remembered that the Macedonians and Greeks were very much a minority in many of the new lands. While they controlled the governments and the choice positions in social and economic life, most of their subjects were native peoples, bearers of the traditional cultures and religions of the areas. In this state of affairs, a process of syncretism went on, a blending of two strains, which resulted in the Greeks adopting many of the ideas held by their subject peoples.

We have already seen one instance of this process: the deification of Alexander the Great in Egypt during his lifetime. This event would have been unheard of among the Greeks of the fifth century B.C., but it made a good deal more sense (at least, apparently, to Alexander) in the alien environment of Egypt. Alexander also adopted Persian costume after his conquests there, and he called attention to the new marriage of East and West by a real marriage of several thousand Macedonians to several thousand Asians in 324 B.C. This ceremony no doubt merely legitimized many relationships which had already been established, but it was intended to have a greater significance.

In brief, the nature of Alexander's empire and its successor states was twofold. While Greek culture was spread over most of the known world, it was "Asianized" in the process, becoming an amalgam of West and East. And while many surviving artifacts and documents give evidence of this syncretic process, none do so more eloquently than coins. Here, we must talk of several elements and their meaning, most importantly portraiture, increased standardization, and introduction of non-Greek pictorial elements and modes of expression.

In the case of portraiture, it must be recalled that the Greeks of the classical era did not depict living persons on their coins. Several possible reasons have already been advanced, among them the basically democratic nature of the Greeks themselves. With Alexander's conquests, the wheels were set in motion that would change all this, which would make a royal portrait the dominant type on Hellenistic coinage over the next several centuries. Alexander never appeared on his own coinage, although some scholars have argued that a number of Alexander's tetradrachms bore a portrait meant to represent

Alexander rather than Herakles. This cannot be substantiated, and the general interpretation is that the portrait represents an idealized young Herakles. The figure of an enthroned Jupiter, holding an eagle and a scepter, dominated the reverse, along with the name of the king and a mint mark. Alexander's tetradrachms were produced in enormous numbers during his reign and for many years after its end. Significantly, they were highly standardized, differing from each other only in minor details and mint marks.

By now, the Hellenistic world was beginning to depict real persons on coins. One of Alexander's successors was Ptolemy I, who controlled Egypt. In 317 B.C., Ptolemy introduced a new obverse type on his tetradrachms, a head of Alexander the Great, with the horn of Ammon. In this land where he had first been proclaimed a god, Alexander the Great was beginning to acquire some of the attributes of a deity. Alexander's headdress was the skin of an elephant, a possible reference to Indian victories. A few years later, Ptolemy put his own name on some silver coinage, along with that of Alexander. This was an obvious attempt to connect himself and the great king in the minds of his subjects. Subsequently, references to Alexander were retired, and Ptolemy's name and portrait appeared on coinage throughout the remainder of his long reign (323–285 B.C.). Thus, shortly before 300 B.C., the likeness of a living king was being placed on his own coinage. The new practice spread widely, and it soon became the norm for coins minted during the Hellenistic period.

As mentioned earlier, the collapse of Alexander's empire eventually led to the establishment of a number of smaller Greek kingdoms. One of these was Pergamum, located in western Asia Minor. If Ptolemy's coins realistically portrayed an aging military leader, those of Pergamum were positively unflattering in their depiction of the founder of the dynasty, Philetaerus (282–263 B.C.). The portraits of Hellenistic kings on coinage tend to be realistic, not idealistic, as was so often the case on earlier Greek coins. Perhaps this is an indication that to the Greeks these people were still men, whether they were kings or not. And in the case of a ruler of no physical attractiveness whatsoever, such as Antiochus I, who ruled Syria from 281 to 266 B.C., idealization would have been a wasted effort. In any case, Hellenistic portraiture achieved a degree of realism perhaps equaled on some Roman coins, but not matched by issues of any other ancient people. And in many instances, the portrait of a Hellenistic ruler may be the only clear, immutable information we have about him.

Still, why did the kings choose to place portraits of themselves on their coins? What was the background of this development, and why should it have taken place when it did? One reason for a king electing to honor himself on the coinage was quite simply that he *was* king, and could do so if he liked. And there were several good arguments in favor of his doing so. First, he would naturally desire to be taken seriously by his subjects. What better way was there of demonstrating to them the ubiquity of his rule than by sending coins with his likeness to all parts of the kingdom? The people would become convinced that there was a strong king in command and, by inscriptions and portraits, that he was that king. This factor assumes a greater importance when we remember that many of the Hellenistic kingdoms were large entities, frequently with unruly populations and primitive communication systems. In many cases, the ruler and his government were virtually all that a kingdom's people had in common. The production of a large coinage with a royal portrait might act as a

bond among ruler, government, and subject. And any bond, however, modest, was of benefit to the state.

    Another argument in favor of the new portraiture grew out of the meeting of East and West which distinguished the Hellenistic era. The kings of Egypt, Syria, and other areas ruled over peoples who had been taught to believe that their monarchs were divine or semidivine. When Ptolemy, a Macedonian by birth, put his portrait on the coins of his kingdom, he was implicitly carrying on a long-standing Egyptian tradition that Pharaoh was divine. One might say that the Egyptians *expected* Ptolemy to follow the tradition if he was in fact their new king. The political benefits to be reaped were obvious—his subjects were less likely to revolt if they could be convinced that he was a god. So Ptolemy had himself portrayed on coinage, and people

were allowed to draw their own conclusions. The new portraiture spread throughout Alexander's former empire, both to regions with a tradition of a god-king, such as Persia, and to places where no such tradition existed, such as Macedon. Even in the latter regions, royal portraiture served a dual purpose: it reminded subjects of the presence and power of a king, and it set him slightly apart from the rest of mankind. So an idea that originally began in the East (the divinity of a monarch) survived the Greek conquest and eventually found expression in the West, on Greek coins of the Hellenistic era.

Not all Hellenistic portraiture was excellent. The great days of realism and artistry occurred during the third and second centuries B.C. After that, portraiture declined, as did the fortunes of the Greek world in general. Still, even coin portraits from the end of

**Below. Bactria. Clockwise from top: square bronze,
c. 150 B.C.; tetradrachm, c. 150 B.C.;
tetradrachm, c. 190 B.C.
Bottom. Top l: Armenia, tetradrachm,
83–69 B.C.; top r & bottom: Thrace, tetradrachms, 323–281 B.C.**

the Hellenistic period have great value, for they are often the only records left of the physical appearance of the rulers of the day.

The increased standardization in Hellenistic coin design is another indication of change. From the time of Alexander the Great, obverse and reverse types became increasingly limited to a few basic subjects: the head of a god (or, later, the king) on the obverse, and the depiction of a seated or standing deity or animal on the reverse. Once adopted, a coin type was likely to be retained for a number of years or even, as in the case of Egypt, through many reigns. In brief, much of the variety and spontaneity present in Hellenic coinage is absent in Hellenistic.

Examples of this standardization are abundant in the coinage of the Hellenistic period. It will be recalled that Alexander's silver tetradrachms featured a portrait of Herakles in a lion skin on the obverse, a seated Zeus on the reverse with the name of the king. The point to be noted here is that this coinage extended over a long period of time, continuing even after Alexander's death, and that it was issued in an essentially identical form by a large number of mints scattered all the way from Macedonia to Babylon. A similar repetition of basic types is found in Alexander's gold staters.

Such a monolithic uniformity of types was matched, perhaps even exceeded, in the coinage of the Ptolemaic dynasty in Egypt. Ptolemy I introduced the basic types for the tetradrachm, a portrait of himself on the obverse, an eagle on a thunderbolt on the reverse. His son and successor, Ptolemy II (285–246 B.C.), introduced a new design for gold coinage: a portrait of his deceased wife Arsinoë on the obverse, double cornucopiae on the reverse. By the time of the next ruler (Ptolemy III, 246–221 B.C.), the bronze, too, had become standardized, with Zeus (now disguised as Ammon-Ra) on the obverse, the

Ptolemaic eagle on the reverse.

Once established, these types continued virtually unchanged for many years. In fact, so standard had the types become by the second century B.C. that it is difficult to tell the coinage of one king from another, a problem augmented by the fact that the dynasty followed the disagreeable habit of naming most of its rulers Ptolemy (there were eventually fifteen of them).

Why should this uniformity of coinage, running so directly counter to earlier Greek practice, have been the rule for the great Greek kingdoms of the Hellenistic period? The answer lies in part in the fact that they were large political entities, many of them larger than anything the Greeks had ever dealt with before. When subjects, numbering in the millions rather than in the thousands, were under the rule of one man, the ruler in question would be likely to strike a coinage of a standard type throughout his domains, due to the large numbers of coins needed and due to his desire to get his name and likeness across to as many people as possible. If the formation and maintenance of great kingdoms ruled by Greeks owed much to Eastern precedents, the new uniformity of coinage seen in those kingdoms was a logical development.

Another result of the blending of East and West which characterized the period was the choice of subjects portrayed on coinage and, frequently, the manner in which they were depicted. For example, when Zeus, a Greek god, is pictured with the horns of Ammon, an Egyptian deity, it is obvious that a process of cultural blending is taking place.

There are many instances of this sort of syncretism in the choice and mode of subject portrayal. Turning again to Egypt, a series of gold coins were struck bearing the portrait of Ptolemy III with the attributes of three major gods, Helios, Zeus, and

Poseidon, an expression of the traditionally close relationship that Eastern peoples postulated between a ruler and the gods. Ptolemy III's son and successor, Ptolemy IV (221–204 B.C.), depicted two major Eastern divinities, Serapis and Isis, on some of his tetradrachms. Incidentally, the worship of these two deities later gained prominence in the Roman world, an indication that religious syncretism was not restricted to the Hellenistic period.

Eastern influence on Syrian coinage reached its zenith during the reign of the Armenian Tigranes (83–69 B.C.), whose issues portrayed the usurper-king in an Armenian headdress on the obverse and local deities on the reverse. Mithridates III (255–185 B.C.) of Pontus included a star and crescent on the reverses of some of his coins, indicating the Persian ancestry claimed by his dynasty.

Closer to the center of the old Greek world, Lysimachus of Thrace (323–281 B.C.) struck coins in both gold and silver that show the best blendings of Eastern and Western imagery. On the obverse, there appears a splendid head of the deified Alexander (Lysimachus' former commander) complete with the horn of Ammon. The reverse bears a figure of the goddess Athena in the act of crowning the name of Lysimachus. This portrayal of the patroness of a formerly proud and free Hellenic polis paying homage to the name of a Hellenistic king says a great deal about the spirit of the new age.

Some of the most direct examples of the blending of cultures appear on the coins of Bactria, commonly called Greek India. Bactria was one of the later conquests of Alexander the Great. Following his death and the dismemberment of his united empire, Bactria came under the sway of the Seleucid kings of Syria. About 250 B.C., Diodotus I, a local ruler of Bactria under the Syrians, revolted against Antiochus II. This revolt succeeded, and an independent Bactrian king-

dom was set up. It struck coins until approximately 40 B.C.

Early Bactrian coins closely resemble those of other sections of the Hellenistic world: the ruler is on the obverse, a seated or standing god on the reverse. But Eastern, in this case native Indian, influence soon became manifest. The coinage of Demetrius (c. 195–150 B.C.) frequently depicted the king in an Indian-elephant headdress. Demetrius extended the Bactrian state deep into India, only to witness some of his many conquests and all of Bactria itself fall to a rival, Eucratides (c. 175–155 B.C.). Henceforth there were two independent states in the region, both of whom struck coins. Significantly, each territory began minting *square* coins in bronze and silver. Square coinage had been fairly common in India from perhaps as early as the sixth century B.C., but its adoption by nominally Greek rulers in northwestern India affords significant evidence of the penetration of Eastern influences into Western culture. Indeed, many of the coins from this area are perfect examples of cultural hybrids. They are struck, have inscriptions in Greek, and frequently feature Greek gods. On the other hand, they may be square and frequently carry reverse inscriptions in Kharoshthi, the local native language.

If we can imagine a map of the ancient Hellenistic world, we would have Greece, Asia Minor, and the Greek islands on the nearer rim and Greek India on the farther. In the center would lie the vast reaches of the former Persian Empire. We must turn to Persia now, for the region produced three distinctive sets of coinage in ancient times, that of the Persian Empire itself and those of its two successor states, Parthia and the Sassanian Empire.

Persian coinage seems to have been an outgrowth of the earlier Lydian series. At least, the rulers of Persia do not appear to have struck any coins until after they had conquered Croesus' kingdom in 545 B.C. The first Persian coins seem to have been struck about thirty years later, no earlier than 515 B.C., during the reign of Darius the Great (522 –486 B.C.).

These coins were minted in gold and silver, and they are very similar in appearance. In all cases, the king is portrayed on the obverse, in a variety of poses. On the silver *siglos*, he is shown half length, shooting an arrow, or running with a bow and spear. On the gold *daric*, the king is depicted in the second or third position, but not the first. Persian sigloi and darics are crude affairs, rather archaic-looking when compared to Greek coins. They are bean-shaped, and the reverses of both denominations contain only an oblong punch mark. During the two centuries of Persian regal coinage, these basic types remained essentially static. The absence of inscriptions makes Persian coins extremely difficult to date accurately, and the numismatist is forced to rely on stylistic differences, variations in portraiture, and to hoard evidence to achieve a relatively accurate chronology.

Persian coinage tells us two things about the people who made it: they were extremely conservative in outlook, and the king occupied a central place in their thinking. Both elements would carry over into the coinages of their successors, the Parthians and Sassanids.

The conservative nature of Persian culture is attested to by the monotonous nature of the coinage. Any people who can be in more or less constant contact with Greek ideas and culture for almost two hundred years, while producing a coinage that looks about the same at its end as it did at its beginning, may be said to have little interest in change—or in art, for that matter.

The Persians were, however, interested in the power and majesty of king and kingdom, as seen in the inevitable appearance of the ruler on coinage. From the absence of inscriptions as to which ruler was currently being portrayed, one might hazard the guess that this consideration was not of primary importance to the Persians and that the institution of monarchy was more important than the monarch himself. And it is true that the conquest of Persia by Alexander the Great was one reason for the spread of the concept of a great, semidivine monarchy during the Hellenistic period.

One final aspect of Persian coinage should be noted. It is not enough to depict a king on all coinage; he must also be portrayed as a warrior, a hunter. Hence the constant inclusion of a bow and arrow or a spear on Persian coins. This finds expression in earlier Persian art, such as bas reliefs, and it betrays the military preoccupation of the Persian state.

In 331 B.C., Persia was conquered by Alexander the Great, who made Babylon the capital of his short-lived unified kingdom. The region passed to Seleucid control after Alexander's death, and then it was ruled by Greeks until the mid-third century B.C.

The natives deeply resented this alien rule. Around 250 B.C., the people living in the area to the southeast of the Caspian Sea rose in revolt, led by Arsaces (c. 250–c. 211 B.C.), a local military chieftain. The revolt succeeded, and much of the former Persian state became newly independent, under the name of Parthia.

The Arsacid kings ruled Parthia for about five hundred years. Parthia's greatest expansion came during the reign of Mithridates I (171–138 B.C.), who added parts of Bactria and Babylonia to his holdings. Later, a long, slow decline in power set in, arrested for a time by the activities of Mithridates II (123–88 B.C.). After his death, the decline resumed, as Parthian dynasts had to contend

Opposite. Top, l to r: Persia, siglos, 5th century B.C.;
Persia, siglos, 336–330 B.C.;
center: Parthia, drachms, 171–138 B.C.;
bottom, l to r: Parthia, tetradrachm, 171–138 B.C.;
Parthia, tetradrachm, 10–40 A.D.

with a number of restive native peoples, with the Scythians (a barbaric people to the north), and in time with the rising power of Rome. The last ruler was overthrown and killed in 226 A.D., and the kingdom of Parthia came to an end.

Parthian coins illustrate the innate conservatism, respect for royalty, and military emphasis which we saw earlier in the coinage of the Persians. The most common Parthian coins are silver drachms, bearing the king's portrait on the obverse and a seated figure of the ruler holding a bow on the reverse, a type derived from earlier Seleucid coinage. The inscriptions are especially significant. In one respect, the Parthians followed Persian tradition on much of their coinage. That is, the actual ruler striking a coin was not specifically named on it. Rather, the inscription ordinarily made reference to the founder of the kingdom, Arsaces I, adding a descriptive epithet of one sort or another. Not until the first century A.D. was the name of the reigning king given on his coins. The establishment of a chronology for Parthian coins is easier than for those of the Persians, however, since portraits are large enough to permit basic identification of successive rulers. The fact that Parthian coins are often dated (from the beginning of the Seleucid era) also helps. It should be noted that most Parthian coins have a reverse inscription that largely or completely surrounds the seated figure. These inscriptions are in Greek, or later in Pehlvi, a native language.

In brief, Parthian coins speak of the nature of the Parthian state. It was a mixed, multicultural affair, as evidenced by the Greek inscriptions and the Scythian dress worn by the reverse figure, the Scythian cap or Eastern diadem adorning the obverse portrait. It was oriented toward the military; the seated figure with a bow is a constant reminder of that. It took the institution of mon-

archy very seriously, and as with the Persians, the institution of the monarchy itself was probably of greater importance than the glory of any individual king.

But the Parthian state was not as rigid, not quite as conservative, as its Persian predecessor. Again, the coins it made bear this out. Inscriptions of individual rulers eventually do make their appearance, and royal portraits change from reign to reign. Moreover, the reverse design is not always that of a seated king. A tetradrachm of Mithridates I has a standing Herakles as its reverse type. A much later ruler, Musa (3 B.C.–4 A.D.), put his portrait on the obverse, that of his mother on the reverse. Artabanus III (10–40 A.D.) issued tetradrachms with his portrait full-faced rather than in profile, with a relatively complicated reverse on which a goddess is presenting him a wreath.

Parthian coinage gives one final indication of change. As the fortunes of this country declined, so did the artistic quality of its money. The treatment of the king's portrait probably suffered more than any other element. The hair became stylized, and at the same time that kings were beginning to put their own names on the coinage, their portraits were becoming so unrealistic that a differentiation of rulers on that basis is impossible. A series of lines were used to depict both obverse and reverse figures; modeling in depth, a legacy of earlier Hellenistic times, disappeared. Finally, inscriptions became blundered, virtually unreadable in some cases. In this decline of the coinage, we can make out the parallel decline in the Parthian state itself, preparing the way for its Sassanian successor.

The story of the four-century-long rule of the Sassanians begins in Persis, a semi-independent kingdom on the Persian gulf. In 224 A.D., Ardashir, a local prince of the dynasty of Sasan, revolted against the

Opposite. Parthia. Top to bottom: drachm, 123–88 B.C.;
tetradrachm, 147–191 A.D.
Below. Sassanians. L & r: drachms, 240–271
A.D.; center: aureus, 292–301 A.D.

Parthians, who were the overlords of Persis. His revolt paralleled that of Arsaces against the Seleucids almost five centuries before, and the results were similar. He established a new empire on the ruins of an old.

Artabanus, last king of Parthia, was defeated and killed in 226. Ardashir began his reign as "King of Kings," a rule that lasted until his death in 240. Early in his reign, the last supporters of the old regime were driven from power with the help of the people, many of whom regarded the Parthians as alien overlords. Far more than the Parthian empire, the Sassanian state was a national creation of the Persians themselves, as evidenced by the fact that all inscriptions on Sassanian coins are in Pehlvi, while Greek lettering was the rule on most Parthian issues.

This sense of regained nationality is present in one form or another on most Sassanian coins. While the earliest issues of Ardashir bear an obverse portrait of the king with a Parthian-style domed tiara, this is soon replaced by a more distinctly Persian

headdress or diadem. An inscription in Pehlvi gives the king's names and titles, and a second reference to the ruler forms part of the reverse inscription. The dominant reverse type is a fire-altar, usually flanked by two figures, the king and his son. The fire-altar was an essential element of Zoroastrianism, the religion of the Persian people at this time. Its choice for a reverse design is another example of resurgent Persian feeling under the Sassan-ids, while the addition of a standing figure of the king in close proximity signifies the interrelationship between the Sassanid church and state. It also betokens the piety of the ruler, witnessed by his attention to religious rites important to his subjects.

The Sassanian kings struck coins in gold, silver, and bronze, although gold issues were rare and copper ones fairly scarce as well. The mainstay of the Sassanian mone-

this encouraged *clipping*, i.e., an individual's removing part of the silver from the edge of the coin and then returning it to circulation. Kavad I (488–531) and most of his successors adopted the practice of placing four equally spaced crescents on this blank margin, presumably in an attempt to render clipping impossible.

By now, the coinage was in a state of artistic decline, paralleling the political troubles of the day. Just as the Parthians had been constantly engaged in war, so too were the Sassanians. Almost from the beginning, the Sassanids fought the Romans and their successors, the Byzantines, in a contest for dominance in the Middle East. The effects of this warfare eventually proved fatal to the Sassanian monarchy. By the seventh century, it had been so weakened by recurrent strife that it was unable to resist the rise of a new, strong, deeply fanatical force from the south. This was Islam, and the story of its rise and the coins it produced will be told elsewhere.

Reviewing the numismatic history of the great eastern states, it must be concluded that developments here left an indelible mark on the history of coinage as a whole. The portrayal of a living ruler became commonplace, as did standardization in the objects portrayed on coinage. In many instances, coinage became marked by an extreme conservatism, both as to objects depicted and the ways in which they were portrayed.

A thousand miles to the east, another coinage experiment was taking place in China. The birth of coinage here and its spread to adjacent lands was an independent development, owing nothing to the Lydians and Greeks. As time went on, Far Eastern coinage would be marked by an even greater conservatism and standardization than that seen in Persia or any other of the great eastern empires.

tary system was the silver drachm, whose name and size are muted reminders of the Greek conquest of Persia centuries earlier. As time went on, the drachm became flatter and thinner, so that while the size of the die originally coincided closely with the size of the planchet, by the late fourth century it was considerably smaller than the planchet. Because of this, a wide, unstamped margin was left around the struck portion of the coin and

3

Preceding pages. Japan, oban, 1860.
Below. China, sycees (fifty and one tael
ingots), 19th century.

The Oriental Coinage Experiment

The Chinese call their land Chung-Kuo, which means "Middle Nation" or "Middle Country." In ancient times, this choice of names was an indication of the widespread Chinese belief that the country occupied a central position in human affairs, and that whatever went on to the east or west of it was of secondary importance.

In the case of coinage, the Chinese definitely did *not* occupy a central position. While they were pioneers in the coinage concept, their products did not occupy center stage in the development of coinage as a whole. On the contrary, Chinese coinage grew up independently of, and parallel to, Western coinage. While it enjoyed an independent life of 2,500 years, it did not affect the nature of money in the West and, indeed, was itself reshaped at last as a result of Western penetration.

Even to the untrained eye, Chinese coins present very obvious differences in comparison with Greek or later European ones. They are cast, rather than struck, and they tend to be fairly thin. Almost all of them have square center holes. They are entirely given over to inscriptions, not portraiture. Virtually all of them are of copper or bronze. Let us briefly examine each of these differences.

Typical Chinese coins were made by pouring molten metal into a mold, frequently made from baked clay. This mold tended to have a central channel, down which the metal was poured, and several branching ducts, each one leading to a representation of the coin to be cast, executed in reverse. Each mold had two halves. These two halves were clamped together, and the molten copper or bronze was poured in at the top. Once the metal had cooled, the two halves of the mold were separated, and the cast coins were removed. At this stage, the resulting object looked rather like a tree, each

"branch" ending in a coin. The coins were broken off, their edges filed, and they were now ready for commerce. The rest of the "tree" would be recycled to produce more coins.

Why cast coins rather than strike them? The answer may lie in the fact that the Chinese had had long experience in casting statuary, utensils, and other copper or bronze objects. This would have been a logical method for them to extend to the coining process.

The decision to cast coins rather than to strike them may help explain another anomaly of Chinese coinage. As mentioned above, Chinese coins tend to be thinner than their European counterparts. From a technological viewpoint, it is easier to cast a thin object than a thick one, where air bubbles become a problem.

Most Chinese coins have center holes. Those on early issues are round, those on later ones—the vast majority of all Chinese coins—are square. This square center hole has been thought by some scholars to have had religious significance: a symbol of the four corners of the earth under the round dome of heaven, a circular coin. A more probable explanation for the square hole arises from the manner in which these coins were made.

As they came from the mold, they were slightly irregular in shape, with a rough projection where they had been attached to the "tree." The simplest way to remove these irregularities was to fit the coins onto a square metal bar, which was turned in a simple hand lathe. By using a file or a chisel, one could make a fair number of coins perfectly round all at once. As to why they should have had holes in the first place, these coins had very little individual worth, and they were often traded in large numbers. A central hole enabled them to be permanently strung together in batches of, say, one hundred or one thousand. They were easier to handle and, incidentally, strung in this fashion they received very little wear. The latter may account for the fact that Chinese coins often circulated for hundreds of years.

The outstanding difference between Chinese and Western coinage is that Chinese coins are given over entirely to inscriptions, whereas Western issues ordinarily include some sort of artistic rendering of a god or king, an animal, a building, a heraldic device. Indeed, the inscriptions on Western issues may be secondary to the device, or they may even be entirely lacking, as was often the case on early Greek coins.

Furthermore, these Chinese inscriptions are fairly limited in their choice of content. They may state the weight or denomination of the coin, or merely that it is the current money of a particular Chinese ruler. Unlike Islamic coinage, inscriptions have neither a religious content nor a propaganda intent. They only state what the coin is or when it was made.

One possible explanation for brief inscriptions on Chinese coinage instead of portraiture may be that the casting method used in ancient times was not a particularly good way of faithfully reproducing a detailed design. Minor points of the artwork would be lost, and the entire design would emerge soft and indistinct. As a matter of fact, some early Western peoples, including the Romans, experimented with a cast coinage with pictorial elements, and the results left much to be desired. Obviously, the casting process had its limitations, and for the Chinese it would have been easier to eschew an ordinary design in favor of simple inscriptions.

But there is more to it than that. The Chinese certainly had the technology to produce a Western-style coinage, had they wished to do so. The absence of this type of coinage through most of China's history must indicate a conscious choice on the part of the Chinese as to what they wished to place on their coins, as to what they wanted their money to mean to the ordinary citizen.

A coin meant different things to a Chinese, a Greek, or a Roman. The Greek would produce a coinage with beautiful renditions of gods, heroes, etc., in part because he believed that beauty and artistic excellence should be present on all objects, large or small. The Chinese, masterworker in jade, textiles, and pottery, was able to keep things designed to please the eye and spirit separate from things designed solely to buy other things. The Roman struck his coins, as we shall see, in part to create beauty, but also with an eye to civilizing non-Romans—to propagandizing, putting across a certain point of view to a captive audience, the people of the Roman Empire. The Chinese was so convinced of the inherent superiority of his culture that he did not need to proclaim it on his coins. And the Chinese Empire did not include several dozen contending nationalities, all of whom had to be converted to the same outlook if domestic peace were to be maintained. The Roman Empire did.

These hypotheses may provide some clues as to why the Chinese preferred inscriptions over other designs, and why they favored the inscriptions they did. We can never be certain, of course, and it might be safest to say merely that Chinese and Westerners were very different peoples, a fact reflected in their coinages.

The metals used for Chinese coinage are significant. While the Chinese experimented with gold, silver, even iron, virtually all of their issues were cast in copper, bronze, or brass. This was due in part to natural limitations—a lack of gold deposits, for instance. It was due much more to the Chinese concept of the nature of money itself.

The Chinese never entirely abandoned the barter concept of money, wherein precious metal was a commodity like any other. As a result, it tended to be cast in an ingot of one form or another, the boat-shaped silver *sycee* being especially popular. A respected local individual then measured and stamped the ingot for weight and purity. The basic weight unit was a *tael*, which corresponds to about an ounce and a quarter (35.4 grams) in our reckoning. Once processed, the ingot was then traded as bullion, rather than circulating from hand to hand as a coin.

In the use of these ingots, we see two examples of the archaic nature of Chinese money: silver was being treated as a commodity; and private individuals, not governments, were weighing and validating it for trade. Moreover, there was no fixed relationship between the tael and ordinary coins. Depending on time, circumstance, and silver purity, a tael could be worth anywhere from seven hundred to two thousand of the round, square-holed coins, called *ch'ien* in Chinese, *cash* in English.

One final generalization must be made concerning the nature of ancient Chinese coinage. It was remarkably conservative, changing very little from century to century. Indeed, no other coinage in the history of the world approaches it in this respect. Consider the facts. Round coinage may have been devised by the sixth century B.C. The third century B.C. saw it replace other forms of coinage. By now it is round, has several characters on the obverse, and has a square hole in the center. It is reformed in 118 B.C., and again in the early seventh century A.D., and it then remains virtually unchanged down to the opening of this century—a time span of thirteen hundred years! It would not be too much to say that this extreme conservatism in China's money stems from an innate conservatism in Chinese people themselves.

This stability, the retention of a basic monetary form through many centuries, was not always the case in China. In the beginning, there was a good deal of experimentation in the *form* given to coins. A variety of shapes was adopted for China's money, and in the choices employed we can see clear vestiges of the original barter system, traces which are more obvious in China than anywhere else.

We can postulate the development of coinage as occurring in three stages. The first is barter, in which various objects are traded for each other. In the second stage, metal replicas of trade items are used, due to greater durability and convenience. In the third stage, barter is abandoned and metallic coins have taken the place of trade objects. In the development of coinage elsewhere, only the third stage has survived. China's coinage is unique in that the second stage is also represented.

China's first coins were not coins at all, in the modern sense of the word. Instead, they were pieces of metal cast in the form of cowrie shells (not native to China, and valuable in trade for that reason), spades (in an essentially agricultural nation, a spade was always valuable), and knives. It is not known when this "barter coinage" was first made, but some scholars have postulated a date sometime in the Shang dynasty (1766–1122 B.C.), and bronze cowries were certainly in use well before 700 B.C. The knives and spades may have come into use by the eleventh century B.C. Spade money evolved into what experts call *pu*, or weight money (so called because it bears characters indicating its weight). It resembles spade money but is much smaller. It has a flat handle (the spades often have hollow ones), and it tends to exhibit a prominent indentation at the foot. As with the other Chinese "coins" of the period, pu money apparently originated in north

China.

In all of these types of money, there is a definite progression from no inscriptions to characters giving weight, value, or place of mintage. An outstanding example of this evolution is the *i pi ch'ien*, or "ant-nose money," which resembles its simple cowrie ancestor only in general shape. Its uniface inscription is incuse and vaguely resembles an ant or a large nose—hence the name. I pi ch'ien dates from the fourth to third centuries B.C., by which time the more orthodox round money was coming into prominence.

Chinese tradition carries the invention of round money back as far as 1200 B.C., though the true date should probably be put at the sixth century B.C. at the earliest, perhaps much later. In any case, round coinage does not push aside earlier forms until the reign of the first Ch'in emperor, Shih Huangti (221–210 B.C.), who built the Great Wall, unified China for the first time in its history, and, as an adjunct of that, gave China a unified coinage. He demonetized the old spade and knife coins, and round coins with square holes were made universal. These were the *pan liang*, so called because of their inscription, which stated that each coin weighed twelve *shu*, or one-half of a Chinese ounce (pan liang). These coins bore only two characters on the obverse. Chinese coinage would follow the practice for the next eight hundred years.

The replacement of the Ch'in dynasty by the Han in 206 B.C. did not occasion any radical changes in China's coinage. Pan liang continued to be cast in large numbers. As time went on, however, they suffered a gradual debasement and reduction in weight, an indication that inflation could be a problem in China, just as it was in the West. By 187 B.C., the pan liang weighed one-third of a Chinese ounce, rather than the half-ounce stipulated on the coin itself; by 179 B.C., its weight had fallen to one-sixth of an ounce; and by 140 B.C., to one-eighth.

Another reform of China's coinage was in order, and it was effected by the emperor Wu Ti in 118 B.C. He recalled the earlier coinage, replacing it with a piece that weighed five shu. It bore two characters on its obverse, as had the pan liang, but it also had a raised rim to prevent filing or clipping. This *wu shu* coinage was a great success, and it remained the standard Chinese denomination for the next seven-and-a-half centuries. Since the simple inscription never changed, any chronological arrangement of this coinage depends on variations in calligraphy. Scholars are not in universal agreement as to which wu shu coins came first and which later; all that can be said with certainty is that they were issued by some nine official Chinese dynasties and twenty-three rebel counterparts, and that they were minted in all parts of the empire.

The only interruption in this long-lived series was the attempt by the usurper Wang Mang (7–23 A.D.) to revive the old knife and weight money. His coins are easily distinguished from original issues, for they are smaller and more carefully made. This experiment in monetary retrogression was abandoned following Wang Mang's overthrow.

Under the T'ang dynasty (618–907 A.D.), the coinage of China received the form it would retain until modern times. The first T'ang emperor, Kao Tsu, issued a new round coinage with a square center hole, ten of which weighed a Chinese ounce. The new coin's rim was wider than before, and the obverse contained four characters rather than two. The characters to the left and right read *tung pao*, or current money. Those at top and bottom give the *nien hao*, the name the current emperor assigned to distinguish his reign from earlier ones. This formula for the obverse of Chinese coins would continue in

use down to the dawn of the twentieth century. The reverses of Kao Tsu's coins were ordinarily blank, although some of them bore a crescent-shaped mark, others a single character indicating the place of mintage.

Kao Tsu's successors introduced some modifications into the coinage, although the four-character obverse was retained. The issues of the Sung dynasty (960–1280) were produced with several styles of writing, among them seal, orthodox, and running hand character. Since Chinese calligraphy reached its height during this dynasty, it is only natural that it should have found some expression on the coinage. One of the Sung emperors, Hsiao Tsung (1163–1189), included numerals on the reverses of his coins to indicate reignal years. This is one of the few instances of a specifically dated Chinese coinage. Parenthetically, the regular dating of coins in the West would have to wait for another four hundred years.

The Sung dynasty eventually fell to

the Mongols, led by Jenghiz and Kublai Khan. They issued coinage only in limited amounts, inscribed with Mongol characters. For most transactions, paper money was used. The Chinese seem to have invented paper currency several centuries earlier; it formed a financial mainstay of the Yüan (Mongol) dynasty and its Ming successor down to about 1400. Traveling in China shortly before 1300, the young Marco Polo observed its usage and duly reported the fact back to Europe. European employment of paper money lay several centuries in the future, however, and it would be invented independently rather than borrowed from the Chinese.

The Ming dynasty (1368–1644) represented a high point in China's cultural and political development. The arts flourished, particularly painting and ceramics. The empire added Assam, the modern Burma, to its already huge holdings. None of this was reflected in its coinage, however. The ch'ien (cash) continued to be China's basic coin, and the obverse design layout was always the same. Greater utilization was now being made of the reverse, however, which frequently had a character indicating the place of minting. Coins in larger denominations were also issued (valued at two, four, five, and ten ch'ien), and this value would also be stated in characters on the reverse.

These minor changes were retained in the coinage of the last ruling dynasty, the Ch'ing (1644–1911). The typical Chinese coin would now have the usual four characters on the obverse, indicating that it was current legal tender in a particular reign. The reverse would bear the name of a mint and, if applicable, the value. The inclusion of the value became an important feature on Chinese coins in the mid-nineteenth century, as the central government inflated the money supply to pay the expenses of putting down the calamitous Tai Ping rebellion (1850–1864). By the mid-1850s, coins were being cast in denominations ranging all the way up to one thousand ch'ien, although their purchasing power was far less.

The Tai Ping rebellion highlighted a serious problem faced by the later Chinese Empire—the penetration of China by Western influences and their effect on the traditional life of the country. In the case of the Tai Ping rebels, the Western influence in question was Christianity, espoused by many of their leaders and a notable percentage of the ordinary soldiers. The influence of the West first made itself felt in the mid-sixteenth century, when the Portuguese obtained a trading concession at Macao, off Canton. As the years went by, the Westerners became more and more persistent in their desires to evangelize, make money from, and, eventually, to acquire pieces of Chinese territory. The Portuguese were followed by the British, who acquired Hong Kong by treaty in 1842, by the French, who gained control over Indo-China later in the century—even by the Japanese, who took Taiwan in 1895. As the nineteenth century drew to a close, a half-dozen nations were busily carving out colonies or spheres of influence for themselves, Christianizing the natives, building railroads, developing mining and manufacturing—in short, bringing the conservative Chinese, willingly or not, into the modern age.

It soon became apparent that a majority of Chinese did *not* will it. Xenophobia—fear and hatred of foreigners and foreign influence—found expression in the Boxer Rebellion of 1900. And the Ch'ing dynasty itself was overthrown in 1911 in part because an increasing number of Chinese doubted its ability to defend China from further incursions from the West.

But along with this hatred of the West, there ran a parallel desire to emulate it.

From the mid-nineteenth century onward, more and more Chinese came to the conclusion that the only way to create a China strong enough to withstand the new currents was to borrow the best elements from those currents—in short, to modernize the country.

This modernization went on in many fields in the last years of the empire, and one area where it had permanent success was in coinage. By 1900, China had a new coinage system, in which one thousand cash equaled one *yuan*, or dollar. In direct contradiction to twenty-five hundred years of tradition, the new coins were struck by machine, not cast. They lacked holes, and they all bore an actual figure rather than merely Chinese characters. The design selected was the flying dragon, symbol of the Chinese empire.

This Western-style coinage was not adopted all at once, however. The first machine-struck copper coins afford a perfect transition between old ways and new, between the deeply conservative nature of late nineteenth-century China and the crusading zeal of the reformers. For the first machine-struck cash were of a design identical to the old cast issues, with a square center-hole, four obverse characters, etc. The struggle between modernization and tradition, as seen in these coins, would typify China for the next half-century. Indeed, it endures in China to this day.

By the turn of the century, the long, native Chinese coinage experiment had come to an end, abandoned in favor of money based on the Western pattern. Many centuries before this, however, coinage inspired by the Chinese model had spread to other areas of the Far East, notably Japan and Korea. It was to have a long, flourishing career in both places, but there, too, the Oriental coinage experiment would eventually be set aside in favor of new ways from the West.

Japanese coinage only began in the

eighth century A.D., and it never went through the barter-coinage stage experienced by the Chinese. Instead, the first issues, dating from around 708, were cast, had square holes, and bore four characters. They are called *wa do kaiho*, and they show a very close resemblance to contemporary issues of the T'ang dynasty in China. In fact, the emperor brought Chinese workmen to Japan in 720 in order to improve the workmanship on these coins. Significantly, this first Japanese issue included a limited amount of silver coinage along with the regular bronze. This highlights one important distinction between Japanese and Chinese coins. The Japanese were more ready and able to experiment with precious metals than were the Chinese.

The Japanese government continued to cast bronze coinage for the next two and a half centuries. Later issues show a progressive deterioration in weight and execution. After 987, official coinage ceased entirely and would not be resumed for six hundred years. This lack of coinage reflected the political realities of that age: the period from the tenth to the sixteenth century was Japan's Middle Ages, during which there was an absence of any central government capable of making coins. Power was in the hands of local warlords. Trade and economic development declined. The parallels between this period of Japanese history and the Dark Ages in Western Europe are striking, and the effects on coinage were fairly similar in both places. As a result, Japan reverted to a barter system. The only coins found in circulation were a few well-worn issues of the previous period, local counterfeits of this coinage, and a sprinkling of bronze coins from China and Korea, which had found their way into Japan through trade.

Coinage was resumed in the late sixteenth century, particularly after the beginning of a long-lived military dictatorship by the Tokugawa clan (1599–1867). This era of Japanese history is known as the shogunate, and, while it represented a very conservative period in many ways, particularly in the matter of Japanese relations with the rest of the world, it was a time of great experimentation in coinage.

The military dictators issued gold in fairly large amounts, in a form unique to Japan. These gold pieces were struck—or at least stamped with official governmental seals—and the mint superintendent inscribed each piece with the value and his signature, in india ink. If the ink wore off in circulation, one could have a gold piece revalidated by the government upon payment of a set fee. These gold coins, resembling thin, oval plates, are known as *obans*. Smaller pieces, without a guarantee in ink, were also manufactured. They are called *kobans*, and along with the larger coins they were made down to the middle of the nineteenth century.

Japanese gold issues partook something of the nature of bullion during the shogunate, as can be seen by the fact that they had to be weighed, inscribed as to value, and signed. This bullion nature of Japanese gold coinage becomes even more obvious on silver issues of the shogun era. In effect, these issues are silver ingots, quite similar in concept to the Chinese sycee, except that they were official rather than private productions.

They occurred in a variety of shapes. One type, called the *chogin* (*gin* means silver in Japanese), was an oval block of silver two to three inches (5.1–7.6 cm) long. The obverse bore stamps guaranteeing its purity and telling the royal era during which it was issued. A second type was bean-shaped, with a representation of Diakokusama, God of Plenty, on the obverse, and, frequently, with a stamp indicating the date on the reverse. This type of silver coin is called *mame gin*, and it bears a certain resemblance to

63

Below. Europeans in China. Top l & r: Hong Kong, dollar, 1867;
center: Hong Kong, cash, 1863.
Bottom. Japan. L to r: wa do kaiho, 708–714; kengen taiho, 958–987.
Opposite. China. Clockwise from top l: cast ch'ien, 1875–1908;
machine-struck ch'ien, 1890; yuan or dollar, 1907.

**Below. Korea. Clockwise from top: 3 chon, 1882–1883;
5 fun, 1895; cash, 1097.
Opposite. Japan. Clockwise from top l: ichibu gin, 1837;
mame gin, 1829–1848; nami sen, 1769–1772;
tempo tsuho, 1830–1853; chogin, 1596–1614.**

some early Greek silver issues. Later silver coinage included the *ichibu gin*, again rectangular, from the end of the shogun period.

In contrast to gold and silver issues, Japanese bronze coinage remained remarkably static during these years. Through most of the shogunate, the basic bronze coin was the *nami sen*, produced from 1626 to 1863. It bore four characters on the obverse, a series of wavelike lines on the reverse. As with the contemporary Chinese coins that it closely resembled, it had a square center-hole and was cast.

This traditional coinage came to an abrupt end in the late 1860s, an indirect result of Western penetration. An American mission to Japan in 1853 did not immediately open up the country to occidental influences, but it did serve to convince many in Japan that the old military dictatorship was not

strong enough to prevent later, and perhaps more serious, incursions from the West. Modernization was in order, and an essential step in this process would be the ending of the shogunate and the restoration of imperial authority.

In 1867, the last shogun was overthrown and the first of a series of reforming emperors took his place. This was Meiji, and his long reign (1867–1912) saw the adoption of many Western ways, first in order to prevent Japan's becoming a colony of a Western power, later as an aid in acquiring colonies for Japan herself. Meiji brought in railroads, factories, occidental dress—and a modern, decimalized monetary system. One hundred *sen* would now equal one *yen*, at par with the American dollar. The first coins on the new standard were struck in 1870, using machinery imported from England. These coins resembled later Chinese issues, and they served notice that Japan had abandoned the Oriental coinage experiment and with it a good many other aspects of its cultural heritage.

Korea's coinage may be more briefly described. The peninsula was under Chinese control until the early fourth century A.D., and Chinese influence continued to be strong in succeeding years. Thus, it comes as no surprise that when the first Korean coinage was introduced shortly before 1100, it closely resembled contemporary Chinese issues of the Sung dynasty. Early coins had four obverse characters and a blank reverse, were made of copper or bronze, and were cast.

Chinese influence was replaced by Japanese in the seventeenth century, but this brought no radical alteration to the coinage. By the late eighteenth century, Korean coinage was being produced at a number of mints, which resulted in reverse characters to indicate the mint responsible and the date of issue. A limited amount of silver coinage, very similar to the bronzes, but without the center hole, was produced in the early 1880s under the emperor Tai (1864–1907).

Toward the end of his reign, Korea abandoned her centuries-long commitment to traditional coinage in favor of a machine-struck, Western-inspired one. Unlike the earlier reforms in Japan, changes in Korean coinage were not part of a general desire to borrow from the West in order to strengthen the country. Rather, they indicated that Korea had lost the opportunity of doing so as a free nation. By the time of the reform, Korea was being carved into spheres of influence by two countries more modern than herself, the Russian Empire and, surprisingly, Japan. Indicative of the general train of events was the fact that Korea's new decimal coins were struck by Russian or Japanese officials at the ostensibly national Korean mint, depending on whichever power dominated the country at the time. The Russo-Japanese War was fought in 1904–1905, in part to decide who would control Korea. Japan won, and the peninsula was incorporated into the Japanese Empire in 1910.

Those in the Western world are apt to see the Oriental coinage experiment as a curious but essentially dead-end affair, something of only secondary importance in the history of money as a whole. This viewpoint is inaccurate in one significant aspect. Any type of coinage that can satisfy the basic needs of one-third of the world's people for thousands of years is not unworthy of our consideration. On the contrary, it must be rated as something of the highest importance and, by its very conservatism and longevity, it can only be viewed as a distinctly successful experiment. For if Oriental coinage had not satisfied the needs of the people who used it, it would have been abandoned in favor of something else.

69

4

Preceding pages. Antoninus Pius, sestertius, 140–144 A.D.
Below. Rome. Top to bottom: didrachm, 269–266 B.C.;
aureus, 112–117 A.D.; as, 14–37 A.D.

Rome

If Chinese coinage faithfully mirrored the great conservatism and the strong sense of continuity of an Eastern people, the coinage of Rome reflected change—the enormous political, economic, and social upheavals of the late classical Western world. Roman coinage can give us a surprisingly accurate look at the ups and downs of an ancient state, if we know how to read it. The view it presents is unique: more than any other classical people, even more than most modern ones, the Romans stated who they were, what they believed, how they thought of themselves—all through the medium of coinage.

Rome's beginnings were humble. The Romans themselves, who were extremely fond of recalling important events and anniversaries, put the date of their city's foundation precisely at 21 April 753 B.C. Any date that exact has to be viewed with suspicion; historians now put the date of Rome's birth at shortly before 800 B.C. The city was founded at a convenient ford on the River Tiber, a small town growing up to supply the needs of the traders and travelers who crossed there. There was nothing mythological about Rome's foundation, although later Romans attempted to bring the gods into it.

Like other Italians of the period, the first Romans were divided into families and clans. This attachment to a local group, the members of which were related to each other, would be a permanent characteristic of the Romans and it found its way onto Roman coinage as well, where ancestors were sometimes depicted. A gold coin of Trajan, for example, honored his father.

Almost everthing about early Rome is shrouded in myth, subject to differing interpretations. Early Rome appears to have been a monarchy, the first rulers of which were natives. Later kings were imposed from outside by the adjacent Etruscans, a non-Latin people of much greater power and a

higher degree of civilization than the Romans. The last Etruscan king was ousted by a nationalistic rebellion around 500 B.C., and Rome became a republic.

Rule by kings, particularly Etruscan ones, had a great effect on Rome's future. The monarchical experiment had not been a happy one, and it imbued the Roman people with a long-lasting distrust for the forms and trappings of monarchy. It helps explain a peculiar characteristic of the early Roman Empire. While the emperor had absolute power as head of the state, he did not dare to say he did. No emperor ever took the hated title *rex* (king), and Rome in theory remained a republic for many years after it became an empire in fact.

From the beginning, the Roman Republic was an oligarchic state. By 500 B.C., there were two free classes in Rome: the patricians, descendants of the original founding families; and the plebeians or plebs—people of lesser importance—descendants of the retainers of the old patrician families as well as some of the later arrivals to Rome. Most of the political and social powers and privileges were reserved for the patrician class, and the inability or unwillingness of patricians to extend full equality to plebeians produced great political stress and played a large part in the downfall of the republic.

Rome's outward expansion helped delay the day of reckoning, however. Among the many factors in the growth of Roman dominion, two stand out. The first was land hunger. Most early Romans were farmers, and they were also members of the plebeian class. As the patricians occupied most of the nearby arable land (and of course had no intention of giving it up), these aristocratic leaders of the republic saw expansion into adjacent districts as a way of providing land for the poor without dividing up holdings of the rich. It would also bind the plebeian class more closely to the republic, which gave them the land.

A second factor was also at work. More than any other people, the Romans were imbued with the idea that they had a divine mission in life, which was to go out and Romanize (to them, "civilize") the non-Roman world. This missionary concept was more than a mere pious justification for taking other people's land. The Romans firmly believed it, and the idea, and the high heroism involved in carrying it out, were constant features of Roman life and thought from the very beginning to the very end. Roman coins sometimes reflect the concept: a copper coin with a Roman eagle seated atop a globe hints at Rome's concept of its mission and role in life.

Logically, early Rome expanded into adjacent territories in Italy. The republic paid back old scores by occupying Veii, a major Etruscan center, around 396 B.C. A long series of wars between Italians and Greeks ended in the 260s B.C. with the victorious Roman Republic now in control of the southern three-quarters of the Italian peninsula. Appropriately enough, the earliest Roman coins date from this period.

The republic's territorial expansion encouraged the adoption of coinage in two ways. First, Rome was becoming large enough to need a coinage of its own. Barter and the occasional use of Greek coinage was no longer sufficient to meet its economic needs. Second, as the Romans expanded south, they incorporated a people who had long experience in making and using coins—the Greeks of the southern Italian city-states.

Early Roman money assumed several forms. The first "coins" were merely cast lumps of bronze, which must have been treated as bullion. These lumps later acquired designs and finally metamorphosed into the so-called *aes grave*, or large round cast bronze coins of several denominations. They weighed roughly three-quarters of a Roman pound, that is, nine ounces, in this denomination (an *as*, the basic unit of the cast coinage). On the obverse they carried a crude head of Janus, a god of great importance in the Roman pantheon, and on the reverse a badly rendered ship's prow, perhaps a reference to Rome's growing role as a naval power.

This unwieldy bronze coinage is of native Italian inspiration. Greek influences are evident on the first Roman silver coins, a series of double drachms, or *didrachms*, struck—not cast—from around 290 to 220 B.C. Except for their designs, these coins can hardly be distinguished from contemporary Greek issues of the same denomination. This seems to have been the coinage with which Rome fought the first Punic War, which heralded the republic's coming of age in the Mediterranean world.

The First Punic War (264–241 B.C.) started as the result of a clash between two young, aggressive powers, Rome and Carthage. (The Romans referred to the Carthaginians as *Poeni*, Phoenicians, hence the modern name for Rome's wars with this city.) Carthage had begun as a trading entrepôt about the time of the foundation of Rome. By the third century B.C., she controlled much of North Africa and Sicily, and a collision between her and Rome was inevitable. The resulting war was something of a draw: while Carthage lost Sicily, that island now becoming Rome's first overseas province, she retained her position in North Africa. Preparing for the inevitable war of revenge, Carthage turned coastal Spain into a base for a second attack on Rome.

The attack duly arrived in 219 B.C. under Hannibal, perhaps the ablest enemy general that Rome ever had to face. The Second Punic War was underway, and it would go on for the next eighteen years. Hannibal crossed the Alps into Italy, raised some local tribes who were disgusted with Roman rule, and very nearly succeeded in capturing Rome itself. Hannibal was forced to leave Italy at last, not so much because he was overcome in battle but because Roman tactics of retreat and delay gradually wore his army down. Hannibal returned to Africa and was defeated at Zama in 202 B.C. Peace followed but at great expense to Carthage: Spain was lost, a huge war indemnity had to be paid, and Carthage's sovereignty was effectively restricted to the city itself.

The Roman didrachm had helped finance the First Punic War. A new coin, the *denarius*, helped pay for the second. Unlike the didrachm, the denarius would survive for several hundred years, becoming the most common coin issued under the Roman Republic, and a prominent feature of early and middle imperial coinage as well.

The denarius dates from shortly before 211 B.C. It was made of good quality silver, and it varied in size between an American dime and an American cent. It had a fixed value in relation to Rome's coinage in bronze, ten (and later sixteen) *asses* equaling one denarius.

Early denarii tended to be very conservative in style. Roma, patroness of the city, appeared on the obverse, along with an X to indicate the value (ten asses). The Dioscouri appeared on the reverse, along with the name of the city. (The Dioscouri are better know as Castor and Pollux, guardian deities of Rome.) Other reverse elements would be adopted as time went on, such as Jupiter, Luna, or, most commonly, Victoria, the personification of military success, driving a chariot. Here is an early example of Roman coinage being used for propaganda purposes.

Early Roman denarii are anonymous—that is, there is no way of determining which government official made them. By the early second century B.C., the low-ranking bureaucrats responsible for the coinage were beginning to put their initials or monograms on their work, and later still, their names. By about 130 B.C., the moneyers were making reference to distinguished ancestors (real or imagined), and a wide variety of specialized types became common on the denarius. The moneyer Sextus Pompeius Fostlus depicted the legend of Rome's beginnings on one of his coins: we see his putative ancestor, the farmer Faustulus, in the act of discovering the twins Romulus and Remus, who would found Rome. This type of coinage, which will be very common during the last century of the Roman Republic, tells us two things about ancient Romans. The first is that they have a strong sense of family, of clannishness in the literal sense of the word. It was this sense of belonging to an ongoing *gens*, or family, which produced the odd Roman funeral custom of exhibiting wax masks of the ancestors of the deceased. One's family or clan was very important to the average Roman, as were the rights associated with fatherhood, the position as head of the family. This familial preoccupation reaches its logical conclusion when the emperor declares himself *pater patriae*—father, or head, of the entire Roman clan—indicated by the letters PP on his coins.

Secondly, Republican denarii with reference to ancestors are early examples of the Roman penchant for self-advertising. These early moneyers were depicting scenes from their family history with a definite purpose in mind: they wanted to show the public how important, wise, or virtuous they themselves were. In a sense, this is already coinage for propaganda, and we shall have much more to say about it shortly.

There is a final item to note concerning the denarius of this period: it underwent several reductions in weight in the mid-

Opposite. Top l: Etruscans, gold, 5th century B.C.; top r: Brutii, silver stater, 282–203 B.C.; center: Rome, didrachms, 280–276 B.C.; bottom: Carthage, gold stater, 320–310 B.C.

Above. Rome. Top and bottom l: anonymous denarii, c. 211 B.C.; top r: denarius with mint master's signature, 150 B.C.; bottom r: denarius of S. Pompeius Fostlus, 137 B.C.

Left: Italy, Social War, denarius, 90 B.C.

dle of the second century. By about 125 B.C., it was stabilized at four grams (roughly one-seventh of an ounce), and it would retain this weight for the next two hundred years. The reduction of the weight of Roman silver coinage was paralleled by a similar reduction in the bronze. An as now weighed only one-twelfth as much as it originally had. Both of these developments reflected the beginnings of a problem that would become much worse in the later Roman world, that of inflation. As many peoples before and since, Romans were beginning to discover that it cost money to wage wars and to administer the territories they won.

And the wars continued. Rome literally erased Carthage from the map with the conclusion of the Third Punic War, in 146 B.C. By the same year, she had become mistress of Greece. By 100 B.C., the Romans were well on the way to becoming what we think of them as today, masters of the known world. By this time also, the Roman state was in deep trouble. The convulsions were underway which would eventually turn the republic into an empire, where supreme power rested in the hands of one man rather than in a representative body.

These changes were largely effected during the last century B.C. Early in that period, the Social War convulsed Italy, a struggle between Romans and their fellow Italian allies (*socii*). The latter desired the rights and privileges of Roman citizenship, and they made war for three years in pursuit of full equality. Their coins reveal their aspirations. A denarius from the beginning of the war shows a bull (Italy) trampling a she-wolf (Rome). The Italians made their point, and they were granted Roman citizenship. Unfortunately, the Social War brought two Roman leaders of opposing philosophies to the fore: Marius, who was an idol of the plebs; and Sulla, champion of the aristocratic Senate, the law-

making body of the Roman Republic. These two politician-soldiers threw Rome into a new period of unrest that lasted until 82 B.C. Sulla and the aristocrats defeated the Marian party, but the latter had the last word, as far as future Roman history was concerned. Shortly before 100 B.C., Marius, faced with a Germanic invasion of Italy, had introduced a proletarian volunteer army. This reform created a new facet of Roman life, one which would survive for centuries: a group of soldiers who served for their own benefit, and who were primarily loyal to their leader, looking to him for rewards.

The stage was set for the eclipse of the republic. Plebeian soldiers fought on both sides in the struggle between Marius and Sulla. Then, under the brilliant Pompey, who started his career as one of Sulla's lieutenants, they turned their attentions to fighting foreigners rather than fellow citizens. Pompey conquered much of the East, advancing the Roman frontier to the Euphrates. Returning to Rome in 61 B.C., he found much internal dissension between the patrician and plebeian factions, the latter led by a rising young aristocrat, Gaius Julius Caesar. Factionalism was settled for a time when Pompey and Caesar, along with one of the wealthiest men in Rome, Crassus, united to rule the republic. This was the famous First Triumvirate (from the Latin for rule by three men). Like most arrangements among strong, ambitious men, this one lasted only until one of them became more powerful than the others.

In this case, the man was Caesar. Reasoning that Pompey's power was based on his military reputation, Caesar decided to build a military name of his own. He conquered and pacified Gaul (roughly, modern France) by 51 B.C. In so doing, he had made himself into a legend. Caesar was probably the greatest military leader in all of Roman history.

1. Top: supporters of Pompey, denarius, 46–45 B.C.; bottom l: Julius Caesar, denarius, 49–48 B.C.; bottom r: Julius Caesar, aureus, 46 B.C.
2. Top: Julius Caesar, denarius, 44 B.C.; bottom l & r: Brutus, denarii, 43–42 B.C.
3. Top: Octavian, large bronze, c. 38 B.C.; bottom l: Sextus Pompey, denarius, 42–40 B.C.; bottom r: Antony, denarius, 32–31 B.C.

Naturally, the success of his colleague alarmed Pompey. A civil war between the two leaders and their armies broke out in the beginning of the year 49 B.C. and lasted for four years. A triumphant Caesar returned to Rome, undisputed master of the Mediterranean world. He did not live long to enjoy his triumph, however. Six months after his return, he was murdered.

Caesar was killed by a senatorial faction because, in a political climate of opinion that still considered Rome a republic, he was acting increasingly like a king. He had acquired limited dictatorial powers in the autumn of 49 B.C. This was not unheard of, since Rome's constitution provided for such an office in the event of a national emergency, for a short, strictly limited period of time. But he received this office again and again. By 46 B.C., he had been proclaimed dictator for ten years; early in 44 B.C., he was given the office for life. This was plainly against the forms of the republic, although absolute rule by one man was an increasingly common political reality by that time.

Caesar gathered other powers to himself as well. While he was a dictator with *imperium* (roughly, the power of life and death over individual citizens), he was also a consul (one of the two chief executives of the republic), and a tribune (the legal spokesman for the plebs). There is evidence that during the last few months of his life he was considering making himself king in name as well as in fact, and that he wished to be worshiped as a god by Romans, as he already was by some Greeks, Orientals, and barbarians. In his bid for absolute power, Caesar failed to take into account the ingrained prejudices of an important segment of the population, who detested kings in name, but not necessarily in fact. His reach for an institutionalized rule by one man failed. A final civil war erupted, and the ultimate beneficiary of it would be Cae-

sar's own nephew, Octavian. He would take advantage of his uncle's mistakes and, in so doing, would lead Rome in the transition from republic to empire, in that institutionalization of rule by one man which had eluded Caesar.

Octavian was nineteen when his uncle died. He naturally inherited many of Caesar's former supporters, and he did his best to keep the connection between himself and the departed popular leader alive in the public mind. Nevertheless, if he were to survive politically, it seemed expedient to ally himself with the outstanding leaders of Caesar's old party. This was achieved in 43 B.C., and the Second Triumvirate was born (Octavian, Antony, and Lepidus). A purge of the senatorial class responsible for Caesar's murder followed. After that, the arrangement quickly degenerated into a contest for power between Antony and Octavian, decided in the latter's favor by the Battle of Actium in 31 B.C. Like his uncle a generation before, Octavian was now master of the Roman world. Historians date the beginning of the Roman Empire from this year.

Roman coins faithfully mirror the political events of the last century of the republic. We have already mentioned Italian coinage of the Social War. The great effort made by Rome to put down the rebellion is indicated by the large number of coins produced to pay for it. Some Roman coins of the period bear the head of Salus, a guardian spirit believed capable of preserving the state, an appropriate motif for the times.

The ensuing civil war between Marius and Sulla is not directly reflected in the coinage, although there are several issues from Asia Minor and Greece either bearing Sulla's name or his figure in a quadriga. Athens has been suggested as the mint-site for some of these coins, and they date from the late eighties. The inclusion of a dictator's name and a representation of his figure first appear in a Roman province rather than in Rome itself. It will be several decades more before this becomes a feature of coinage made in Rome.

During the seventies and sixties, there is little reference to contemporary events on Roman coinage. Moneyers are again selecting types from their family pasts. There is, however, a tendency towards celebrating recent ancestors rather than more remote ones, which paves the way for honoring living men and events later on.

Coins are becoming more faithful witnesses to the times than before, as we move into the period of the First Triumvirate. A rare *aureus* (the basic Roman gold coin, introduced some years earlier, equal to twenty-five silver denarii) from 61 B.C. depicts Pompey celebrating his military successes. Three years later, Caesar invaded Gaul, and this resulted in a number of military issues struck by a traveling mint which accompanied him on his campaigns. There is a good deal of self-advertising on these coins: an elephant, representing Caesar, tramples a dragon, symbolizing Gaul; Venus, the legendary source of Caesar's family, is depicted on silver and gold coins; and Caesar's role as Pontifex Maximus, chief priest of the Roman state religion, is also mentioned.

As the Roman world slid into another civil war, the coins began to reflect contemporary events with still greater immediacy, greater accuracy. Pompey's forces struck money in Rome and elsewhere between 49 and 45 B.C. The coins allude to Pompey's military victories, and after his death in battle in 46 B.C., his portrait appears on denarii struck by his diehard adherents in Spain.

Caesar and his supporters struck coins of their own. One of the most interesting dates from 48 B.C. and shows the head of the Gallic leader Vercingetorix, who was defeated by Caesar at the end of the Gallic Wars. The titles of Caesar's offices also appear on the coinage. An aureus from 46 B.C. reminds us that he is consul for the third time (seen abbreviated to COS TER in the inscription). But he now took a step that no living Roman had ever taken before, one that lent credence to the idea that he wished to be a king: he put his own portrait on the coinage. Caesar was shortly assassinated, as we have noted. It was perhaps fitting that one of his assassins, Brutus, placed *his* portrait on the obverse of a famous denarius, and on the reverse a liberty cap flanked by two daggers, and the inscription EID MAR (The Ides of March)—all references to Caesar's assassination and Brutus' role in it. The fact that a man struck down a ruler who wished to be king, and then celebrated his attack with a coin bearing his own portrait, is interesting. Romans had always regarded living portraiture on coinage as an Eastern, monarchical practice; Brutus' use of his own portrait may have been an indication that the republic was moving towards a monarchy, no matter who the eventual ruler turned out to be.

All factions in the civil war following Caesar's death made their mark on coinage. As we have just seen, Brutus, a leader of the senatorial party, minted coins. So did Sextus Pompey, son of Caesar's old enemy and inheritor of much of his support. The younger Pompey's coinage shows either his father or himself. By now, self-portraiture was becoming general. The Second Triumvirate issued coins of their own, on which the heads of the three leaders appeared prominently. When Antony and Octavian began their struggle for sole mastery, each struck coins to pay for it. One of Antony's most common issues celebrated the Roman legions and fleet who fought in his support. Those of Octavian commonly bore his portrait, along with the inscription DIVI IVLI F on several early issues. Translated, this means "the son of the deified Julius," and it refers both to Octavian's adoption by Caesar as son and heir and to Caesar's deification. By this and other references to his late uncle, Octavian sought to curry favor with the old Caesarean party. He was successful, partly due to his own shrewdness, partly due to the ineptitude of his adversary, Mark Antony.

By 31 B.C., Octavian was in sole command of the Roman state, and he would remain in power for the next forty-five years. But he accomplished all this in a curious fashion. While he or his friends held all power, the old republican offices were all retained. They were now safely under the control of one man, himself. He made no moves to have himself declared king, mindful of Caesar's fate. The only official indication of his new power came in 27 B.C., when the by-now-servile Senate voted him the title of Augustus (august, or magnificent one). This is how he is henceforth known to history, and it is this title which appears on most of his coins.

Let us examine one of these coins, a copper as, for it will tell us much about the appearance and reality of the new Roman state. Copper and bronze coinage had been scarce or absent during the middle years of the republic; they become common again during Augustus' reign. On one side the coin in question bears Augustus' head and on the other a long inscription surrounding the letters SC. It is the inscriptions which chiefly concern us here. The obverse legend informs us that this is a coin of Augustus, a member of the Caesar gens. PONT MAX reminds us that he is chief priest of the state cult; TRI-BVNIC POT, that he has the power of a tribune, to act as guardian of the Roman plebs.

The circular reverse inscription is given over to the name of the moneyers; this was a holdover from republican days, and it

was later dropped. The large SC stands for *Senatus Consulto*, by decree of the Senate. That is, Augustus gave the Senate power over the minting of base-metal coinage. He retained control over silver and gold, and, in practice, also had the final word about the designs used on the copper and bronze.

But at first glance, there is no sharp break between this type of imperial coinage and earlier issues of the republic. The use of a portrait was no longer controversial. The Senate, at least in theory, controlled the coinage, and here were the names of its moneyers. So the form was still there. It is only when we remember that Augustus in fact controlled the offices listed on the coin—and the Senate itself—that we begin to see that Rome was no longer a republic, but a monarchy.

But there is something more. Recall Octavian's earlier coin with the inscription DIVI IVLI F. Consider this one, with its references to the Caesar name. Augustus was wrestling with a dilemma that plagued him and his successors for centuries. The problem was a simple one: granting that Rome had become a monarchy again, granting also that no ruler would dare call himself king, how could he make it clear that he had a legitimate right to rule—indeed, that he should be the ruler, rather than someone else? Augustus attempted to solve the problem by references to himself as the legitimate heir of the great Caesar. A denarius from around 18 B.C. affords another example of Augustus' efforts to connect himself with the deified Caesar in the public mind. Augustus appears on the obverse, on the reverse is a spectacular comet which the state said was Julius Caesar himself.

Augustus ruled until 14 A.D. His immediate successor, Tiberius, had been adopted late in the reign, and Tiberius naturally attempted to stress his own right to rule by issuing a large series of coins, part of

whose inscriptions ran TI CAESAR DIVI AVG F (Tiberius Caesar, son of the deified Augustus). Tiberius had the Senate declare Augustus a god, just as Augustus had been instrumental in deifying Julius Caesar years before. Later emperors followed suit; it imparted stronger legitimacy to one's rule if the inhabitants knew that the man who had adopted you as his successor had been declared a god by the Senate, still theoretically the voice of the Roman people. Parenthetically, as an extra reminder that his "father" was now officially divine, Tiberius struck a series of coins with Augustus' portrait and the inscription DIVVS AVGVSTVS (the divine Augustus) on the obverse and an altar on the reverse. Later rulers often followed this practice, too.

The desire to impress the people with the legitimacy of a ruler leads to a central attribute of Roman imperial coinage. Certainly more than any of its predecessors, probably more than any of those who succeeded it, the Roman imperial state used coinage as a propaganda medium. For it was not only necessary to tell people that an emperor had the right to rule, but also to tell them exactly what he was doing by way of backing up his claim. If one could convince the population that a certain man was doing an excellent job running the state, they might not be inclined to question whether or not he had an inherent right to the office, and whether or not he was a dictator.

Coins were ideal vehicles for official propaganda. Since they had value, people would tend to retain them and would attempt to get more. They could carry messages far and wide, and did, in fact, for the empire formed one vast Common Market. Coins were durable; the message would last, being read and reread. Coins were mass-produced. Indeed, they were one of the few items in ancient times that *could* be turned out in large quantities, for they were fairly simple to manufacture. Best of all, in using coins as bits of propaganda, the ruler had a captive audience—the inhabitants of the Roman Empire, a hundred million of them at one point, who had to use something for daily transactions. Since the state had a monopoly on coining money, they would have to use its product.

So coins could be used to inculcate loyalty to a ruler, either by references to his glorious antecedents, or to what he was doing to earn his keep, or both. Coins could also stress the glories of Rome, of being a Roman; they could state Rome's great civilizing mission—in brief, they could be used to say things dear to the average Roman. We must remember this fact about Roman imperial coinage: the ideas it expressed were not entirely self-serving, and many people took them very seriously.

The imperial choice of subject matter for coin propaganda depended on the predilections of the individual emperor. As we have seen, Augustus' coinage stressed the continuity of the political form of things. That of Tiberius (14–37 A.D.) recalled his close connections to the now-deified Augustus, both by means of inscriptions and by frequent use of Augustus' portrait as a main type. Tiberius' mother, Livia, is also thought to have been represented on both the silver and the bronze. Since Livia had been instrumental in securing the throne for her son, her inclusion on Tiberius' coinage may have been an oblique reference to her role.

Tiberius was followed by Gaius, commonly known as Caligula (37–41 A.D.). Fancying himself a brilliant military leader, Caligula projected an invasion of Britain, then lost his nerve at the crucial moment. The invasion never took place, but we do have pieces with the emperor addressing his troops, just as if he *had* led them into battle.

Caligula was quite mad, and he was eventually assassinated by members of the

crack Praetorian Guard, who chose his elderly uncle, Claudius, to succeed him, then cowed the Senate into accepting their choice. They were duly rewarded by the new emperor. An important precedent had been established for the future: the military was once more a political factor to be reckoned with.

Claudius ruled from 41 to 54 A.D. A recurring type on his copper coinage is a standing figure of Liberty. This may refer to the new emperor's restoration of personal freedoms after the reign of terror which distinguished the last part of Caligula's rule. It might also be a veiled indication of something which several ancient historians say Claudius wished to do: to restore the republic. This interpretation is unlikely, and whatever his ultimate desire, his coinage types are similar to those of other first-century emperors. Rome invaded Britain in 43, and Claudius actually made a visit to the war zone (after it was safe to do so). His conquest of Britain is immortalized in an aureus, with his head and titles on the obverse, a triumphal arch with the inscription DE BRITANN on the reverse. Claudius frequently honored members of his family, a practice which would be common through later imperial coinage. By this time also, rulers were not only celebrating their accomplishments, but their virtues. This was achieved by depicting allegorical figures on the reverse, with accompanying inscriptions to indicate that this was a virtue of the ruler. Claudius' use of Libertas was an early instance of such a practice. Other virtues portrayed would include Providentia (clear-sighted imperial planning), Aequitas (Justice), and many more as time went on.

These attributes were emphasized by fairly good rulers, such as Claudius, as well as by those with nothing in particular to say, such as his successor, Nero (54–68). In addition to stressing his virtues, Nero was fond of praising his accomplishments as a builder. A large bronze *sestertius* (a quarter of a silver denarius) shows the harbor of Ostia, which Nero completed. Since Ostia was the entrepôt for the grain supply which fed Rome, Nero's building activities here were of prime importance to the average citizen. So was the *macellum*, the public market he built, shown on a *dupondius* (half a sestertius). Nero was also a devotee of the arts, and, on an as from around 65, he portrayed himself as Apollo, patron of the arts, playing a lyre.

The public's image of this ruler was on a somewhat lower plane than his image of himself. By 68, he had become a deranged megalomaniac, and a military revolt induced the emperor to commit suicide. Nero was the last of the Julio-Claudian line, descendants of Julius Caesar. Two important facts were emphasized by Nero's death and the ensuing civil war, which lasted for a year and a half. The first is that there still was no universally recognized and acknowledged method of imperial succession. The emperor was *not* a king, however often his face appeared on coinage. He could be replaced by a new ruler completely unrelated by blood. The second fact is that the military now saw itself as a determining factor in the selection of an emperor. All the claimants in the civil war following Nero's death were soldiers, whose troops felt that their leader alone should wear the purple of a Roman emperor. The fact that these troops would be richly rewarded by their chief if they were successful was a primary consideration governing their actions, of course.

None of this touched the daily life of the average Roman, however. Despite periodic civil wars and border skirmishes, this was the period of the Pax Romana, two centuries of almost uninterrupted peace, lasting from the accession of Augustus into the late

Opposite, above. Top row, l to r: Trajan, denarius, 103–111 A.D.; Trajan, denarius, 112–117 A.D.; center, l to r: denarii of Nerva (98 A.D.), Trajan (112–117 A.D.), Hadrian (118 A.D.); bottom row, l to r:

denarii of Antoninus Pius (143–144 A.D.), Marcus Aurelius (166–167 A.D.), Commodus (183 A.D.). Opposite, below. L & bottom: Hadrian, sestertii, 119–138 A.D.; r: Antoninus Pius, sestertius, 159–160 A.D.

second century A.D.

Emperors came and went. Vespasian, the ultimate victor in the civil war of 68–69, ruled for ten years. Roman portraiture reached a high point during this period and throughout the last third of the first century. A war against the Jews, from which Vespasian had been called to wear the purple, ended in triumph in 70, and a famous series of coins commemorates the victory: a weeping Jewish woman sits beneath a palm, with a captive Jew in the background and the legend, IVDAEA CAPTA (Judea captured). Vespasian and his sons ruled until 96. Two years later, the energetic Trajan became emperor. Trajan's active nineteen-year reign saw Roman military triumphs abroad (the empire now reached its greatest size, the emperor leading his armies into Central Europe and the East), and building programs at home, both of which are commemorated on his coinage. Victories in Central Europe are celebrated on a coin with a bound figure seated on a shield; a later coin shows Trajan's Column, which endures to this day.

Trajan was one of several so-called adoptive emperors. As a way of providing for an orderly succession, the ruler would now adopt a colleague, an heir of excellence and widespread popularity. Hopefully, if the heir was of sufficient prestige and the ruler who chose him was loved and respected by the people, the transferral of power would be peaceful. The system worked well enough under Nerva (96–98), Trajan (98–117), Hadrian (117–138), and Antoninus Pius (138–161). It broke down after the death of Antoninus' successor, Marcus Aurelius (161–180), for the latter chose his worthless son, Commodus, to succeed him. Commodus was murdered in 192, and a period of anarchy, lasting on and off for a century, set in. As it did so, Rome entered a period of decline, one from which she never recovered.

All this lay in the future, however. Neither Hadrian nor Antoninus was much involved in war, and their coins depicted them as virtuous rulers, engaged in peaceful pursuits. From Hadrian's reign came a series of coins showing the emperor and a representative of a province greeting each other, as well as personifications of provinces themselves. These coins are a reminder that Hadrian traveled more than any other Roman head of state, visiting and inspecting virtually every important area of his sprawling domain. Antoninus' coins are more likely to depict an abstract attribute of the emperor, such as his sense of justice (IVSTITIA) or his piety (PIETAS). Antoninus also placed members of his family on the coins, especially his deceased wife, Faustina the Elder, held up to the world as a paragon of matronly virtue (which apparently she was not), and his heir, the future emperor Marcus Aurelius. As one can see, coinage was being used to advertise and popularize the imperial heir-apparent. A rare issue of sestertii depicting Britannia dates from 143–144, witness of a military campaign on that island. It is about the only warlike reference to appear on the coinage of Antoninus.

Unfortunately, the same cannot be said for the issues of his successor, Marcus Aurelius. Designs referring to military campaigns and victories abound on Marcus' coinage, and with good reason: the reign of this most peace-loving and philosophical of Roman emperors was filled with barbarian incursions and attacks from Rome's hereditary enemy, Parthia.

As the coins tell us, Rome won the Parthian war, which lasted from 161 to 166. But returning Roman soldiers brought with them a mysterious Eastern plague, perhaps malaria, which decimated the population of several provinces at a time when the empire could ill afford it. The wars with the northern barbarians (the Marcomanni, Quadi, and

other Germanic tribes) were more of a draw. Roman coins with military trophies piled high obscured the reality; the fact that Marcus died in 180 in a military camp preparing for a new campaign against the Germans is a more faithful indication of the truth. These barbarian attacks never ceased entirely during the remainder of the empire, and they were a prime factor in its demise.

Military problems abroad were paralleled, even dwarfed, by problems at home. Commodus was murdered in 192. Insane, he had increasingly identified himself with the god Hercules. Coins from the last years of his reign sometimes portray him as the god himself, complete with lion-skin headdress and a club, both attributes of Hercules.

Commodus' assassination plunged the empire into a civil war similar to that following the death of Nero. This one lasted for five years, however, and it reached a low point of sorts when the Praetorian Guard auctioned off the throne to the highest bidder. The wealthy recipient, Didius Julianus, lasted for three months.

By 197, the Roman world had been reunited under the control of one man, Septimius Severus (193–211), the founder of a new dynasty, the Severan. Septimius' coins reflect his prowess as a military commander, for this ruler warred successfully against the Parthians and barbaric tribes in Britain, who had taken advantage of the Roman civil war in order to raid Roman territory. On an early issue of coins of the type depicted, Septimius pays tribute to the Roman legions, the guardians of empire and, incidentally, instrumental in his own rise to power.

The Severan dynasty lasted to 235. The coins of its rulers reflect individual tastes and historic events. Caracalla, Septimius' surviving son (212–217), conducted campaigns in Germany and his coins mention that fact in the letters GERM (short for Germanicus) on obverse inscriptions. His eventual successor, Alexander Severus (222–235), struck coins with references to military activities against the Parthians and later the Germans. Some of his coins also depict the Eastern sun god, which under the official patronage of this more Eastern than Roman dynasty had come into prominence.

The coinage of the Severan dynasty is of great historic importance, not because of what it says about political events of the day, but rather because of what it tells us about economic ones. As in earlier centuries, inflation was again becoming a problem for the Roman state. But this time it would never be fully resolved.

Rome's basic silver coin had been the denarius. For the first three centuries of its existence, it had remained remarkably stable, made of good quality silver. As time wore on, however, it encountered greater and greater stresses, as Rome found itself with an empire to rule and defend, a large, indigent population to feed, and an ambitious public building program to fulfill. Inevitably, the denarius was debased, beginning with the reign of Nero. Debasement continued for the next century and a half. By 215, what had started out as virtually a pure silver coin now contained about fifty percent alloy.

In that year, Caracalla introduced a new "silver" coin, naming it after himself, the *antoninianus* (Antoninianus was his given name; Caracalla was originally a nickname). An antoninianus was theoretically worth two denarii, though it was actually only fifty percent heavier than the standard denarius. It was struck in forty percent silver at this time. Its silver percentage would drop radically over the next fifty-odd years, and by 270 it would contain less than three percent of the precious metal. By then, they were striking antoniniani from copper and then silver-plating them.

What had happened? A series of interrelated events came into play which brought Rome to the lowest point in its history up to that time. These events were both internal and external. Alexander Severus' death in 235 initiated a period of wild military anarchy, in which there were more than twenty "official" emperors, only one of whom died of natural causes. This was not counting a host of usurpers, pure and simple. The armies now held full sway over who should or should not rule Rome. The peoples surrounding the empire took advantage of its distress. The Sassanids, successors of the Parthians, invaded Syria and Asia Minor several times, capturing and killing a Roman emperor (Valerian 253–259) in the process. New barbarian peoples, such as the Goths, and older ones, including the Franks and Alamanni, overran the northern frontiers. Disgusted with the turn of events, Britain and part of Gaul withdrew from the empire itself. They established a state of their own, which ruled these areas from 259 to 274. A final factor in the problems of the third-century Roman state was a decline in its population. Scholars do not agree as to the reasons for the drop in the Roman birth rate, but it does seem to have been a historic fact. This meant that there were fewer people to till the land, weave cloth—and that there were fewer taxpayers, who, after all, were the ones who had to shoulder the rising expenses of domestic and foreign wars.

Faced with these dilemmas, the emperors of Rome increased taxes in an attempt to bridge the widening gap between income and expenses. And when that proved insufficient to pay the bills, they turned to coinage. The group of three antoniniani pictured on page 94 date from around 215, 255, and 270, respectively, and they graphically illustrate the downward slide in the silver content of the antoninianus. Something similar occur-

red with bronze and copper coinage, which became lighter and lighter as time went on. Smaller denominations disappeared entirely and larger ones were much smaller than they had been in the days of Augustus and were issued only sporadically. The decline of these coins bears witness to the declining fortunes of Rome itself.

What else can coins from the period of military anarchy (235–284) tell us? First, that Roman art was also in a state of decline. Portraiture is crude in comparison to that found on earlier issues. Reverse figures become almost barbaric—as on a coin of Gallienus (259–268), which honors a Roman legion, the source of his power. The coins of Britain and Gaul are interesting exceptions to this rule. The emperors of this so-called Gallic Empire took great pains to achieve artistry on their coinage, as witnessed by the excellent portrait on an issue of Postumus (259–267). That Roman coinage elsewhere should have been so unattractive may have been due in part to the fact that the coins were hastily executed. The tenure of office of a Roman emperor in those days was not a long one—indeed, Marius, a Gallic usurper of 268, is reputed to have ruled for a grand total of three days! But he still struck coins, as did most other aspirants to the throne. Remember that coins were one of the few available means of informing subjects that a ruler existed; if a would-be emperor minted coins—even if they were only useful for paying his own troops—they would lend added authenticity and legitimacy to his cause.

Roman coins of the period were becoming less faithful witnesses of contemporary events than they had been, in terms of their designs. Gods, goddesses, and personifications of one sort or another assumed an increasingly important place on Roman coin reverses. There are numerous exceptions, of course. Philip I celebrated Rome's thou-

Opposite. Top, l to r: Marcus Aurelius, sestertius, 172–173 A.D.;
Commodus, as, 191–192 A.D.; center: Septimius Severus, sestertius,
193 A.D.; Alexander Severus, denarius, 231 A.D.; Caracalla, sestertius,
215 A.D.; bottom, l to r: Caracalla, denarius, 215 A.D.;
Caracalla, antoninianus, 215 A.D.
Below. Top, l to r: Trajan Decius, antoninianus, 249–251 A.D.; Philip
I, sestertius, 248 A.D.; center, l to r: Claudius II, antoninianus,
268–270 A.D.; Aurelian, antoninianus, 270–275 A.D.; Probus,
antoninianus, 276–282 A.D.; bottom l & center: Diocletian, folles,
c. 298–299 A.D.; bottom r: Maximian, follis, c. 298–299 A.D.

Opposite, above. Inflation in ancient Rome. Top row, l to r: antoniniani of c. 215, 255, and 270 A.D., respectively; bottom, l to r: Augustus, as, 7 B.C.; Gallienus, as, 253 A.D. Opposite, below.

L: Valerian, antoninianus, c. 255 A.D.; center: Postumus, antoninianus, 259–268 A.D.; top r: Gallienus, antoninianus, 253–268 A.D. (honoring a Roman legion); bottom r: Marius, antoninianus, 267 A.D.

sandth anniversary in 248 with a large issue of coins in several metals. His head and titles appear on the obverse, a variety of animals, those prominent in the games held to mark the great date, on the reverse. The next ruler, Trajan Decius (249–251), emphasized his Illyrian background (Illyria today is Yugoslavia) with a type honoring the Illyrian portion of the Roman army. The fact remains that, after centuries of coinage with a wide range of propaganda types, Roman issues began to become more standardized in the third century, a trait that was intensified in the fourth.

Late in the 260s, Rome's fortunes took a temporary turn for the better. The first in a line of extremely energetic soldiers from Illyria, Claudius II, took and held power long enough to drive the barbarians back, to repair some of the worst damage inflicted on the empire. Claudius received the surname Gothicus from a grateful Senate for his victory over that tribe in 268. Claudius' reign was brief (268–270), but his successors carried on in the same vein. Aurelian (270–274) gave up Dacia, on the northern fringe of the empire, in 270. He recovered Rome's fortunes in the East, however, and the empire would be little troubled by that area for several decades. The Gallic Empire was reincorporated into the Roman state the year of Aurelian's death. Probus (276–282) carried on his work. The coinage of this period sometimes reflects the flow of events. It is better executed than before, and in its frequent reverse type of Sol Invictus (the Invincible Sun God), we have a reference to a popular soldiers' religious cult, imported from the East.

The greatest of these reforming soldier-emperors was Diocletian, who in his desire to stabilize the Roman world introduced another Eastern influence, that of the absolute, divine monarch. Diocletian reasoned that only an Oriental-style, divine emperor could gain and hold the respect of the people and the army. This monarch would be supported by an expanded bureaucracy and army personally loyal to the ruler. The ruler himself would have all the trappings of an Eastern despot—a diadem, royal robes, etc. His person would be divine, accessible only to the favored few, remote from the masses.

While Diocletian saw himself as an Oriental potentate, he was also a practical man of affairs. He felt that the empire was too large, its demands too great, to be met by a single man. So he divided it in two, himself taking the East, assigning the West to a colleague, Maximian, in 285. Each of these *Augusti* would have a junior partner, called a *Caesar*, to be in charge of a part of his particular piece of the empire. Thus, there would be four Roman emperors, which should mean that one would be in close proximity to any foreign invasion or domestic dispute. After a period of twenty years, the two senior emperors would step down and the two junior partners would succeed, choosing Caesars of their own as they did so. Diocletian's political reforms were an ingenious attempt to deal with Imperial defense and the succession problem all at once. They were not particularly successful, but overall his reforms helped add another century to the life of the Roman Empire.

Diocletian attempted to reform many aspects of Roman life during his twenty-one-year tenure (284–305), including the coinage. In 295–296, he established a new coinage system, based on an aureus, struck at sixty to the Roman pound, and a silver coin marked XCVI, to indicate that its weight was one ninety-sixth of a Roman pound. These were supplemented by a large coin of silvered bronze, called a *follis*. Portraiture and reverse types were fairly static throughout the life of this reformed coinage. This may have been an attempt to convey the impression of stability

3   4

5

1. **Constantine I.** L & center: solidi, 335 A.D.; r: follis, 307–310 A.D.
2. L: **Constantine II**, follis, 320 A.D.; r: **Constantius II**, folles, c. 348–350 A.D. 3. **Julian II**, large bronzes, 361–363 A.D.
4. **Magnentius**, large bronze, 353 A.D.
5. **Valentinian I**, solidus, 364–375 A.D.

of the Roman ruler and his state. Portraiture was also deliberately remote, aloof from the concerns of the common citizen. A favorite reverse type was a standing figure with the inscription GENIO POPULI ROMANI (Guardian Spirit of the Roman People).

Diocletian's coinage reforms did not all survive his resignation in 305. The follis decreased in weight as time went on, and the reformed aureus was shortly replaced by a new, slightly lighter gold coin, called a *solidus*. Inflation continued to be a problem in the late Roman world, as evidenced by the failure of Diocletian's attempt to freeze prices in 301.

His political reforms were not entirely successful either. Having four emperors, each with his own court, bureacracy, and army, meant a tremendous increase in the already considerable burdens imposed on the taxpayer. And in any case, the four-emperor system (called the Tetrarchy by Roman historians) failed the first time it was put to the test. Diocletian and Maximian obediently stepped down at the end of their twenty-year terms, in 305. The empire was almost immediately engulfed in a civil war, in which there were no fewer than five claimants in the field. By 312, one of them had emerged to dominate the West, Constantine the Great (306–337). In 324, he defeated his last rival in the East, and the Roman world was reunited for the time being.

Constantine carried Diocletian's reforms to their logical conclusions. Wishing to secure a tax base adequate to the expanded needs of the empire, Constantine froze people —and their descendants—in their occupations. Thus, since the empire needed a certain number of shoes each year, those who were shoemakers would remain shoemakers, and so would their sons. Small farmers were now bound to the land. Many of them had already lost their holdings and were working on the lands of others, where they had to remain. In these events we can see the beginnings of one of the most widespread of medieval institutions, serfdom. Indeed, there was much in Constantine's Roman Empire that more properly belongs to the Age of Faith than to the Age of Rome.

One such element was Christianity. Long a persecuted Eastern-based sect, Christianity acquired new respectability when Constantine himself embraced it in 312 (he was not baptized until shortly before his death, however, because during his reign he needed the goodwill of pagans and Christians alike).

Christianity gave the emperor an important boost upward in his ascent to more-than-human status. It was helpful for an emperor to be protected by specific gods in the Roman pantheon, but it was much more advantageous to be the favorite of the sole God of the entire universe. Constantine and his successors found that they could use the Church to give their regimes an extra aura of legitimacy, and the Church found that official favor had advantages of its own. A pact for mutual benefit was reached, and Christianity, which preached love and obedience to established authority as one of its tenets (see Romans, Chapter 13) became an integral part of the machinery of the Roman state.

All of this found its way into the coinage. Constantine's coins continued to use pagan motifs: Sol Invictus is a frequent type, as are depictions of Victory and defeated barbarians. Christian imagery makes its appearance shortly after Constantine's death, however, and its usage becomes increasingly frequent as time goes on. Constantius II (337–361) employed a Christian banner accompanied by two captives on some of his coins, a most unusual juxtaposition of types. He is better known for his FEL TEMP RE-

1

PARATIO reverses, featuring a Roman warrior spearing a fallen horseman. This design, intended to indicate that prosperity and good fortune had returned to Rome, became such a popular motif that later the barbarians themselves adopted it.

The use of Christian motifs increased as time passed. One of its most striking applications on coinage occurred during the reign of the usurper Magnentius, who in 350 overthrew Constantine's son, Constans, and ruled over parts of the Roman West for the next three years. In the last year or so of his reign, Magnentius introduced a large bronze coin with a purely Christian design: a Chi-Rho (cross), or *Chrismon*, the monogram of Christ, flanked by the Greek letters Alpha and Omega (the Beginning and the End), two of Christ's attributes in the Book of Revelation. In passing, one might note that a common pagan practice, that of putting a god's attributes on money, had been extended into Christian coinage. Magnentius was defeated and killed in 353, but the use of Christian symbology on Roman coinage would live on.

Constantine the Great had attempted to set up a ruling dynasty made up of members of his own family. The last representative of that line was Julian, who was acclaimed emperor by his troops in 360 and whose position was solidified by the death of his uncle, Constantius II, the following year.

Disgusted with the sectarian wrangling of the early Christian Church, Julian at-

2

3

tempted to revive the old pagan Roman religion. Christian historians dubbed him Julian the Apostate for his pains, and he is supposed to have been struck and killed by a lightning bolt hurled by an enraged Almighty in 363. (Actually, he seems to have died from wounds suffered during a war with the Persians and anyway one suspects that Christians were attributing Jupiter's punitive practice to Jehovah.) Julian's attempts to restore old religious ways were singularly unsuccessful. His coinage makes little reference to this policy, except insofar as Christian symbols are lacking. A large bronze coin with a bull design on the reverse may have been intended to pay homage to Apis, an Egyptian deity. In any event, most of Julian's coinage extolled the virtues of the Roman Army, the eternity of the Roman state, the glories of the Roman people—the sorts of things that had been mentioned by his immediate predecessors and would be celebrated by those who followed him. These are the kinds of messages one might expect from a declining state, aware of its condition and attempting to hide the fact from its subjects.

Julian's successors reintroduced Christian symbology on their coins. The use of the Chi-Rho quite often was combined with another major design. A solidus of Valentinian I (364–375) had a reverse type featuring a standing soldier, perhaps the emperor himself, receiving a wreath from a smaller figure. Originally, the latter would have represented Victory; now it was beginning to turn into a Christian angel. The large figure held a standard with a Chi-Rho on its banner, and the entire design was surrounded by the inscription RESTITVTOR REIPVBLICAE, referring to the reconstruction of the Roman state.

By now, the number of types and legends employed was becoming fairly limited. A silver coin, the *siliqua,* had made its appearance toward the end of Constantius' reign. A fair number have survived, because they were buried during the increasing unrest and the unsettled climate which was characteristic of the late fourth century. The designs on siliquae and bronzes are quite limited in scope. Virtually all of them celebrate Rome itself, the amity among the rulers of various parts of the empire (Diocletian's institution of rule by more than one man continued through most of the fourth century), and the political health or security of the Roman state. Types on the gold issues are somewhat more varied; strong Christian influence is shown on a solidus of Valentinian II (376–392), which portrays two seated emperors over which a winged figure hovers. The figure is intended to represent Victoria, or Victory, but by this time she is definitely a Christian angel.

Late in the fourth century, the barbarian tribes on the fringes of the empire again resumed their attacks. In 378, the Visigoths killed the emperor Valens and destroyed his army at Adrianople, today a city in Turkey, and then ravaged the countryside. This brought to prominence the last great Roman emperor and the last man to rule over an undivided empire, the Spaniard Theodosius.

In his sixteen-year reign (379–395), this ruler succeeded in subduing the Goths, settling them on waste lands south of the Danube as *foederati* (official allies of Rome, with an obligation to fight on Rome's behalf). By this time, the Roman army was more barbarian than Roman anyway, and Theodosius' policies with the barbarians were nothing new, although they did ignore the question of where the loyalty of these barbarians would ultimately lie. In addition to his temporary victory over the threat of invasion, Theodosius gradually eliminated those persons standing between himself and sole rule of the empire. The last claimant, the pagan Eugenius, was defeated in 394. Theodosius' reign was marked by a series of decrees dating from around 390, making Christianity the sole legal religion of the Roman state. Theodosius ruled alone for the brief remainder of his life. He was the last Roman emperor to do so; on his death, he unwisely divided Roman domains between his two young sons, Honorius (395–423) and Arcadius (395–408). The split was permanent, creating a Western Roman Empire, whose capital was Ravenna (Rome had ceased to be the seat of the imperial government late in the third century, a result of Diocletian's reforms), and an Eastern one, whose seat of power was Constantinople, the city that Constantine the Great had completed in 330. The Western Empire perished by 476. The Eastern one, better known as the Byzantine Empire, endured until 1453, and will be discussed in the next chapter.

Theodosius' coinage reflects few of these important developments. Types remained fairly static during his reign, and Roman coinage for propaganda had essentially lost the immediacy it once possessed. This may have been deliberate: as we have seen before, by issuing a series of unchanging portraits and limited types, the late Roman emperors may have desired to impress people with the idea that the empire, too, was unchanging, that it would endure forever.

If this was their desire, reality soon made a mockery of it. Theodosius' death was followed by a renewed wave of barbarian invasions, and this time the tribes were coming to settle as well as to loot. The Western Empire received the brunt of the onslaught. The wealthy East was able to buy off the tribes, to pit one against another. The West was not so fortunate—Gaul was taken, Britain lost, Spain and Portugal became barbarian kingdoms. In 410 and again in 455, Rome itself was sacked. In essence, the Western Empire in the fifth century was made up of barbarian peoples, now permanently settled in former Roman provinces, running their own affairs, but still paying verbal homage to the emperor at Ravenna. Emperors were regularly appointed and deposed by barbarian chieftains until 476, when one of them, Odovacar, abandoned the sham, setting aside the last Western Emperor, Romulus Augustus (there is irony in his name, incorporating as it did those of the legendary first king of Rome and the first emperor). Odovacar declared himself king of Italy, ending the political fiction of a Western Roman Empire. The substance had been lost decades earlier.

Fifth-century Roman coinage is almost entirely silent concerning these great events. By now, types were virtually frozen in place, and they had little or nothing to do with contemporary happenings. Gold solidi tended to have an emperor's portrait on the obverse, increasingly rendered three-quarters face rather than in profile. He is adorned in royal robes and wears a diadem. Whether rendered in this manner or in profile, portraiture had by this time degenerated to the point that individual rulers can only be identified through inscriptions.

On the reverses of these gold coins, a common inscription reads VICTORIA AVGGG (the Victory of our Emperors; the Romans often indicated plurals in inscriptions by adding or repeating letters). A popular reverse type was an emperor holding a long cross, treading down a serpent (whether this was meant to be read as defeating the barbarians or as an identification with Christ defeating the Devil, neither was particularly relevant to the times). A figure of Victory (or an angel) was also popular.

None of these fifth-century gold pieces is common, for several reasons. As the barbarians occupied the West, mints closed down, and total coinage production declined. Further, by this time much of the population was moving backward toward a barter economy. The barbarian invasions had disrupted trading activities throughout the West, and people were forced to get along as best they could. Since there was nothing to buy, few coins were required. This may be a partial explanation for an important characteristic of very late Roman coinage in the West: while gold is scarce, silver and copper are almost nonexistent. Gold was still needed for large transactions involving imports, but since cheaper items such as food and clothing were being produced on a local level, they could be traded for locally, using a barter system.

One final note on the last Western Roman coinage. Much of it was minted at Constantinople, capital of the Eastern Empire. This was due in part to the legal fiction that there was actually still only one empire, ruled for convenience's sake by two emperors of equal standing. In the days of Diocletian, the ruler who had divided the empire for the first time, the Augustus in the East struck coins in the name of his colleague in the West, and vice versa. The fifth-century coins from Constantinople, bearing the names and portraits of Western emperors, carried on this tradition. They also bore witness to the fact that Rome had ceased to be the center of the world and that, in the new Age of Faith which was replacing the Age of Rome, Constantinople would inherit much of the luster of power and learning that Rome had once enjoyed.

101

5

Preceding pages. L to r: England, penny, 870–905; Northern Iraq, dirhem, 103 A.H. (721–722 A.D.); Byzantines, hexagram, 692–695. Below. Top, l to r: Byzantine solidus (Anastasius I, 491–518) and barbarian imitation (Italy, Ostrogoths, Theoderic, 492–518); center, l to r: Byzantine tremissis (Anastasius I) and barbarian imitation (France, Franks, 6th century); bottom, l to r: Spain, Visigoths, tremisses, 6th century.

Coinage during the Age of Faith

The early part of the Middle Ages has often been called the Age of Faith. This is usually in reference to the Christian successor kingdoms in Western Europe, inheritors of pieces of the shattered Roman Empire. But the term can be applied to two other areas as well—the brilliant Eastern Roman or Byzantine Empire, and the dominions secured by the adherents of a new faith, Islam. In all three places, religion played an important role in the life of the individual and of the state. And the coins of all three regions—Western Europe, the Byzantine Empire, and the new Islamic lands—reflected the importance of religious faith. Indeed, it would be difficult to find another period when the links between religion and coinage were stronger.

Why this close connection between religion and other aspects of life, such as coinage? In fact, why should religion have been a dominant concern during the early Middle Ages? The answer is suggested by the nature of the times themselves. Throughout the former Roman world, and well beyond it, the centuries we call the Age of Faith were ones of immense uncertainty. Wave after wave of barbaric peoples swept across Europe. The old verities of civilized life, such as the city, communication over long distances, international commerce, and in some cases, safety of persons and their property, could no longer be taken for granted. Cities became ghost towns. Rome, which had boasted a population of a million during her peak, counted less than ten thousand by the eighth century. Roads and trade routes fell into disuse: the splendid Roman roads of Britain were partially dismantled, their paving stones used to build houses and churches. Learning declined, and some things were simply forgotten, others became the concerns of a priestly minority. The decline of learning, at least in the West, is graphically illustrated by the contrast between two outstanding rulers, one

a Roman emperor, the other a king of the barbaric Franks. We have met the first man before: he is Marcus Aurelius, emperor of Rome from 161 to 180. While in military camps fighting the German barbarians, Marcus Aurelius wrote a book on philosophy, the immortal *Meditations*. The second ruler, who reigned from 768 to 814, was Charlemagne, king of the Franks (cousins of the Germanic tribes plaguing the Roman Empire in Marcus Aurelius' time). Charlemagne was unquestionably the most outstanding early medieval king, and he effected numerous reforms. Charlemagne's contemporaries considered him learned because he was able to read. He was unable to write, however—his biographer, Einhard, tells us that he kept writing materials under his pillow at night, in case he ever learned how.

At least as far as the former Roman West was concerned, there had been a dramatic decline in almost all aspects of the quality of life with the onset of the Middle Ages. When times are unsettled and growing worse, the natural tendency is to cling to something, usually something larger than oneself. This is where Christianity entered the picture. By promising heavenly rewards, Christianity made life on this earth somewhat more bearable. A man might be a serf in life, working for a harsh master, but in the afterlife, master and man would stand before God as equals.

It was inevitable that Christianity would play an important part in the life of the West. Its role was strengthened by the zeal and activities of the Christian priesthood. Interpreters of the one safe thing in an unsafe world, the Catholic priests had an essential place in many aspects of life during the Age of Faith. They gave the barbarian kings, now baptized as Christians, an important aura of legitimacy in a time when most political conventions had been swept away.

Any surviving knowledge was their province also. Gathered in large monastic communities, they amassed power and wealth to themselves. As a reflection of both, they frequently minted coins—indeed, some of the earliest coinage of Western European countries, such as that of Switzerland, was a product of the Church. And the Church's—or Christianity's—influence was evident on most early Western medieval coins, no matter who minted them. The Cross predominated everywhere, on coinage as in life.

Christianity's influence was equally strong in the Byzantine East. This area had escaped much of the barbarian onslaught suffered by the Western Roman Empire. But times there were also uncertain, especially as the empire seemed always under attack from one enemy or another. Christian feelings ran deep in the East, where the tradition of a Savior-God was an old one. And in the East the new religion had gained its first converts. So the Age of Faith was alive and well in the Byzantine East, just as it was in the barbarian West. Eastern Christianity was gradually assuming a different form with a different emphasis, however, one based in part on the pagan past, and we shall see this divergence reflected on Byzantine coins.

Another component of the Age of Faith was Islam. This new religion was born in Arabia early in the seventh century, and Mohammed and his followers undertook a lightning career in conquest and conversion which in less than a century would take them from the gates of China to the Pillars of Hercules. Inevitably, their victories would be won at the expense of others. Islam would eventually conquer all of the Byzantine Empire, but much of the Christian West also fell under the sway of the new, nationalistic religion. Spain and North Africa were prime examples. Parts of Spain were occupied from 711 to 1492, and North Africa remains Moslem to this day.

In the world of the Islamic conquerors, religion played a part at least as great as it did in the Byzantine Empire or the West, but it was a different sort of role. In the latter two areas, the Christian faith was looked upon as a bulwark against bad times. In the former, Islam was seen as an expression, as a harbinger of good times. For example, the early medieval Frank put a cross on his coins because he hoped for God's favor. His counterpart in Baghdad made references to Allah on his coins because he *knew* he had his God's favor, and he wanted everyone else to know.

Despite these differences in how people viewed their God, all would have agreed that he was immensely important in the general scheme of things. He was a part of daily life, to a degree incomprehensible to later peoples. Many surviving artifacts from the Age of Faith underline God's importance to medieval man. None do so more strikingly than coins, the most plentiful survivors from the Age of Faith. Let us examine coins from the West, from the Byzantine Empire, and from Islam, in that order.

Of the three coinage components of the period, Western coins are by far the least numerous. We have discussed some of the reasons for this situation earlier. Wealth in those days lay elsewhere, as in Constantinople. We would be safe in saying that for every surviving coin from Western Europe, we can count at least a hundred from the Byzantine East, perhaps as many more from Islamic areas.

Nevertheless, coins were made in the West. Logically, the first ones were strongly imitative of earlier Roman and more-or-less contemporary Byzantine issues. Western barbarian moneyers fabricated Roman and Byzantine look-alikes in part because they had no native coinage tradition of their own for design inspiration, in part be-

1

2

3

4   5

**Below. L: England, penny, 1042–1066; top & bottom r:
Castile, dineros, 1073–1109. Opposite. Early Byzantine copper coinage.
Above: folles, or 40-nummi pieces; below, l to r: 20, 10, and
5 nummi coins. All from the reign of Anastasius I.**

cause they hoped their imitations would be accepted in trade as readily as were the originals.

The coins most widely copied were the Roman-Byzantine solidus and a new coin, worth one-third of a solidus. The latter was called a *tremissis*, and it had been introduced during the reign of Valentinian II. In the beginning, the solidi and tremisses of barbarian manufacture adhered quite faithfully to their imperial prototypes: a solidus of Theoderic (493–526), Ostrogothic king of Italy, carries the portrait of the current Byzantine emperor Anastasius (491–518) on the obverse, a traditional Victory type on the reverse. It can be distinguished from its Byzantine counterpart only by some stylistic differences. The same might be said of some early tremisses from France, which closely resemble those minted in the East by Anastasius, with the exception of a mint mark. Likewise, the earliest Visigothic coinage in Spain is an

imitation of early Byzantine gold. As in France, the most common denomination here is the tremissis, with the head of the ruler on the obverse, a figure of Victory or occasionally a cross on the reverse.

As time went on, coinage in the West began to acquire a sense of individuality. While Roman and Byzantine coins still served as inspiration, they were not copied quite as slavishly as before. Names and portraits of native rulers began replacing those of Byzantine ones. In passing, it should be noted that one reason for the earlier use of Byzantine legends, portraits, and types had been the political fiction that, whatever the real state of affairs, Western Europe still owed fealty and was subject to an emperor of Rome—who happened to reside in Constantinople at this time. As the barbarian kingdoms became more-or-less established, it was no longer necessary to render homage on the coinage to a far-away ruler—whose actual po-

litical power over the West was minimal, anyway. Western Europe became a definite entity with a mind of its own. And coinage here would now begin to evolve along lines of its own, while remaining heavily influenced by Roman and Byzantine practices for some centuries to come.

This mixture of native development and Roman-Byzantine inspiration is illustrated by a bronze issue of the Ostrogothic king of Italy, Theodahad (534–536). The coin bears his titles and his head rendered in profile, not in three-quarters as was currently in vogue in the Byzantine Empire. At the same time, the reverse is purely Roman in style, with a figure of Victory with a wreath and the letters SC prominently displayed on either side of the figure. The fact that the Roman Senate had been moribund for decades, had had no real power for over five hundred years, did not deter Theodahad from including this reference to it on his coins.

Elsewhere, coins were becoming more native, less imitative. The issues of Visigothic Spain are a good example. As mentioned, early coins closely resemble Byzantine tremisses—in fact, they tend to be catalogued in terms of which Byzantine emperor's issues they imitate. By the late sixth century, it is evident that native tastes are taking over. Portraiture is no longer fully modeled and is more likely to be a collection of lines and dots. Lettering may be blundered. All the same, the people portrayed, however crudely rendered on the coinage, are the current rulers of Spain. The coins bear their names and the names of the mints responsible for the issue. And we are moving from the classical type of coinage, which is relatively thick in proportion to diameter, to what we tend to consider the distinctly medieval type of coinage, which is broad and thin. On some later Visigothic issues, a Christian cross is prominently displayed on the reverse. This

Opposite. Above: Justinian I, solidi, 538–565.
Below: Justinian I, new dated folles, year 12, 538–539.

was already the case on much coinage elsewhere, including issues from Italy and France.

In Britain, coinage was somewhat different. A native British gold coinage, inspired by the issues of the Merovingian Franks (who were in turn influenced by Roman and Byzantine models), seems to have begun sometime in the sixth century. This gold was replaced by or degenerated into a coinage of small silver pieces, called *sceattas*. Historians disagree as to when the sceat was introduced: a date as early as 575 has been postulated, and they were certainly dominant in the British monetary system of the seventh and much of the eighth centuries.

Sceattas, like the earlier British gold, were influenced by older coinages. Roman influence is heavy: an entire series of sceattas imitates Roman bronze coinage of the period of Constantine the Great, with a diademed profile bust on the obverse, the reverse an abstract rendering of what had originally been a Roman standard with an inscription. Other sceattas imitated a popular reverse design on Byzantine solidi, a cross on steps. At that point, the fertile Anglo-Saxon imagination took over, and complicated designs and grotesque renderings of birds and animals became the norm. England's sceatta coinage, as we have noted, was in silver, and the widespread use of silver for money was virtually restricted to the British Isles at this time. It shortly became general, however, and it gave the Middle Ages its most common denomination, the penny *(denarius, denaro, dinero, denier,* depending on where you were).

The penny was a small, thin, silver coin. It was introduced as a coinage reform, first in France in the 750s, then in England, by about 785. Over the years, the Western European solidi and tremisses had become progressively debased, to the point where public confidence in them had nearly vanished.

Under various names the penny would be the dominant coin in Western Europe until the opening of the thirteenth century. In effect, Europe moved from a gold standard to a silver one. The longevity of this humbly named coin may be gauged from the fact that it remained the basic unit of reckoning in Britain until 1971, a time span of nearly twelve hundred years.

We must examine the penny in some detail, for it can tell us much about the nature of the medieval world which gave it birth. First, it was fairly standardized, both in terms of weight and of design. A portrait of the king and his titles appeared on the obverses of many coins, his monogram on others. Reverses tended to have the city of mintage, the name of the moneyer responsible, and some religious symbol, most commonly a cross, but at other times a church or saint. There was relatively little deviation from these basic designs, and this, along with a good deal of attention as to a standardized weight, gives evidence of an important historic fact: by the eighth and ninth centuries, much of the political anarchy that had characterized the very early Middle Ages had become a thing of the past. New, semiunified states were emerging, particularly in England and France, states with enough political power to produce a consistent coinage, states large enough so that to do so became economically and politically advantageous.

Another point to consider is that, in comparison with earlier medieval coins, the penny was produced in fairly large numbers. Charlemagne's issues were quite plentiful, for example. From this, and from the fact that an English penny was convertible to a French denier and vice versa, we may conclude that trade was experiencing at least a modest increase. If there were no commerce, as was virtually the case a few centuries earlier, why mint coins? And if commerce between re-

gions did not exist, why strike a convertible coinage? In fact, trade *was* increasing. Its rise would be slow at first, but it would increase after 1000, as Europe moved towards the Renaissance.

The beginnings of this commercial rebirth may be seen in another aspect of the penny—the manner in which it was made. As with all other coins up to that time, the penny was struck by hand from two dies. But the manner in which those dies were fabricated had changed. Many people consider medieval coins extremely ugly, particularly as regards portraiture. Faces are rendered by means of a series of curved lines, dots, and the like, and there is no attempt to give the design any dimensionality. But part of this abstraction is due to a new die-production practice. Instead of laboriously cutting each portrait, each die-type by hand, why not *stamp* the types into the coins, along with the letters of the titles? In fact, why not use the same collection of curved elements and dots to do both? The result would not be the most beautiful coin-die ever engraved, but the process would yield more dies per man-hour than the older method and the dies would be easier to fabricate. This practice was adopted in various parts of the medieval West by 1000, and the most logical reason for its usage was that more coins were needed than before. Since dies broke after repeated impressions, any situation requiring more coins necessitated more dies. Hence the adoption of the new practice, hence the abstract, even bizarre nature of some coinage design at this time.

By 1000, Western European coins indicate that the region was moving away from the Dark Ages, out of the Age of Faith, on to a path that eventually led it to the Renaissance. A stable coinage denomination, the penny, had been devised. It was much the same in many places, which would aid commerce. And it could be produced in larger quantities than before, as indicated by the new minting techniques. At least in economic matters, Western Europe was on the road to recovery, and with economic improvement could come amelioration in other fields, including cultural and political areas. Much of this lay far in the future, of course, but there was a ray of light that promised a better future for the West.

To the East, in the Byzantine Empire, there had been light, brilliant sunshine in comparison with the Western darkness, but this light was beginning to falter in the East, just as it was growing stronger in the West.

We have seen the antecedents of this Byzantine Empire. Politically, it was born as a result of the division of the old Roman Empire in 395. But the roots of its individuality go back much further. Essentially, in the late classical world there were two cultures, each with a style of its own. The Western one was centered in Italy; its members tended to think of themselves as Romans, spoke Latin, and embraced what would later be called a Catholic brand of Christianity. The Eastern cultural area, whether paying homage to a Roman emperor or not, was a Greek-speaking blend of Eastern and Greek cultural traits. There was a thin Latin veneer, of course, but members of this group tended to think of themselves as Greeks (or Syrians, etc.) They adhered to a brand of Christianity which was already showing divergences from the Western variety in terms of how it saw Christ, its view of the relationship between Church and State, and so forth. These differences would in time lead to the Schism of 1054, from which there would emerge two distinct branches of the Christian Church—the Catholic and the Greek Orthodox.

The barbarian invasions and settlements in the old Roman West tended to heighten, not diminish, the differences between the Greek and Latin cultural centers. Before, Greeks and Romans had shared a more-or-less common degree of civilization. But the barbarian West had very little in common with the civilized Byzantine East, and both sides knew it. The Byzantines looked upon the Franks and Saxons as unlettered barbarians, and the latter viewed the rich, cultured Byzantines as effete Greeks, who were probably heretics. The West was jealous of the East, of its power and culture. Their differences must be taken into account. The Byzantines were *not* Westerners, and their history, culture, and coinage manifest many things not seen in Western Europe. As far as coinage is concerned, however, there is a point of definite similarity. Like money in the West, Byzantine coinage manifests a heavy preoccupation with religious matters. The Age of Faith left its mark on coinage here, just as it did on coinage elsewhere.

In the case of the Byzantines, the use of religious symbols, figures, and titles was even stronger than it was in the West. In addition, Byzantine coinage reflected contemporary events more faithfully than did coinage in Western Europe—indeed, much of it was even dated, a practice that had totally disappeared in France, England, etc.

Byzantine coinage began as a simple outgrowth of late Roman coinage. The same types and denominations were issued from Constantinople and other Eastern mints as were being struck elsewhere. The beginnings of Byzantine coinage proper took place during the reign of Anastasius. He reformed copper coinage in 498, introducing a new, large denomination called a *follis*. It was worth forty *nummi* (the nummus was a tiny copper coin, about the only copper issue in the fifth century; an indication of its value was that it took 16,800 nummi to equal a single solidus). The denomination, forty, was indicated by a large M (Greek symbol for that number) on the reverse. Pieces worth twenty, ten, and five nummi were also issued, their values indicated by the letters K, I, and E, respectively. The forty-nummi piece had a Christian cross atop the M and a star on each side, with CON below, short for Constantinople, the place of mintage. With the exception of the five-nummi piece, all coins of the series bore a cross on the reverse.

Their obverses were taken up with a profile bust of the emperor, along with his titles. With local variations, these coins were struck at Nicomedia and Antioch, as well as at Constantinople. Anastasius' reforms extended only to copper coinage. In the area of precious metals, solidi and their subdivisions continued to be struck with tried-and-true designs and on a standard identical to those of earlier rulers. Silver coins were produced in minute quantities, a common characteristic of general Byzantine coinage. While there are coppers in huge quantities and a considerable amount of gold, silver coinage is absent most of the time. This was the exact opposite of what was going on in the West.

Anastasius' reforms were augmented by his eventual successor, Justinian I (527–565), probably the greatest of the Byzantine emperors. Justinian inherited an Eastern Empire including Greece, Asia Minor, part of the Near East, and Egypt. His reign witnessed great military victories against the barbarian West, resulting in the recapture of North Africa, part of Spain, Sicily, and, by 536, Rome itself. Under Justinian, the empire reached its maximum size. Though its ruler could not foresee it, the remainder of Byzantine history would be a long, painful decline, ending in a complete extermination in 1453.

Like many of his Roman predecessors, Justinian was a builder and a reformer. His building program gave us the Hagia Sophia, one of the most famous and beautiful churches in the world. His reforms gave the

world the Justinian Code, which endures to this day as the basis for the legal codes of France, Germany, Italy, and Latin America. His reforms extended to coinage, too, and Justinian gave Byzantine coinage its most typical appearance, the one best known to the collector.

These reforms are more immediately evident on copper coinage than on that of precious metals. On early gold solidi and their divisions, the obverse continued to display a three-quarters-facing bust of the ruler with a spear, shield, and helmet—a type that originated late in the Roman period, as we have seen. Reverse types showed Victory, usually holding a long cross. Early in the year 538, a design reform was introduced for gold. The emperor was now shown completely full-faced, wearing a helmet, holding a cross on a globe in his right hand with a decorated shield at his left shoulder. The reverse type continued to be a facing Victory, with slight variations from earlier designs.

But in the same year, copper coinage saw much greater changes. The new, full-faced bust adopted for solidi was extended to the copper series, and the reverse, while retaining the essential form that Anastasius had given it, received an important new addition—the date, given as the year of the emperor's reign. Alone among coins of this period, these medieval coins can actually be dated down to the year.

We tend to take the dates on modern coins for granted. They are part of the meaning of the coin itself, as much a component of it as the metal in which it is struck and the denomination that it represents. But this was definitely *not* a concept shared by most people in the Age of Faith. Perhaps time and its passage were of lesser importance to them than they are to us. Indeed, one tends to think so, for the early Middle Ages lacked another concept we take for granted today—

the concept of progress, of material and intellectual improvement. And we, at least, tend to link the idea of progress with the idea of time's passage. People of the Age of Faith did not.

In the West, coins were not commonly dated until the fifteenth and sixteenth centuries, or even beyond. In the Byzantine East, they were dated a thousand years before. Did the Byzantines have a different notion of the importance of time than that of their Western contemporaries? The answer is probably no. In Justinian, however, they did have a strong ruler who saw himself as heir to the mantle of the Roman emperors, who had had his generals reconquer Rome itself by way of proving it. He wished to be regarded (as do most reformers) not as an innovator, but as the engineer of a successful return to the glorious past, to the reestablishment of a Roman Empire in the West. And since rulers in the greatest days of the Roman Empire tended to indicate the year of their rule on their coins, Justinian did the same. So, on one side of the large central letter that indicated its value, we seen the word ANNO (year); on the other, a figure in Roman numerals, indicating the exact year of the reign in which the particular coin had been struck.

The dating of coins provided another advantage for Justinian and for those who would follow him in the practice. Along with the inscriptions indicating the mint and the workshop of the mint that had produced a particular coin (shown by a smaller letter below the large one), an addition of the date made it easier to trace shoddy, lightweight coinage to its source so that those responsible could be prosecuted. However, keep in mind that only the lowly coppers were so dated; gold and the few silver coins being struck were not.

As the Eastern Empire reached its

115

Opposite. Top: Justinian II, solidi, 692–695; center,
l & center: Leo IV, silver miliaresia, 776–780;
center r: Leo IV, solidus, 776–798; bottom: Anonymous
Bronzes, 988–1028.

greatest extent during the reign of Justinian, so did the number of its mints. Coins were now being struck in Carthage, Sicily, and perhaps Spain, besides in the traditional Eastern mints. If Justinian brought the Byzantine Empire to its peak, his successors came dangerously close to losing it all. The late sixth and early seventh centuries were times of distress, and the coinage indicates as much. Many coins were crudely struck, as if there were no time to prepare carefully finished dies. The size of the copper coins diminished during this time, as if inflation were becoming a problem. Two developments, both during the reign of Justin II (565–578), pointed toward the future of Byzantine coinage. On many copper issues we see both the emperor and his consort, not merely the ruler alone, and the figures are nimbate, i.e., surrounded by halos. Each of these developments tells us something of the evolution of Byzantine culture and thought.

The depiction of more than one person on the coinage is easy to explain. It was an outgrowth of the earlier Roman practice in which family members were honored on the coinage. The halo motif is somewhat more important, for it shows us two things: first, the concept of monarchy in the Byzantine world was tinged with the older, Eastern concept of a divine ruler; second, in the Byzantine scheme of things, the ruler was closely identified with the Eastern brand of Christianity, eventually to be known as the Greek Orthodox Church. In Christian imagery, Christ wears a halo, saints wear halos. In the Byzantine Empire, so does the emperor, with increasing frequency. Often he is associated with a saint, or with Christ, or with the Virgin Mary.

What does all this say about the nature of Byzantine church-state relations? Primarily, it is an indication of a fact we know from other historical sources: that in Byzantine thinking, the ruler was head of both church *and* state. He did not accept the increasingly vocal assumption of ultimate religious authority by the Pope in Rome. Historians use the term *Caesaropapism* to describe the role of the Byzantine ruler in the Eastern Christian Church, and it was one of the bases for the split of Christianity in 1054.

Byzantine political and military reverses came to at least a partial halt with the accession of Heraclius (610–641). While he was unsuccessful in ejecting the barbaric Lombards from nothern Italy (they had invaded the area about the time of the death of Justinian I), Heraclius did throw back a determined Persian attack, the last major war launched by the decaying Sassanian Empire. The early part of the war had gone well for the Sassanians. By 610, they controlled most of Egypt and the Byzantine East, and they were knocking at the gates of Constantinople itself. Heraclius spent nearly twenty years defeating them, at the end of which period the Byzantine Empire was almost as weak as the Persian state. We can sense some of the urgency of those years in Heraclius' copper coinage. Many of his early pieces were simply overstruck on older coins, which was much quicker and easier than preparing new coin blanks as would ordinarily have been done. Heraclius must have needed money in a hurry, a fact shown by the historical record.

The weakening of the Byzantine Empire as a result of war with Persia unfortunately coincided with and facilitated the rise of a new power, one which would in time inherit Constantinople's role in the East. This was Islam, which will be discussed in detail later in this chapter. Its first major conquests outside of Arabia occurred during the last years of Heraclius' reign. Many of these victories were achieved directly at Byzantine expense. Egypt, Palestine, and Syria, which Heraclius had regained from the Sassanians,

Above. Top row, l to r: John I, tetarteron, 969–976; Constantine IX, scyphate nomismata, 1042–1055 (2nd & 3rd coins); Isaac II, electrum, asperon trachy, 1185–1195; Venice, grosso, 1253–1268; and Byzantine imitation (Andronicus II with Michael IX, miliaresion), 1295–1320; bottom row, l to r: Basil II, histamenon, 976–1025; Romanus IV, tetarteron, 1067–1071; Manuel II, silver hyperperon and its half, 1391–1425.

Opposite. Above: Byzantine follis (Justin II, 567–568), and
Arabic imitation, 7th century;
below: Byzantine follis, Heraclius (612–613), and
Arabic imitation, 7th century.

were lost to the Arabs by 641. During the remainder of its existence, the empire would be confined at most to Greece, bits of Italy, and the heartland, Asia Minor. In time, these too would be lost.

With few exceptions, these military and political reverses were not reflected on Byzantine coinage for many years. This is not to say that the coinage remained static, for it did not. A different reverse for gold solidi was widely used in the reign of Constantius II (641–668), a Christian cross standing on several steps. The design was a popular one, and it was employed for many years on much coinage of the medieval West as well as the Byzantine East. Some silver was being struck by this time. The basic denomination was called a *hexagram*, and it will appear from time to time through much of the future.

By the seventh century, emperors (and members of their families, if desired) were commonly represented on the copper coinage in a standing position, facing the viewer. This was also the case on much of the silver and gold. By late in the century, the subdivisions of the follis had been lost, and the follis itself was small, usually struck on an irregular planchet, with no pretense of being round.

Byzantine artistry on coinage may have reached a low point during the reign of Constantius II. It began to revive under his successor, Justinian II (685–695, 705–711). Greek began to replace Latin in coin inscriptions. At first, coins contained bits of both languages, but Greek soon predominated, another indication that the Byzantine Empire was much more Greek than Latin at its roots. The chief novelty in Justinian II's choice of coinage types was his introduction of a facing bust of Christ on the reverse of gold solidi, with the ruler's portrait on the obverse. Here was an obvious attempt to connect the King of Kings with the Emperor of Byzantium. Religious representation on Byzantine coinage had taken a major step, and from this time onward, busts of Christ, Mary, or the saints—associated with the emperor or appearing alone—would be the norm.

The artwork on Byzantine coins was at its best from the late seventh to the early eleventh centuries, which roughly coincided with the last good years of the Byzantine Empire itself. A political turnaround began in the reign of Leo III (717–741): an Arab attack on Constantinople was defeated, and the barbaric Slavs, who had overrun the Balkan provinces, were conquered and pacified. It was at this time, too, that the Iconoclastic question rent the Eastern Church. The Iconoclasts, including the emperor, opposed the representation of Christ and the saints in the fear that this would lead to worship of the objects upon which the images appeared, rather than the figures those images represented. For coinage, this meant that religious figures could not be depicted, and Leo and his successors down to 842, when the controversy was finally resolved, regularly portrayed themselves and their relatives on coins, but never religious personages. The Christian cross, however, did continue to appear on coins, as it had for hundreds of years. And Christ, Mary, St. Alexander, and others made their reappearance by the middle of the ninth century, remaining there until the end of the Byzantine state.

During the last quarter of the tenth century and through most of the eleventh, the figure of Christ was dominant. His visage appeared on a very important series of coins, the so-called Anonymous Bronzes. Byzantine emperors regularly appeared on gold and silver coins, complete with titles. But a new design for copper, was introduced, consisting of a haloed, full-faced bust of Christ on the obverse, the inscription "Jesus Christ, King of Kings" on the reverse, in Greek. Coinage of

**Opposite. Above: Byzantines, Heraclius, solidi, c. 639–641;
below: Arab imitations of above coins (Syria, dinars,
late 7th century).**

this type was struck from the 960s to the 1090s, and individual coins can be attributed to specific emperors only with a good deal of doubt.

The Anonymous Bronze coinage may have represented a monetary reform, an attempt to reestablish a good, base-metal coinage. Certainly, some of the earliest Anonymous Bronzes are large, almost the size of the early folles issued in the days of Justinian I. If such a reform were contemplated, it was not particularly successful, and the Anonymous Bronzes (called folles for convenience), soon decreased in size and weight. They are the last good examples of Byzantine coinage portraiture.

For a general decline was setting in. It was first seen in coinage and soon it would appear in other areas, including the fortunes of the Byzantine state itself. The decline in coinage began to manifest itself by the late tenth century. Unlike ancient Rome, the Byzantine Empire had never been greatly troubled by inflation. Copper coinage might shrink in size, but the backbone of the Byzantine monetary system was gold. The basic unit, the solidus, had remained remarkably stable ever since its introduction in the fourth century.

By the 960s, however, the demands of increasing warfare began to be felt on the coinage. Faced with a constantly increasing military budget, the empire decided to make ends meet by debasing the gold coinage. It was not so bad at first, for a new, slightly lighter gold coin was introduced during the reign of Nicephorus II (963–969). Called a *tetarteron*, it was intended to circulate at par with the solidus, even though it was worth less. For instance, it was said that the government collected taxes in solidi but paid out money only in tetartera, pocketing the difference.

Outright debasement had set in by 1030, and it progressed rapidly during the remainder of the century, the theoretically solid gold coin now being made out of a gold-silver alloy, with emphasis on the silver. A curious feature of this adulterated coinage was that it was cup-shaped, concave. This distinguishing characteristic would soon be extended to copper as well. After around 1025, not only did Byzantine coins decline in their intrinsic worth, but their artistic quality fell as well.

These problems in Byzantine coinage were reflections of much larger problems faced by the Byzantine Empire itself. The last great ruler of Constantinople was Basil II (976–1025), whose great northern campaigns subdued the savage Bulgars, safeguarding the Empire from Slavic attack. His successors during the remainder of the eleventh century were largely a collection of nonentities, and one of them, Romanus IV (1068–1071), was defeated at Manzikert by a new wave of invaders, the Seljuk Turks. The Empire never recovered from this disaster, and in the confusion following the great defeat, the Seljuks were able to overrun most of Asia Minor. The Byzantine Empire had lost its heartland, and would soon lose much more.

A century later, it would lose its independence (1204), not to Easterners or to pagan barbarians, but to Christianized Western Europeans. The old factor of Western jealousy of the wealthy Eastern Empire finally found expression in what ostensibly started out as a crusade against Moslems in the Holy Land. It ended as an excercise in piracy, conducted at the expense of fellow-Christians.

The Westerners stayed in Constantinople until 1261, when the Byzantines succeeded in regaining control of their own city, restoring a battered and tarnished Byzantine Empire for almost two centuries longer. The city of Constantinople finally fell to a new branch of Turks, the Ottomans, in 1453.

Little need be said about late Byz-

123

Right. Syria, dinar, 77 A.H. (697 A.D.).
Center. L to r: Sassanian drachm, 590–628, and Arabic imitation, 64 A.H. (683–684 A.D.).
Bottom. Damascus, fals, 87 A.H. (705–706 A.D.).

antine coinage. In its crudity of style, in its metallic debasement, it reflects something of the dwindling fortunes of the people who made it. Much of it continued to be cup-shaped. As a reminder of the fact that Constantinople's position of commercial preeminence in the eastern Mediterranean had been usurped by Venice, which had a strategic location, Byzantine coins were imitating Venetian ones by the late thirteenth century. Gold had completely disappeared by the early fourteenth century, and the last Byzantine coins, still showing the imperial bust on one side, a figure of Christ on the other, were flat again, struck in copper and debased silver. Coinage designs were much cruder than before, an indication that Byzantine eminence in the arts had come to an end, along with any other outstanding qualities once possessed by this people. We should not remember them for the crude, pitiful coins of their last years, however. Recall instead the empire in its best days, the wealthiest nation in Europe and repository of the arts and learning which is inherited from classical times.

In the West and Byzantine East, the Age of Faith was based on a well-established religious creed, Christianity. In many other areas, however, it was founded on a new religion, the last major creed to appear in human history. The new faith was Islam, and from the early seventh century onwards, it left an indelible mark on the Age of Faith, and on the coins produced during it.

Islam was founded by Mohammed, who lived from 570 to 632. He began preaching his new religion around 620, and was driven from his home, Mecca, in 622 for his pains. His flight (Hegira) from Mecca to Medina is regarded by the faithful as the beginning of the Moslem calendar, and the importance of this event is evident in the fact that virtually all coins produced by Islamic peoples bear dates computed from the Hegira.

Islam's tenets are simple, and this very simplicity was an element that made the new faith attractive to its early converts. Islam teaches that there is one God, Allah, and that he is merciful, compassionate. Mohammed was the last and greatest of the prophets, chosen by Allah to explain the true faith to humankind. The will of Allah, as related to Mohammed, is contained in the Koran, whose language is clear, unmistakable, and decisive—the final word on any subject for the practitioner of Islam. The Koran also teaches that there is a heaven and a hell, for like Christianity, Islam is a religion of divine reward and punishment. Finally, every follower of Islam is the equal of every other follower of Islam, regardless of race, color, tongue, or status.

These tenets were simple enough for anyone to grasp, and they were, as mentioned, a major factor in the rapid expansion of the Islamic faith. Historians once believed that the sole reason for the incredible Arabic expansion of the seventh and early eighth centuries was the great religious fervor of the converts to the new religion. Zeal, based on the simplicity and universality of Islam, was undeniably a factor in its early successes. But another basis for Arab conquest was that by the time Mohammed gained his first converts, the Arabian peninsula had become overpopulated. We now know that Arabs had been emigrating to Iraq, Palestine, and Syria for some time prior to Mohammed. Now, with the birth of Islam, they had a new faith to serve as a symbol of newly felt Arabic unity. And the first Islamic expansion out of Arabia was into adjacent areas in which fellow Arabs had settled previously.

So the new faith, at once a religion and an expression of nationalism, gathered momentum very quickly. Its battle cry might be the profession of the Islamic creed, but its ulterior motives seem to have been the age-old ones of conquest for adequate living space, and loot. By the time of Mohammed's death, Mecca had been conquered, and perhaps a third of the Arabian peninsula was Moslem. Within a few years, all of it was conquered, and adherents of the new creed were looking elsewhere.

They looked to Byzantine and Sassanian lands first. Syria, disaffected by some of the tenets of current Byzantine theology, fell easily by 634. Jerusalem was captured in 639, Egypt the following year. The Byzantine Empire had been parted from some of the richest lands it possessed. The Sassanians of Persia received the same treatment at the same time. In 637, Arabs took Ctesipon, the Sassanian captial; by 651, they were the new masters of the entire Sassanian Empire.

Then they turned farther west, and east. In 698, they took Carthage and conquered the native Berber tribes, who had successfully been able to resist the Romans, Vandals, and Byzantines in turn. In 711, they crossed the Straits of Gibraltar, entered Spain, and added almost all of it to their holdings by 718. By 725, they were in France, and here at last they were turned back at Tours (732) by Charles Martel, ancestor of the great Charlemagne. Meanwhile, they had been spreading east from Persia, through modern Russian Turkestan, and by 724 they had reached the Indus River and the western borders of China. A vast new empire, based on military might and religious fervor, had entered the scene. It is still with us today, at least in a religious sense. At a conservative estimate, there are now around five hundred million followers of Islam.

The birth of the new religion gave the world a new type of coinage as well, one impossible to confuse with any other. This coinage evolved during the first century of Islam, and its development occupied two distinct stages.

Prior to Islam, the Arabs had essentially lacked a coinage tradition of their own. Their modest trade was carried on through barter or the use of other people's money, particularly Roman, Sassanian, and Byzantine. But the early conquests did two things: first, they carried the Arabs into large, populated areas with inhabitants that used and needed coinage; second, they brought Arabs into contact with the mints that had produced coins for Byzantine Egypt, Sassanian Persia, etc. Given these circumstances, the most logical thing to do was to simply strike coins closely based on Byzantine or Sassanian models. This was done down to about the beginning of the eighth century, and it became the first stage of Islamic coinage.

Those coins fashioned after Byzantine models by the early Arabs were struck in copper, gold to a much smaller degree, and silver not at all, which more or less reflected the metallic ratios of genuine Byzantine coins at the time. A copper follis, or forty-nummi piece of Justin II, served as a popular model for Arab imitations. The original showed the emperor and his empress seated on the obverse, with an inscription giving their names. This inscription was replaced by a new one in a mixture of Greek and Latin, which simply named the mint that had struck the new coin. The follis of Heraclius received somewhat similar treatment on the obverse; an Arabic inscription was added to the reverse.

As far as Arab copies of Byzantine gold coins are concerned, a solidus of Heraclius served as a popular model. This coin depicted the emperor and his sons on the obverse, a cross on steps on the reverse. The Arabs retained most of the design, but they substituted a globe on a pole for the offending Christian cross.

Arabic imitations of Sassanian coins were struck almost exclusively in silver. They copied the thin, flat drachm, the most

typical Sassanian coin issued during the last centuries of that state's independence. The issues of Chosroes II (590–627) and Yezdigird III (632–651) were struck in very large amounts, and these were the coins most commonly copied by the Arabs.

Arabic issues here were extremely close in types and inscriptions to their Sassanian prototypes. The conventional portrait and inscription remained on the obverse, the fire altar and two attendants on the reverse. Note, however, the addition of a brief Arabic inscription on the margin of the obverse, put there by Islamic conquerors to indicate that this was their coin, not a Sassanian one.

By the end of the seventh century,

Arabic coinage was entering the second stage of its development, a stage in which it would cease imitating other people's coinage and strike out on a radically new, independent career of its own.

As we have seen, the imitative coinage of the first stage included representations of people and objects as part of its design. This was plainly against the tenets laid down in the Koran, which forbids the use of images. In addition, the Koran opposes the exaltation of one individual over all the other members of the Islamic community, and this, of course, had been one of the main purposes for depicting human beings on coinage since the practice was adopted in the time of the Greeks. In brief, a new kind of coinage was required, and, in 697, it was introduced.

This new Arabic coinage bore no imagery at all, only inscriptions. And as evidence of the great importance attached to religion by the Arab people, the majority of the inscriptions were adapted from the Koran. Gold coins, called *dinars*, saw the light in 697, and copper ones, called *fals* (their name derived from the follis of the Romans and Byzantines), appeared a few years later. But the most typical early Arab coin was a flat, thin silver piece, known as the *dirhem*, first minted in 698. Let us examine this coin for a moment.

In terms of its size and fabric, it is clear that the dirhem was inspired by the earlier Sassanian drachm. Both coins are broad and thin, although the dirhem contains somewhat less silver than the drachm. Even the name of the new coin was an adaptation of the name of the old. Most important, however, were the inscriptions found on the dirhem. They comprise a veritable litany of the new Islamic faith. The obverse of a typical dirhem has a large central inscription in three lines, which reads, "There is no God except Allah. He is Alone. (There is) no partner

to Him." The circular obverse inscription gives us the name of the mint and the year, adding that the coin was struck in the name of Allah. On the reverse of our typical dirhem, we again have a central legend, this one somewhat longer than its counterpart of the obverse. It reads, "Allah is One. Allah is the Eternal. He did not beget and He was not begotten, and there was not to Him equal a single one." Paraphrased, the marginal reverse inscription tells us that Mohammed does not consider his religion as having come to destroy other religions, but to supplement them. Allah sent him to perfect the monotheistic faiths, Christianity and Judaism, to reveal at last in full clarity what had only been dimly seen before.

Similar inscriptions appeared on gold and bronze coins of the period. With minor variations, this would be the basic type of Arabic coinage for the next six centuries, through the remainder of the Age of Faith and well beyond. By the late eighth century, the name of the caliph, frequently along with that of a local governor, regularly began to appear, but these rulers were never depicted on the coins, nor was anyone else. The Islamic rejection of imagery on coinage has persisted into modern times, at least on the issues of the stricter Moslem countries such as Saudi Arabia. In this, the modern adherents to Islam are maintaining a tradition started by their forbears almost thirteen centuries ago. The new religion proved to be remarkably tenacious in the mind of its believers. And so were the conquests made in its name: while Spain, Israel, and some Mediterranean lands were eventually lost to Islam, elsewhere, what Islam had conquered in the seventh and eighth centuries it still retained in the twentieth. The spread of this new religion is perhaps our chief legacy from the Age of Faith, and the coins it produced are its best, most enduring reminders.

6

Preceding pages. England, sovereign, 1485–1509.
Below. Top row, l to r: England, penny, 1066–1087; France, denier,
1180–1223; center row, l to r: Antioch, denier, 1136–1149;
Sweden, sterling, 994–1022; Poland, denier, 1034–1058;
bottom: Castile, maravedí, 1223 A.H. (1185 A.D.).

The Age of Awakening in Europe

It has been said that the Middle Ages lasted for a thousand years and was divided into two periods of five hundred years each, the second period being primarily devoted to pulling humankind out of the morass into which it had fallen during the first period. This attitude somewhat oversimplifies and overstates what actually happened. All the same, there is a certain amount of truth in the generalization, and if the early part of the Middle Ages can be called the Age of Faith, the best name for the late Middle Ages might be the Age of Awakening.

This Age of Awakening in Europe occupied the five centuries from 1000 to 1500. The word "awakening" can be applied to several aspects of human behavior during the period. There was an economic awakening, a burgeoning of trade. This was aided by and in its turn fostered the awakening of nation-states. A map of Europe from the period begins to resemble a modern map. France is there, so is Britain; so, shortly, will be Spain. There was a definite cultural awakening and spread. Classical works were rediscovered and used as models for late medieval efforts. Culture unfolded from the religious sector of society, the priesthood, which had had something approaching a monopoly over it for centuries. It became the concern of wealthy businessmen and rulers of emerging national states, and for the first time we can speak of patrons of the arts in the modern sense of the term. The flow of culture out of the churches and into the outer world symbolized the greatest awakening—the rekindling of man's consciousness of, and faith in, himself. His views of God and of the human relationship to Him were becoming a good deal more benign than they had been during the Age of Faith. Perhaps people could even change and improve their previously immutable conditions. With this set of ideas, this greater optimism, people began moving toward a new

philosophy, called Humanism. Humanism will be one of the hallmarks of the chief cultural legacy of the Age of Awakening, the Renaissance.

The important thing to note about these years is the extremely close interrelationship of events. Humanism and a return to the classics could only have come about in a more self-confident age, and the self-confidence was founded upon greater economic and political stability. In sum, just as the end of the ancient world had been based upon an interrelated set of adverse factors, the end of the medieval world was due to a number of intertwined developments working in the opposite direction.

Although the changes bringing an end to the Middle Ages were inextricably bound together, we will divide them into three categories, for purposes of clarity. Each category influenced the others, and, as we shall see, had a large role to play in the story of money during the late Middle Ages.

The first area of concern is the economic, and the major occurrence here was the revival of trade. We have seen that by 1000 a new, convertible coinage denomination had been devised, the penny. New and more rapid methods for fashioning coin dies had also been discovered, insuring that the penny could receive wide distribution when and if occasion demanded. By the eleventh and twelfth centuries, more coins were needed, for trade was experiencing a modest upsurge that would increase through time.

Much of the anarchy that had earlier characterized conditions in Western Europe was abating. In England, a strong Norman monarchy had taken power in 1066, setting aside the Anglo-Saxon dynasty that had ruled the island since the departure of the Romans. In France, the Capetian line was gradually extending regal control, curbing the powers of unruly barons and bringing the

Church under royal influence. There was also a modicum of order in Germany and Italy, although these areas would not see final unification for another eight centuries. This return of political order was a prerequisite for the economic growth of Europe during this period.

In addition, new and fruitful contacts were being made with other, non-Christian parts of the world, especially Islam. The native rulers of Spain had been conducting a crusade of sorts against the Moslems ever since their invasion from Africa in 711. This movement, called *La Reconquista* in Spanish history, would go on for eight centuries, forever changing the Spanish character. But shortly before 1100, other Christian states began a series of holy wars against Islam, which we call the Crusades. There were to be eight of them, lasting all the way from 1095 to 1270. Their ostensible purpose was to recover the Holy Land from Moslem control. In their avowed objective, they would ultimately fail. While Jerusalem and other holy places were taken, the Europeans were eventually ejected. But the Crusades had other, long-lasting effects. They brought Europeans into contact with Islamic peoples and their products, and this in turn stimulated a profitable trade. They also brought Europe back in touch with many of the classical writers of the past, whose works had been preserved in Islamic lands but lost in Christian ones. This latter would have a great effect on European cultural developments leading to the Renaissance.

So, due to a variety of factors, European trade began reviving after 1000, and this, of course, left its mark on the coinage of the time. The penny spread from its original home, and soon it—or something much like it—was being minted all over Europe. We have two graphic reminders of this fact. One is that Western European coins are now common, within reach of the average collector. This is an indication that many more coins were being struck than had been before. The second bit of evidence is that we now have coinage from areas such as eastern Germany, Bohemia, and Poland (all beginning in the late tenth century), Russia and Scandinavia (both beginning around 1000). These issues generally resembled the Western penny, and they were clearly meant for trade. They are also an indication that new sources of precious metals were being opened up. Soon, Central Europe would become the major supplier of silver to the West, a position the region would enjoy until early modern times.

As trade expanded, so did specialization. Towns and regions began concentrating on a few products because it became clear that they could obtain whatever else they needed from outside, often more cheaply and of better quality than anything they could produce at home. So England would produce raw wool for export. France and Flanders would weave that wool into cloth. Italy would trade that cloth to the East, receiving spices and gold in return. The beginnings of a trans-European trade nexus were being set up.

All this trade came together in the great medieval fairs, which became a permanent feature of the economic landscape after the eleventh century. The economic revival brought other advancements, too: the beginnings of modern banking, the growth of cities, and the development within those cities of a merchant class with wealth and leisure enough to patronize the arts. The latter now had the potential of leaving the religious world and entering the secular one, an indication of the new spirit of the times. None of these changes occurred overnight, of course, but by the beginning of the thirteenth century, their roots were firmly in place.

The new times demanded new kinds of money. There were three developments

here. The first was more important for the potential it offered for the future than for any immediate effect. It was the bill of exchange, and in time it would lead to the use of paper money in Europe.

The Chinese had been employing a form of paper currency since the T'ang dynasty (618–907). This was a sensible development, for the individual cash was of very low value, and it took a great many of them to be worth much in trade. So paper money was devised. It was much easier to transport and use for trade than were several thousand copper coins. Marco Polo saw it in use around 1300 and duly reported on it to Europe, though the Europeans did not immediately adopt it. Their coins were worth more individually than were the Chinese cash, and in any event there was not yet enough trade to prompt the governmental issue of paper money. As far as that went, there was no government in Europe strong enough to force its usage.

Still, with the growth in trade, a more convenient and safer method of handling money was desirable, and this need was answered by the private sector, which devised the bill of exchange. The bill of exchange functioned something like a modern bank check. Party A gave Party B a written promise to pay a certain sum of money. Provided A's credit was good, B could use the bill of exchange to pay off his own debts to Party C. And so forth. Eventually, the last holder presented the bill to Party A for payment. The bill of exchange made financial transactions much easier than before, as well as less hazardous. While Europe was becoming less anarchic than it had been, traveling from Britain to Italy with a large amount of coined money was still a dangerous undertaking. In time, goverments would take over the responsibility for issuing and guaranteeing the new monetary medium, and true paper money would emerge. All this

lay several hundred years in the future.

The economic awakening of Europe had two other immediate effects on coinage: larger coins of silver made their appearance, and gold was revived as a coinage medium. By the opening of the thirteenth century, trade was growing sufficiently so that the relatively small penny was no longer adequate for business transactions. Something of greater intrinsic value was needed. The first of a long series of new, larger silver coins appeared at a most logical place and time. The new coin's birth in Venice was logical because the city had already become a major trading center, doing a brisk business with the Moslem East and the Christian West. Its timing— in 1202—also made sense. Venice was embarking on the Fourth Crusade, and it needed large amounts of coinage to pay for outfitting an expeditionary force. So the new coin was introduced, and it soon became known as a *grosso* (Italian for big). The coin spread to the north and west—to France late in the thirteenth century, to Britain by the middle of the fourteenth.

It was introduced in France during the reign of Louis IX (1226–1270), who led the Eighth Crusade and was eventually sainted. In 1266, Louis introduced a general monetary reform in France, with a new, large silver coin, the *gros tournois*, equal in value to twelve of the old French deniers, or pence. The new coin bore a large cross with royal inscriptions on its obverse, a crude rendering of the cathedral of Tours on the reverse. By royal statute, the right of issue of the gros tournois was reserved for the king, an indication that Louis was attempting to curb the landed magnates, who had enjoyed the right of coining their own money as an aspect of their political power. The nobility could still issue deniers, but their rights were being eroded. By the late fifteenth century, the increasing arrogation of power to the throne made French kings among the strongest in Europe.

The gros tournois was an immediate success in France, and coins like it soon appeared elsewhere. There was an abortive attempt to introduce the new coin in England in 1279. It was unsuccessful because it contained so much silver (and was tariffed so low) that it allowed no profit to the private moneyers who struck it in the name of the king. In any case, England's economy was still backward at the time, and the penny served her economic needs reasonably well. The new silver coin, called a *groat*, was withdrawn, but it was reintroduced by Edward III (1327–1377), around 1350. By this time, England's burgeoning trade in wool had made a larger silver coin feasible. The English groat had the king's head in full-face along with his name on the obverse, and a long cross with pellets in the angles on the reverse, with the name of the mint and the responsible mint official. These designs would be standard on English silver coinage down to 1500.

Renamed, the grosso spread to other parts of Europe. It was called a *croat* in Barcelona, where it made its appearance in the last quarter of the thirteenth century, the first heavy silver coin on the Iberian peninsula. Germany knew it as the *groschen*; it made its debut here and in Poland in the fourteenth century, and its name survives to this day on Austrian coinage. As the new, larger silver coin spread from one end of Europe to the other, it stimulated further trade and was itself an indication that commerce was reviving, assuming a greater and greater role in life of the average European. As trade grew and new silver deposits were uncovered, the grosso was dwarfed and replaced by even larger silver coins. By around 1500, the *testoon*, soon to be known as the shilling, was being coined in England, and while the French franc in silver did not appear until

1577, the term was in use for gold coinage by the middle of the fourteenth century. At the very end of the Middle Ages, a huge silver coin appeared in the Tyrol, part of modern Austria. It was one of the earliest European coins to be dated, and it was the largest silver coin struck up to that time. The new coin spread rapidly. It was soon being produced in many parts of Germany and Bohemia. In Bohemia, the Counts of Schlick struck it from silver taken from their mine at Joachimsthal. Their coin became known as a *Joachimsthaler*, and understandably its name was eventually shortened to *thaler*, then applied fairly indiscriminately to any large silver coin. It is the ancestor of the word *dollar*.

The revival of gold coinage followed paths similar to the revival of silver, and for the same reasons. Coins of greater worth became necessary in the expanding economy that characterized the later Middle Ages. In gold also, the Italians were the pioneers of the period. In silver they had introduced the grosso, a heavy coin of higher denomination than the penny. But they virtually reintroduced coinage in gold, and a coinage that was intended as a commercial convenience ended up stimulating business still further.

As might be expected, Florence and Venice, leaders in the new Italian gold coinage, were the preeminent economic powers of the day. Florence introduced its coin, the *florin*, in 1252. It bore a lily on one side (a pun on the name of the town—in Italian, the words for flower and Florence are similar), a standing portrait of St. John the Baptist on the other. The florin was made of good gold, and it was clearly intended for trade. As such, it inspired the Venetian *ducat*, introduced in 1284. The ducat was witness to the strong ties that had existed for centuries between Venice and the Byzantine Empire. The obverse depicted the doge, leader of the city, kneeling before St. Mark, its patron, while the reverse

bore a figure of Jesus Christ. Like the florin, the ducat was an immediate success, its issue in quantity insured by Venice's enviable trading position, as well as by the discovery of large deposits of gold in Hungary, which were pressed into service to produce it.

Both the florin and the ducat had many imitators. Other Italian city-states struck coins of a similar size but with different names and designs, such as the *genovino* from Genoa. Elsewhere in Europe, and well beyond, the florin and ducat were closely imitated in style and weight in such disparate places as Lübeck, southern France, and the Byzantine Empire.

However, Western Europe soon began experimenting with a gold coinage which was less imitative and more native. In England, Henry III issued a gold penny around 1257 (which was not a success due to the fact that it was undervalued in relation to silver), and the French introduced the *ecu d'or* shortly before 1270. This coin suffered the same fate as the English gold penny, and for the same reasons. A new French gold coin, the *petit royal assis*, was introduced around 1290, however. It had a higher official value against silver, and it

survived. Gold coinage was revived in England by 1344, and it was meanwhile making its appearance in Spain, the Low Countries, and Germany.

As the coinage of gold spread through Europe, new and larger coins made their appearance in this metal, just as they were being introduced in silver. The new English *noble*, first coined in 1344, is an outstanding example of a later medieval large gold coin, and it remained the standard gold denomination in England for many years. Similar developments were taking place elsewhere, but the English noble is espe-

cially important because it shows the effects of another group of factors shaping the later Middle Ages. These were of a political nature.

Let us examine the noble in some detail. The coin depicted comes from the reign of Edward III, and it is one of the earliest English nobles coined. It bears the king's figure on the obverse, a cross on the reverse. The inclusion of these basic elements is an indication that we are still in the Middle Ages. But there is more here. The obverse inscription proclaims Edward as king of England and France. As the English

Below. Part of the coining process in 18th-century France.

tried to make good this claim, the French tried to nullify it. At the time this coin was minted, the Hundred Years' War (1337–1453) was raging in France.

The noble's design is of greater importance than the inscriptions it bears, however, for it portrays the king as the embodiment of English nationality, as the most important quantity in the political equation of the times. At the same time, it downplays the role of the Church. Consider the obverse again. We see the king with a sword and a shield, by which he intends to defend and extend English power. The shield, incidentally, bears the British lion and the lily of France, repeating the claim of English rule over both countries. The king is in a ship, which may be a reference to the English naval victory at Sluys in 1340, or simply an apt way of symbolizing the aggressive insularity of the English, as well as a reference to growing English sea power.

On the reverse, we see a Christian cross. But it is significant that this cross is very small in proportion to other elements. Again, there are the lions of Britain and the *fleurs-de-lis* of France, with a royal crown over the lions. The entire design is enclosed in medieval-looking double scalloped lines. It almost seems as though the central cross has been included to produce a pleasing design, rather than for any religious symbolism. And the cross's center has become a convenient place to make a final reference to the king—the letter E, for Edward.

In short, the growing power of kings, the growing sense of nationality, the declining importance of the Church in the medieval scheme of things—all these find their expression on this English noble. England was not an isolated example of these developments. They are reflected on many

143

other coins of the period. While Edward was striking his nobles, his opposites in France were groping toward a similar display of nationality. By the reign of Charles VI (1380–1422), the reintroduced ecu d'or bore a cross device in which the French lily figured prominently on one side, a large shield with *fleurs-de-lis* surmounted by a crown on the other. The Spanish *dobla* of Pedro I (1350–1368) commonly bore the king's head on the obverse (in profile, a new development), the arms of Castile and León on the reverse. Both obverse and reverse inscriptions proclaimed Pedro king. The Spanish monarchs would soon come to be the most powerful in all of Europe. Pedro's coin contains little in the way of Christian symbols or inscriptions, an early indication of a future historic fact. In Spain the monarch would effectively be ruler of both State *and* Church.

Obviously, this type of medieval coin, which glorifies the ruler and nation and ignores more traditional elements in society, is most common in the emerging nation-states. But many elements found their way onto coins from areas that were not sharing in national unification movements. In Italy, the city of Milan depicted its arms on its florins, and in Germany, despite the fact that it was ruled by an archbishop, the design on a florin or *riel* of Cologne was almost entirely devoid of religious content. Both sides of the Cologne florin employed coats of arms. The side with three shields bears the date (1436), rendered here in Roman numerals. The concept of a dated coin, lost in Western Europe since the days of the Romans, was beginning to reappear. Perhaps this was an indication that, as conditions in Europe began to improve, the idea of progress was taking root in the mind of the West. Perhaps if ideas and conditions could change, if progress could occur, then

the passage of time might matter far more than it did before, and time's passing might find its expression on money in the form of a date to indicate when a coin was struck. This is speculation, but it seems borne out in part by the fact that the dating of coinage in the West did not begin until the later Middle Ages, by which time Europe was improving and growing.

By the waning of the Middle Ages, coins tell us of the great political events that took place in Western Europe. Principalities coalesced into national states, with a newly acquired sense of common culture and destiny. The power of the king grew, as that of the Church declined. The new, larger coins of the period, occasioned by economic growth, made fit vehicles for the expression of new national ideals, for the glorification of the monarch. But there was something else occurring here. The image of the king himself underwent change, both in terms of how he saw himself and how he wished his subjects to see him. These changes in royal imagery were projected onto coinage.

Through most of the Middle Ages, Western thought saw the ruler as an essential part of God's plan. But the *idea* of the king was most important. Any individual ruler was not all that significant in the whole scheme of things. To put it another way, while everyone knew that a king was a necessary part of the complete plan, it was not particularly important who that king was, or what he was like. Since the concept of progress was lacking, the accomplishments of any specific ruler were relatively unimportant.

All of this found its reflection on the coinage of the earlier Middle Ages. Kings were depicted full-faced, and there was little if any attempt to distinguish one from another. A graphic indication of this fact is found on English coinage, where the por-

145

trait of Henry II (1154–1189) was used through his reign and those of his successors, Richard I (1189–1199), John (1199–1216), and Henry III (1216–1272), down to about 1250. The real appearance of the king was unimportant. It might be said that portraiture was intended to symbolize the fact that there *was* a king, that God's plan was firmly fixed in place.

By the fourteenth century, however, the scene was changing. New, more energetic rulers were appearing. They were hammering out nation-states in alliance with the burgesses of the towns, in opposition to the nobility of the countryside. Their views of themselves began to occupy a place of central importance in their thinking, and they began to consider ways by which they could turn their subjects into active royal supporters against the pretensions of baron and cleric alike. They turned to coinage as one way of expressing their new identities and those of the states they represented. In this, the kings were aided by the economic upsurge of Europe that called for new and larger coins, which in turn would afford the king more space to bring his portrait and the badge of his state before the public.

In the king's desire for power, in his wish to be taken seriously, he began changing the manner in which he appeared on his coins. More and more frequently, he was surrounded by the trappings of his office, depicted in a manner calculated to inspire loyalty and awe among his subjects. The English noble was an early attempt in this direction. In France, the king was often portrayed as a knight on horseback, the very embodiment of a national leader. Late fifteenth-century English coins depicted the monarch enthroned in majesty on a new coin, the *sovereign*, ancestor of the present British pound.

Earlier rulers had been content to be presented on their coins in a symbolic manner, with no pretense at a realistic portrayal of how they actually looked. For the new, ambitious rulers of the fourteenth and fifteenth centuries, this was no longer enough. It was not sufficient that their subjects were merely aware of the fact that there was a king on the throne. The new type of ruler wanted to show them that *he* was that king, and that he looked thus-and-so. This may be the reason for a most important development in late medieval portraiture. For the first time in a thousand years, the old, full-faced rendition of the ruler was abandoned, and profile portraiture took its place.

This substitution, which has been followed ever since on Western coinage, was due in part to the new cultural tastes of the Renaissance, which were spreading through much of Europe. One of the main features of the Renaissance was a self-conscious return to ancient models for inspiration. The Greek and Roman princes had portrayed themselves on coins in profile; late medieval rulers would do the same. But there was more to it than that. Full-faced portraiture is not an effective way of presenting the individuality of a human face, and late medieval kings found that profile portraiture showed their real appearance much more faithfully.

The use of the profile portrait had been seen periodically throughout the Middle Ages, but it only began to come into favor in the fourteenth century. An early example, the dobla of Pedro I, did not have a completely realistic portrait, but it was a distinct step above the usual. The spread north of the portrait in profile was a leisurely one. It appeared in southern France in the 1360s, but it did not become common in France or England until around 1500. Still, if it were slow in moving north, its po-

Right. Castile, dobla, 1454–1474.
Below. L to r: English pennies
of Henry II (1154–1189); Richard
I (1189–1199); John (1199–
1216); Henry III (1216–1247).
Bottom. England, groats of
Henry VII (1485–1509), showing
full-faced and new profile
portraiture.

tentiality as a weapon in the extension of royal power is suggested by two English groats, made a few years apart in the reign of Henry VII (1485–1509). One portrays the king in the typical medieval fashion; he could be anyone. The other shows what he actually looked like. There is no mistaking that this man was the king of England.

The utilization of profile portraiture on coinage spread south much more rapidly. It was most widespread on Italian coinage of the late Middle Ages and Renaissance. This brings us to a third set of circumstances that had an effect on coinage during the Age of Awakening—cultural factors. The cultural rebirth at the end of the Middle Ages, which we call the Renaissance, was attended by economic and political developments of the highest importance. Had there been no economic upsurge, such places as Venice, Florence, and Bruges would never have risen to prominence, nor would some of their citizens have acquired the leisure time necessary to patronize the arts. In the same way, had rulers not seen advantages in cooperating with these wealthy classes, the development of the strong, monarchical state would have been long delayed, for the urban middle and upper classes formed willing royal allies against the landed nobility. In short, economic and political factors both played their parts in the decline of the medieval frame of mind and in the rise of a Renaissance one.

What were the prime ingredients of the Renaissance spirit? Above all, it was man-centered, not God-centered. Man was viewed a good deal more optimistically than before, God more benignly. This optimism extended to the idea of progress. People had come to believe that things could improve, that God had put nothing in the way of their improvement (this attitude would shortly encourage technological and scientific experimentation, in coinage as in other areas).

Men of the Renaissance were more nationalistic, less universalist than their medieval forbears, and so, probably, were their princes. In this respect, the Hundred Years' War was an expression of a mutual dislike between the French and English that would last to Waterloo and even beyond.

If the new rulers were more nationalistic, they were also more sure of themselves, less patient. They had fixed purposes in mind, and they were not very scrupulous about how they achieved them. In this, they were merely reflecting the prevailing mores of their subjects. The Renaissance was not a particularly good period in which to flourish as a saint.

So the Renaissance spirit was ambitious, nationalistic, enterprising, egotistical, forward-looking. We would call it pushy. In one key aspect, however, the spirit of the age looked backward to classical times. This was in the area of arts and letters, for the Renaissance spirit rediscovered the Greek and Roman past and sought to duplicate it in such disparate areas as sculpture, painting, poetry, and coinage.

As regards coinage, there is a great deal of the Renaissance cultural spirit on money from the period of its greatest flowering, the fourteenth through the early sixteenth centuries. As mentioned, profile portraiture, a typically Renaissance development, represented an attempt to celebrate a ruler by a return to ancient models. The outstanding examples of such portraiture come from Italy.

We catch an early indication of what was to come in an *augustale*, a gold coin from thirteenth-century Brindisi. The coin looks, as was intended, like a Roman aureus. The augustale was a somewhat isolated attempt, however. Profile portraiture did not become common on Italian coinage

Opposite. Top to bottom: Ferrara, Ercole I d'Este,
testone, 1471–1505; Milan, Francesco Sforza, ducato,
1450–1466; Milan, Bona of Savoy, testone, 1476–1481.
Above. Milan, Charles I, testones, 1535–1556.

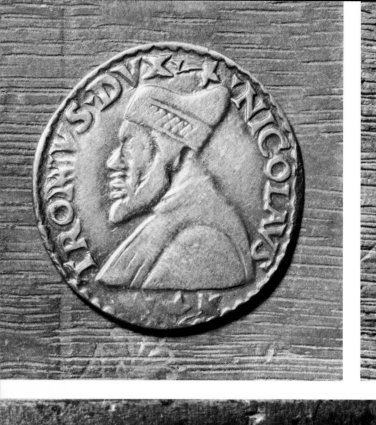

Opposite. Top l: Venice, lira, 1472.
Top r: Ferrara, Alfonso I d'Este, testone, 1505–1534.
Below: Montalcino, ascendi, 1556.

until the fifteenth century. But at that point there was a virtual explosion, giving us some of the best portraiture ever to have appeared on coinage. From Venice comes a silver *lira* of 1472, with a fine portrait of the current doge, Nicolò Tron. The Venetian lira was an unsuccessful coinage experiment, but the name would eventually be applied to the basic Italian monetary unit. Another Italian trading entrepôt, Ferrara, produced a series of splendidly realistic portrait coins. One coin (p. 150) depicts Ercole I d'Este, who ruled this duchy from 1471 to 1505. As the coin shows us, Ercole was not the most handsome of men. His desire to include a realistic self-portrait on his coinage stemmed from the Renaissance trait of princely egotism and from the new spirit of artistic realism.

Milan also produced coins with the realistic profile portraits demanded by the times. The city was ruled by the Sforza family until 1535, and coinage portraits in profile began there during the reign of Francesco Sforza (1450–1466). Almost alone among medieval coinages, that of Milan saw an issue with a woman's portrait, Bona of Savoy, who was regent of the city from 1476 to 1481. Milan is generally credited with having produced the best portraiture of the Italian Renaissance, a model for other states. This reflected the city's prominent role in Italian affairs at the time. Milan lost its independence in 1535, falling under the control of Spain, but artistic excellence continued to predominate on its coins.

A profile of Charles I, king of Spain and new ruler of Milan, was among the most striking portraits ever to have appeared on a coin. In the coin's inscriptions and its depiction of Charles in military armor, it was also following another formula dear to the Renaissance heart. It went back to ancient Rome for inspiration and in fact looked very much like a Roman coin.

This similarity becomes even more apparent on the reverse. The design layout is nearly identical to that of many Roman coins, as are the inscriptions, as is the central figure of Pietas (Piety, a popular motif on second-century bronzes). This coin, a *testone* minted between 1535 and 1556, is perhaps the most obvious example of a return to the classical past for design inspiration, but there are many others. A testone of Alfonso I d'Este of Ferrara (1505–1534) has a seated male figure which closely resembles those found on some Roman coins, while a rare gold *ascendi* from Montalcino has the Roman Wolf and Twins as its central design.

For their design inspiration, the artists of the Renaissance were going beyond the Age of Faith to the Age of Greece and Rome. This is not to say that the religious element previously present on medieval coins disappeared entirely, for it did not. But it did cease to be an essential part of the design on *every* coin struck in Italy and throughout the rest of Europe. This was something new, and it rather aptly symbolized the fact that the new era was more secular than the old, that the Church was ceasing to occupy the central role it had before, and, in a sense, that the Middle Ages themselves were drawing to a close.

By the time Charles I issued his testone from Milan, Europe had definitely left the Middle Ages. For Charles was not only king of Spain and duke of Milan (and, for that matter, ruler of the Holy Roman Empire), he was also sovereign over a vast new territory which, half a century before, no one in Europe had known existed. This was the Americas, of course, and its discovery and exploitation would change world history forever. Among other things, they would cause the beginning of a world-wide spread of coinage of the European type.

153

7

Two Shillings

A Quarter of

Two Shillings

...arter of

...o Shilling

His Bill of Two Shillings, due from the Colony of Connecticut in N. England to the
Possessor thereof, shall be in value equal to
Money, and shall be acordingly accepted by the Trea-
surer & Receivers subordinate to him; and for any
stock at any time in the Treasury.   Hartford July
the Tenth, in the VIIth Year of His Majesty's Reign
Anno Dom. 1733. By Order of the Gen. Court, New-
Haven, Octob. the Ninth, 1735.

A Quarter of

Two Shillings

A Quarter of

Two Shillings

Preceding pages. L to r: Lima, 8 escudos, 1710; Potosí, 8 reales, 1637; Connecticut, 25 shillings, 1735. Below. Top: Spain, Ferdinand and Isabella, 4 excelentes, 1474–1505; center, l to r: Mexico, 4 reales, 1536–1556; Santo Domingo, 4 maravedís, 1535–1556; bottom l to r: Lima, 8 reales, 1568–1598; Potosí, 8 reales, 1684.

The Expansion of European Coinage

In the Year of Grace 1492, two key events took place. Granada, the last Moslem city in Spain, was captured by the forces of the Catholic Monarchs, Ferdinand and Isabella, as the year dawned. Spain was now Christian from the Pyrenees to the Straits of Gibraltar. In October, a somewhat down-and-out gentleman adventurer named Christopher Columbus, who happened to be sailing under Isabella's aegis, touched land on an island off the coast of a huge area which he decided was India. Columbus duly claimed the region for Spain, and then sailed back to tell the Spanish monarchs about it.

These two events were to touch off a feverish period of European development and expansion, one which would see greater changes in Europe over the next two hundred and fifty years than had occurred during the previous two thousand. In the process, Europe would move from the Middle Ages to the dawn of modern times. But there was more to it than that. From 1500 to 1750, European influence, ways of life, and culture would appear in areas that had never seen them before. The years from 1500 to 1750 would see the outward spread of Europe to a position of world dominance which has only recently been relinquished.

The late Middle Ages and Renaissance provided the bases for these events. Had it not been for the new, questing spirit of the Renaissance, Columbus would never have received the backing he needed for his first voyage of discovery. Indeed, without the intellectual spirit of the times, it is unlikely he would have conceived of it in the first place. Moreover, had Spain not been unified under strong monarchs, symbolized by the capture of Granada, she would not have been strong enough to take advantage of Columbus' discoveries. As far as that goes, had it not been for the economic stronghold the Italians had achieved in trade with the East, the Spanish

would not have been interested in Columbus' proposal to reach the East by sailing West, thereby breaking the Italian monopoly over the older trade routes. And the Italian monopoly and the desire of enterprising Spaniards to get around it—these, too, were products of the later Middle Ages and Renaissance.

Of all the changes which took place during the two and one-half centuries of the Age of Expansion, two are most important in the story of money. The first was the discovery of new and more efficient ways of striking coins. Since the birth of coinage, two thousand years before, Western coins had been minted in essentially the same way: they were made by hand, by placing a piece of metal between two dies and striking the top one with a hammer. This method was slow, and the results were sometimes indifferent, but it had worked reasonably well over the centuries.

It was not good enough for the new spirit of the Renaissance, however. Earlier in the period, people had primarily been concerned with literary and artistic matters; by 1500, they were beginning to turn their attentions toward scientific and technological pursuits. Leonardo da Vinci is a perfect example of an individual interested in both worlds. He was one of humankind's greatest painters; at the same time, his writings are crammed with drawings and technical descriptions of new inventions springing from his fertile mind. Leonardo devoted some thought to an improvement of the coining technique, and so did many others.

The results of all this speculation were a number of new machines which, taken together, revolutionized the coining process. A heavy rolling press was devised, which pulled bars of metal through a series of rollers. This produced a wide, thin sheet of metal from which coin blanks could be cut. A machine to punch out those blanks was perfected, one that could produce planchets many times more rapidly than the old medieval process. By 1573, a restraining die collar, which encircled the coin blank as it was struck, had been invented. This insured the coin's roundness and made an edge border possible, a protection against clipping and counterfeiting.

But the essential advance was in the development of a machine used for the striking of the coins themselves, the screw press. This device literally squeezed the design into the face of the coin blank, using far more pressure than was possible with the old sledge hammer technique. The first practical screw press seems to have been invented by Donato Bramante, a prominent Italian medalist of the early sixteenth century.

The new inventions spread north and west. The screw press was used in France by the 1550s, in England by the beginning of the 1560s. A different sort of coining machine, the roller press, saw service in Austria at about the same time. The roller press was a logical extension of the device used to produce thin sheets of metal. In this case, thin sheets of gold or silver were passed between two rollers with obverse and reverse dies engraved on them, and the resulting coin impressions were then punched out separately with cutters. The roller press was extensively used in Austria, Germany, and Central Europe, but it was eventually superseded there and elsewhere by the screw press.

None of these coining developments became popular overnight. They tended to put coiners out of work, and opposition to them was so strong that, to give one example, the screw press was banned in England in 1573, not to reappear there for almost a century. Still, the potentials of the new methods are graphically shown by two coins illustrated on page 161, both shillings of Elizabeth I. The second specimen was minted some thirty years after the first, yet it is unquestionably the more primitive of the two. Despite initial opposition, the mechanized coining process came into its own by the middle of the seventeenth century, and it was standard practice throughout Europe from then on.

It was one thing to devise machinery making it possible to mint larger numbers of coins. It was quite another to come up with the precious metals necessary to make those coins. At this point, Columbus' discoveries entered the picture, for they would lead to undreamed-of amounts of gold and silver, ensuring that the new ways of minting money would receive maximum employment. This was the second major legacy given to the story of money by the Age of Expanison.

Columbus was searching for a new route to Asia, a new way of bringing the wealth of the East to the coffers of the West. He never found that route, and toward the end of his life became dimly aware that what he had discovered was not Asia at all, but a new, hitherto unsuspected land mass between Europe and Asia. Columbus found small amounts of precious metal on his voyages—not enough to make them paying propositions, but sufficient to whet the appetites of Spanish adventurers with a different sort of vision from that of Columbus. Perhaps, they reasoned, the new lands might contain enough wealth to make their conquest worthwhile. Perhaps the search for Asia ought to be deferred, the potentials of this new land more fully investigated.

There resulted one of the most spectacular stories of expansion and conquest in the history of the world. In 1500, only a few of the Lesser Antilles and the larger island of Hispaniola were under Spanish dominion; by 1580, Spain had conquered all of Mexico and

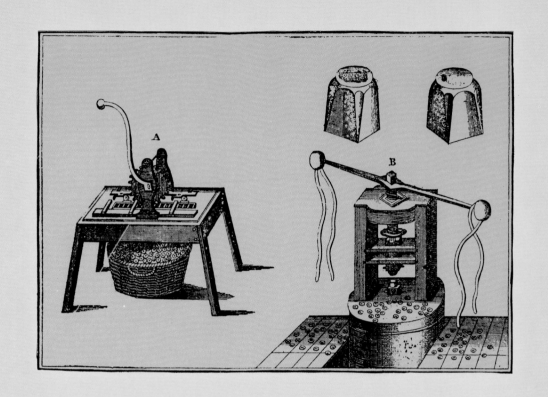

Above. L to r: France, teston, 1552; Austria (Tyrol), thaler, 1564–1595.

Central America and had brought the most productive regions of South America under its control. In the north, Spaniards were moving into the future American Southwest; in the south, they were colonizing Argentina and Chile. The world had never seen anything like this before, nor would it again.

Spanish hopes of finding wealth were richly rewarded. In Mexico, they subdued the Aztecs by 1521. In Peru and Bolivia, the Inca fell under their control by 1538. Both Indian nations had amassed huge quantities of gold and silver, which were promptly sent back to Spain. They soon made Spain the richest country in Europe.

But this was merely a taste of what was to come. By the 1540s, Spaniards were discovering incredibly rich veins of precious metal in Mexico, Peru, and Bolivia. In Bolivia, an Andean Indian found what might have been the very symbol of the new wealth of the Indies, a cone-shaped mountain, called Potosí,

which was essentially solid silver. Over the next three hundred years, that one mountain provided Spain with almost a billion pesos' worth of silver. On today's price scale, that would amount to perhaps twenty billion dollars. The new lands were indeed a paying proposition.

This huge increase in the world's supply of precious metals had a logical effect on coinage. We have seen that by the sixteenth century coins could theoretically be mass-produced. Now, they were. The result of all this was an economic revolution, dominating this Age of Expansion. Wars were fought because of or using the new influx of metal. Capitalism's development received an essential forward push. Banking was revolutionized. The growth of the absolute monarchy was stimulated. But in addition to all this, the new metallic wealth had an immediate effect on coinage. For the first time, coinage of a European nature spread far be-

Above. England, L to r: machine-struck shilling, c. 1561–1566; hand-struck, c. 1592–1595.

yond the boundaries of Europe, into the New World and the East.

This phenomenon sprang from several factors. With the rumor of wealth, there was no shortage of colonizers from the mother country, people who were accustomed to using European coins for their business transactions. They demanded that coinage be provided in New Spain, just as they had in Old Castile. Furthermore, the turning of previous metallic ore into coinage had obvious advantages for the metropolitan nation. It would be far easier to ship as coins than as ore, and it could be used to pay bills as soon as it reached Europe, instead of having to be turned into coinage first. These considerations brought about the spread of European-style coinage.

The Spanish pioneered the concept, just as they were leaders in the actual processes of colonization. In 1536 the first mint in the Americas was set up in Mexico City. It

was shortly joined by a temporary one at Santo Domingo, and by two permanent establishments, one at Lima and the other at Potosí. These latter two mints date from 1568 and 1575, respectively.

The American mints struck coins on the Spanish *real* standard, a piece of eight *reales* being the equivalent of a thaler. These large "Pieces of Eight," particularly, were struck in enormous quantities, and they became the best-known, most widely accepted trade coins in the world. Their designs were crude—ordinarily the Spanish shield on one side, the arms of Castile and León (or later, the Pillars of Hercules and the date) on the other. If their designs were crude, the method by which they were struck was primitive in the extreme. This coinage was not manufactured by the improved techniques devised during the sixteenth century. A semiround ingot was cast, cut into more-or-less round sections, then struck by hand. As a result, part

161

or much of the designs are commonly lacking on these coins, and unblemished specimens are rare. But the men who coined them were not concerned about the fine points of esthetics or technology. They wanted a coin of good silver fineness to ship back to Spain, or, if necessary, to use locally. As long as silver content was high, the appearance of the coin did not matter. And crude or not, the Piece of Eight and its subdivisions had a tremendously important role in the history of the world.

Impressed with the success of the Spanish colonization experiment, other European nations soon joined in the scramble. In reality, Spain's Iberian neighbor, Portugal, had originally started the entire train of colonial events. The Portuguese had attempted to reach India by sailing around Africa; with the epochal voyage of Vasco da Gama (1497–1498), they succeeded, and they shortly set up trading stations along the Indian coast. They were also the first to strike a European-style coinage there, beginning with the reign of Manoel I (1495–1521). Portugal's colonizing and coining activities in India were followed by several other European nations in time: the Danes by about 1650; the British, Dutch, and French somewhat later. Most of these latter countries issued coins which were more Indian than European, however.

The Portuguese also got into the Americas fairly early. Cabral, a Portuguese sailor, accidentally discovered Brasil in 1500. By the 1530s, struggling Portuguese settlements were scattered along the Brasilian coast, none of them as remotely important as the Spanish settlements to the north and west. No large sources of gold or silver were found for several generations (although the Portuguese exerted every effort to find them), and what commerce existed was primarily carried on through barter, by the use of the ubiquitous Piece of Eight, and whatever Portuguese coins entered the fledgling colony.

Brasil's first coinage appeared in 1695, at about the same time as precious metal deposits were found in Minas Gerais. The new coinage was closely modeled on the Portuguese, was struck by means of imported presses, and was probably intended more for local consumption than was that of the Spanish-American mints.

Elsewhere in the Americas there was relatively little coining activity, a reflection of political and economic realities. The Spanish Empire was the foremost military power of the day, easily able to ward off any colonization attempt in a critical area by an outside power. Further, Spain had a virtual monopoly on gold and silver deposits in the Americas, so that any non-Spanish colony that was set up would be unlikely to have access to bullion for coinage. As events developed, two of Spain's traditional enemies, France and England, *did* establish colonies in the Americas; both were confronted with a shortage of precious metal for coins, and each resorted to various expedients to overcome the problem.

For France, the matter was somewhat less onerous than it was for England. New France, the core of the present-day French Canada, was established as early as 1608, but the infant colony offered little in the way of economic allure, and few colonists came. An attempt by Louis XIV to interest Frenchmen in emigrating to Canada met with some success, however. By 1670, the new colony contained enough inhabitants to prompt a distinctive Canadian coinage, struck in France on behalf of the French colonials. This issue was a modest one, but it, along with French coins and frequent recourse to barter, satisfied the colony's basic monetary needs until the end of French control there (1763). Put more simply, French Canada never attracted enough inhabitants to necessitate a determined coinage effort, and no mint was

1

ever set up in that colony.

However, the same could not be said for the English colonies farther south. Established in the years between 1607 and 1733, these English creations grew rapidly, their economies based on agriculture, modest manufacturing, and trade. Their populations were made up of religious and political refugees from England and other parts of Europe. Boston was established by 1630; within twenty years, it was the center of a prosperous trade with England and the Spanish colonies to the south. By this time, it had evolved to the point where barter, wampum, and infrequent shipments of British coins were insufficient for its monetary needs. Since the region lacked gold or silver to make its own coins, the problem appeared insoluble.

Shortly after 1650, however, a way out of the dilemma was found, and the first coins minted in the English colonies made their appearance. These coins were based on the English shilling and its subdivisions, and they exist in four different basic designs. The best known has a pine tree (perhaps a reference to New England's wealth in forestry resources) on the obverse, the denomination and date on the reverse.

This coinage is interesting in two respects. First, it was made from Spanish-American silver; Massachusetts authorities simply removed underweight Mexican and Peruvian coins from trade, melted them down, and used them to strike their own coins. The problem of the lack of native precious metals was thus evaded. The second point of interest was an evasion of a different kind. The date on the coin illustrated on page 162 (bottom right) is 1652. It was actually minted around 1670. Why the date 1652, which appears on almost all Massachusetts silver? Very simply, it was to get around the law, to provide a coinage, legal or not. By British law, such a coinage was definitely *not*

1. L to r: Sweden, 10 daler, 1717; Sweden, riksdaler, 1707; Rhode Island, 6 pence, 1746.
2. Dutch Brasil. L to r: 3 guilders, 1646; 6 guilders, 1646.
3. Spain, Philip II, 8 reales, 1588.
4. L to r: Bremen, reichsthaler, 1743; Lübeck, thaler, 1731.
5. L to r: Spanish Netherlands, philippusdaalder, 1561; Netherlands (Deventer), siege rijksdaalder, 1575.

**Right. Louis XIV on his coinage.
L to r: écu, 1643; louis d'or, 1652; louis
d'or, 1672; écu, 1711.**

legal: the king, not the authorities in a faraway colony, enjoyed the right to coin money. But if there were no king, the law might be null, and in 1652, there *was* no king. Charles I had been beheaded three years before, and a Parliamentary dictatorship led by Oliver Cromwell was in command. So the Massachusetts authorities put that date on their coinage, even though it was struck well into the 1680s. Charles' son and eventual successor, Charles II (1660–1685), took a somewhat dim view of the proceedings, and he ordered the coinage stopped. It was stopped, and the needs of the colonists for a circulating medium of exchange became acute once more. But they soon found another way out of their difficulties. They employed a new form of money, one whose development was made possible, even inevitable, by the great flow of Spanish-American wealth into Europe. This new circulating medium was paper money.

The vast influx of wealth from the Indies occasioned better ways of keeping track of it. Such homely skills as double-entry bookkeeping now found general use, and the bill of exchange, a medieval recipe for safely transferring funds from one place to another, was now perfected. Great banking houses arose all over Europe, lending large sums to king and commoner alike. In 1661, one of them, the Stockholms Banco in Sweden, put together several obvious components and issued the first European paper money. Very simply, its notes were promises to pay the bearer a specified sum from funds of the bank. The good name of the bank in question stood behind its notes.

Here, indeed, was a revolution. Large sums of money could be safely and easily transported, used to pay bills, etc.—in short, paper money could have all of the advantages of coinage with none of the annoyances or risks. The new system spread rapidly.

The Bank of England was set up in 1694, issuing its first notes the following year. In France, John Law established his Banque Générale in 1716, which issued notes in place of the current large silver coin, the *écu*.

It should be noted that all of these pioneering, note-emitting banks were *private* concerns. Their issues were very close to our concept of paper money, but they were not identical. It remained for the struggling English colonies in America to take the final step, to issue paper money produced and guaranteed by a legally constituted government. This occurred in 1690, in Massachusetts, always the economic leader of the English colonies.

Massachusetts was perpetually short of coinage, as were the other colonies.

The 1652-dated silver could no longer be minted due to English law, and the local inhabitants were dependent upon whatever English or Spanish-American coinage came their way. This was insufficient, and, in any case, most of it went to England to pay for imports. In 1689, the situation worsened. England and France began the first of a drawn-out series of wars over Canada. Massachusetts, along with other colonies, was expected to arm, train, and pay colonial militia. Under ordinary circumstances, this would have been impossible, but colonial authorities devised a way around their quandary and in doing so created the first truly modern paper money.

In lieu of coins to pay troops and purchase supplies, the General Court (the co-lonial legislature) authorized the printing of paper money in several denominations. These bills would be given out to pay the militia, etc. Of essential importance to the whole scheme, the notes could be redeemed for specie (coinage). Massachusetts could make such a guarantee because England had promised to reimburse the colony for her expenses at the conclusion of the war. This guarantee of convertibility was the key: as long as people realized that in accepting the notes they would be able to cash them in later, they would embrace paper as readily as coinage, and paper would circulate. The new system had obvious advantages for both the government and its people. Since the citizenry knew that sufficient cash reserves existed to redeem the bills, these notes could remain in circu-

lation, where they could be of great benefit to colonial development. And the people now had enough money in circulation to render barter unnecessary, except in limited circumstances. As noted, Massachusetts issued its first paper currency in 1690, to finance a war. South Carolina followed suit in 1703, to finance another war. By 1755, all of the original thirteen colonies had issued or were issuing paper—to fight wars, to pay regular expenses, to finance building projects, or simply to make everyone's lives a bit easier.

There were problems inherent in the new medium, and they were felt both in English America, with its government-issued currency, and in Europe, where private emissions long continued to be the norm. Paper was much easier to counterfeit than coinage, and authorities and forgers began a duel that has continued to the present, with neither side winning, neither side showing any disposition to give up the fight.

Of greater importance, however, is the fact that paper money has always possessed value primarily because people believe that it does. In effect, we accept paper because we believe that we can buy as much with it as we gave to purchase it. When faith in paper's stability diminishes, its value goes down, and inflation results.

This faith can be attacked by several means. Counterfeiting is one such way, although, with a few exceptions, it has never been as large a problem as is commonly supposed. A much more serious concern arises from the nature of the authority printing the notes, whether private or public. If the issuer is of known fiscal probity, problems are minimal. But if the source of this currency has a bad financial record, is bankrupt, is about to or has lost a war, its notes will circulate with difficulty or not at all. The entire matter revolves around public faith, and public faith is incredibly delicate, easy to shatter. The Eng-

lish colonies had problems with public acceptance of their currency from early in the eighteenth century onward, and, in the private sector, John Law's Banque Générale came crashing down in 1720, from the same set of circumstances. These problems were nothing compared to twentieth-century developments, but they were an indication of an inherent problem in paper currency: people have to believe in it for it to work. Nevertheless, problem-ridden or not, paper's use expanded as time went on. If it presented difficulties, it also offered great possibilities in the way of public finance.

Through much of this book, we have talked about the influence of historical events on money. But there have been periods in human development when money had an influence on historical events. The Age of Expansion was definitely one such period. The key to money's role in history during these years lies in the fact that, due to the wealth of the Indies, more money existed in Europe than ever before. This increase in the European money supply had an important part to play in European and world economic and political events.

We have already examined some of the economic effects, such as the development of new banking and fiscal practices and the birth of European paper money. But the influx of new wealth left other long-ranging economic legacies. It led to a shift in the economic balance of power from southern to northern Europe, and this in turn assisted in the development of modern capitalism.

In the beginning, virtually all of the new-found wealth, whether in the form of bullion or of coinage, flowed directly from the Americas to Spain. By 1503, the Spanish government had devised a closed trading network with its trans-Atlantic possessions. Under this system, all gold, silver, and other American products were to be channeled di-

Right. England, George II, crown, 1739. Opposite. Above: Prussia, reichsthaler, 1771. Below: A screw press at work.

rectly to Spain, and Spain in turn would furnish her colonists with manufactured goods and other commodities that they could not produce in the New World. Unfortunately, Spain could not keep up her end of the bargain. She had never been much of a manufacturing nation anyway, and the lure of wealth in the Americas was far more compelling to the average Spaniard than a prosaic employment operating a loom. So Spanish manufacturing could not expand to meet the needs of American colonials or, for that matter, of native Spaniards.

Faced with this problem, the Spanish government turned to areas which were primarily specialists in the manufacturing of goods. They came to depend especially on the Netherlands, which were Spanish possessions at the time, but they also traded with France and, infrequently, with Britain. Spain in effect became a conduit: wealth poured into the country from the Indies, and it flowed right out again, to the north. Relatively little of it remained in Spain itself. These events heralded a shift in the economic balance of power from southern to northern Europe, for something similar occurred in Portugal at the same time, and Italy, too, declined in prosperity with the discovery of the new Portuguese and Spanish trading routes.

The gold and silver coins of Spanish America ended up in the coffers of merchants in Amsterdam and other cities on the North Sea and the Baltic. These places were often infected with the hard-driving work ethic of the new Protestant religion, yet another development of these crowded times. The work ethic encouraged the hoarding and reinvest-

ment of wealth, rather than its immediate expenditure on luxury items. More wealth now existed in concentrated form than ever before and new methods of banking and transferring money were developed. These factors came together to produce a new economic phenomenon, capitalism. Capitalism would be the driving spirit of this enterprising age and of those to follow. It still enjoys a dominant place among the world's economic systems, and the two other economic arrangements we know today—socialism and communism—were born as a reaction to it. And at the bottom of all of this activity were those freshly minted coins entering Europe from the Spanish Indies.

The new coins had other effects, too. They were not only responsible in part for shifting the economic balance of power, but they had a similar influence on political matters. The coins were a manifestation of the richness of the new Spanish-American lands. As such, they naturally whetted the appetites of other European nations, who hoped that they, too, could find wealthy new lands to exploit, or, barring that, perhaps could wrest

170

them from the Spanish. These desires on the part of England, France, and Holland prompted much exploration and some settlement in areas overlooked by Spain, such as New France and New England. Of greater immediate importance, however, was the fact that Spain and Portugal were already in possession of the richest of the new lands. In consequence, the latecomers would have to take these lands from the control of the Iberian nations if they were to secure a rapid return on their colonization endeavors. The result was a series of colonial wars, beginning in the 1550s, and lasting, in one sense, all the way to the Spanish-American war of 1898. Non-Iberian attempts to raid or colonize Iberian areas were not notably successful, and they were more of an annoyance than a threat for the Spanish and Portuguese empires.

Money was at the root of much of the trouble. The have-not nations were jealous of the wealth of the haves, and the have-nots proposed to do something about it. The accident of colonial wealth was no fault of Spain, and in all fairness one cannot accuse that nation of responsibility for the colonial warfare that went on.

But for another series of wars, European ones, which were going on at the same time as the colonial friction, Spain bears much greater responsibility. The colonial warfare lost Spain relatively little, but her European adventures lost her much more, including her preeminent role in Europe.

Here again, those Spanish-American coins came into play. As mentioned earlier, most of the wealth from the Americas passed through Spain as payment for northern European commodities. But enough of it was left behind to embolden the Spanish monarchy to set out on a number of disastrous crusades intended to turn back the tide of the new Protestant faith and to maintain Spain's dominant role in Europe in the days

of Charles I (1516–1556). These wars ended badly for the nation. By 1600, Spain was beginning to show definite signs of decline; by 1700, she counted so little in European affairs that France and England fought the War of the Spanish Succession (1701–1713) to determine whose candidate would mount the throne of Spain. (The French contender won, inaugurating a period of French influence over Spanish affairs which would help in time to bring about Spain's loss of the Indies.)

Spain's new wealth brought about her participation in costly wars, and this in turn helped to shift the center of political influence northward to England, France, and Holland. The influx of vast amounts of gold and silver shaped the policies of those countries, too. England and France, at least, were strongly unified under ambitious kings by the opening of the sixteenth century. These monarchs sought to augment the power and glory of their countries and themselves. The flow of Spanish-American coinage into their nations provided them with a way of doing so. With the revenues they secured from this trade, they could hire and equip large mercenary armies to fight their wars. The mercenary soldier, who fought for the highest bidder, became an apt symbol of the new times; several smaller European states would turn the hiring out of able-bodied men as mercenaries into something approaching a national industry. All in all, the new wealth from the Americas helped increase European warfare after the middle of the sixteenth century—no matter who was fighting those wars, no matter what the reason.

The American coinage probably had one final political effect in Europe. While it is impossible to prove the point, it seems likely that the new money fostered the growth of the absolute monarchy, hindered the development of the parliamentary state. For it soon became apparent that if kings could purchase soldiers with the new wealth, they could also buy whatever else they needed to assure their complete control over government and nation. They could hire bureaucrats to streamline the conduct of public business, and, since they paid the salaries of those functionaries and were the sources of the wealth and honors which rewarded faithful servants of the monarchy, they could keep the reins of bureaucratic control firmly within their grasp. They could build a loyal following among the nobility or the middle classes (or both), by a judicious application of money where it would do the most good.

As they did all of this, they were building up strong, devoted supporters. At the same time, they were undercutting the growth of popular participation in government, as expressed in the form of a deliberative body, a parliament. For the simple fact was that the kings no longer needed parliaments to conduct their affairs. Enough money was now available to them so that they could purchase what they wanted rather than having to beg for it from a parliamentary body, as had previously been the case. They no longer needed to make concessions to popular rule in order to gain their objectives. They could go around it, and, indeed, they had already purchased the loyalties of some of the key elements in the society.

Louis XIV (1643–1715) stands as the prime exponent of the new absolute European monarch. Perhaps he never said *"L'Etat, c'est moi"* (I am the State), but he certainly could have. The fact that succeeding generations credited this monarch with that statement tells us something about the monarch in question and about his royal colleagues elsewhere in Europe. They *were* the state, and they wanted everyone to know it.

Their coins tell us as much. The coinage of Louis XIV is in effect a long portrait gallery, with depictions of the king from childhood to old age. There can be no doubt of who is in command here. The king dominates his coins, as he dominated seventeenth-century France. On the reverse of Louis' coins, regal or French national symbols are prominent. The reverse of a 1711 écu is reasonably typical. There are three crowns, intermixed with three *fleurs-de-lis*, an apt combination of the symbols of king and country. There is little religious content to Louis' coins: a cross appears on some of them, but it is composed of several Ls, which, of course, referred to Louis. The cross is an element of decoration by this time, and it bears little or no religious significance.

The basic elements present on Louis' coinage may be found on money throughout Europe at this time. Royal portraits predominate, often in armor, as on Roman coins. While there is an attempt at realistic portraiture, the main point to be put across is the dignity and majesty of the king. This would lead to some unattractive results. Even the English kings, who were among the least absolutist in Europe, insisted in having themselves portrayed in this way. Unfortunately, members of the new Hanoverian dynasty were uniformly homely, and no engraver's skill in the world could veil that fact. A 1739 crown of George II (1727–1760) is a prime example of what the die engravers were up against. Still, the artisans strove for majesty where there was none, and the monarchs strove to become more absolute.

A reaction to all of this and many other aspects of the Age of Expansion was in the works, however. By 1750, that era was beginning to be replaced by another, aptly called the Age of Revolution (1750–1900). During this new period, political, technological, social, and economic changes would go on more rapidly than ever before. And money, too, would change rapidly, reflecting new stresses and needs.

Preceding pages. Coins, l to r: England, penny token, 1811; Congo Free State, 10 centimes, 1888; France, 2 sous, 1793; bills, l to r: Italy, 2 lire, 1866; United States, 3 dollars, 1776.
Below. Top: England, 2 pence, 1797; center, l to r: Sierra Leone, penny, 1791; England, penny, 1797; bottom: United States cents, 1835 and 1836.

The Age of Revolution

The last half of the eighteenth century and all of the nineteenth were times of almost incomprehensible development and change throughout the world. Consider the differences between a man living in 1750 and his counterpart in 1900. The average man of the mid-eighteenth century was probably a small farmer (indeed, if he lived in many parts of Europe, he was still bound to the soil). He was illiterate, had no concept of other lands and cultures, and was born, grew up, married, had children, and died within an area of a few square miles. He was unlikely to have any political power whatsoever. He had an average life expectancy of about thirty-five years.

Now consider his 1900 counterpart. This man was likely to work in a factory. He was literate, at least somewhat so, and he was aware of events taking place around the world. He lived in a city and traveled from place to place by train or even underground transportation. If he still lacked many basic political rights, he was becoming increasingly aware of that fact and had made up his mind to do something about it. His major attachments now lay with the nation, not with the village where he was born. He might expect to live to be fifty.

These changes in the life of the average person were the reflection of much greater changes in the world at large. Between 1750 and 1900, the bulk of what we accept as our current way of life was firmly set into place: mass production, rapid transportation, the modern city, nationalism, total war.

We must speak of revolutions in three distinct fields of human development, all of which left lasting imprints on man's history and money. These areas are the technological, the economic, and the political. It must be noted that in all three areas, extensive groundwork for change had been laid years, sometimes centuries, before. Once this groundwork had been laid, change could be rapid and spectacular, developments feeding upon each other in a kind of snowball effect. For example, had the useful machines of the Age of Expansion never seen the light, the Industrial Revolution could not have taken place. Further, were it not for the earlier revolutions in banking and money, the full flowering of capitalism would have been deterred. And the spread of nationalism and, later, of imperialism were firmly based on the late medieval/early modern concept of the nation-state. None of these observations detracts from the revolutionary nature of the late eighteenth and nineteenth centuries; they are merely indications that in history nothing springs out of a vacuum.

We call the cluster of technological changes during this period the Industrial Revolution. Its effects were first felt in Britain around 1750, and from there it spread to the rest of the world. It may well have been the most important of the three types of revolutions occurring during these years, for it greatly influenced developments in the other two. As an example of its influence, the Industrial Revolution gave us the railroad, the steamship, the telegraph. All these inventions helped to bind states together more closely than ever before; to that extent, they fostered nationalism, a key element in the political revolution of these times.

In essence, the term Industrial Revolution refers to the invention and adoption of new ways of manufacturing commodities, and, of great importance, of manufacturing more of them with greater rapidity than ever before. In effect, the perfection of the steam engine by James Watt in the 1760s and its first application in manufacturing by the 1770s and 1780s meant that, given enough raw materials, an almost infinite quantity of any commodity could now be manufactured.

Coinage is a commodity, a product

Opposite. The evolution of nineteenth-century paper money. Top to bottom: South Carolina, Bank of Camden, 10 dollars, 1849; Georgia, Southern Bank of Georgia, 2 dollars, 1858; Uruguay, 20 pesos, 1871.

like anything else, and it was only a matter of time before the new techniques of mass production were extended to it. In fact, coinage was one of the earliest products to be mass-produced, as the new concept of steam power was applied to coining money.

The steam-powered coining press was the result of a collaboration between James Watt and Matthew Boulton, who became partners in 1768. In 1770, Boulton designed a steam-operated coining machine, and then, in Birmingham, England, he set up an entire plant devoted to the mass production of money. His concern was soon busy producing coins for the Sierra Leone and East India companies, British colonial enterprises in West Africa and southern India. Boulton also manufactured a vast number of tokens during the British coin shortage of the 1780s and 1790s and finally, in 1797, he was awarded a contract to coin money for the British government itself. His resulting penny and twopenny pieces were not universally popular, for they were extremely large and heavy, the idea being that they should be worth their weight in copper. All the same, they were more perfectly struck than any previous coins had ever been. Later, somewhat lighter coins made by Boulton's firm did find widespread acceptance. Mechanization had become the norm for British coinage by 1800.

From there, the new techniques spread rapidly. France's first steam-powered coins date from around 1805; by the 1820s, several other European nations were employing steam presses. The new method crossed the Atlantic in the 1830s. The first steam-powered coining presses were set up at the mint of the new United States of America in 1836, and they would eventually be found throughout both North and South America. Late in the nineteenth century, the steam press appeared in Japan and China, revolutionizing coinage in both countries. (This was also an indication of economic and political penetration of the East by the West.)

Coinage was directly influenced by the technological aspect of the Age of Revolution, though the maximum application of new minting practices would have to wait until the discovery and exploitation of new sources of metals. These came about from the 1830s onwards, as vast deposits of copper were found and mined in Michigan, gold in California, Australia, South Africa, and the Klondike, and silver in Nevada and Mexico. The technological revolution touched these aspects of human endeavor, too. One reason for the dramatic rise in the world production of precious metals was that new ways had been invented for getting them out of the ground. By about 1850, as many nations had or were adopting the steam press, the metals necessary for the full utilization of that machine were being found. This would result in greater numbers of coins being minted than ever before, and the new, abundant coinage would have much to say in a second aspect of this Age of Revolution, its economic phase.

The concentration of wealth which we saw in the preceding chapter continued and increased during this period. The new manufacturing techniques of the Industrial Revolution made vast amounts of money for some members of the upper and middle classes. These people reinvested their new-found wealth in railroads, more factories, and other trappings of the industrial age. Added to this were the gold from California and Australia and the silver from western North America, which came to Europe as bullion, or, shortly, as new, perfectly manufactured coins. Further wealth led to further economic development and concentration, which in turn led to greater wealth. Capitalism was coming of age.

These revolutionary changes in the economic life of the eighteenth and nine-

THE BANK OF CAMDEN
(SOUTH) CAROLINA
TEN DOLLARS
CAMDEN,

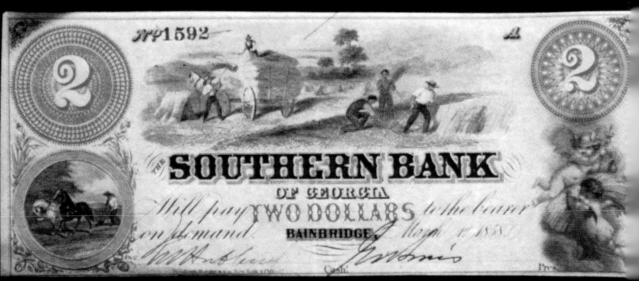

SOUTHERN BANK
OF GEORGIA
Will pay TWO DOLLARS to the bearer
on demand BAINBRIDGE

EL BANCO MAUA & Cía
Nº 092773
VEINTE PESOS EN BILLETES DE CURSO LEGAL
MONTEVIDEO, 1º DE MARZO DE 1871.
VEINTE PESOS
DOBLONES

1 2

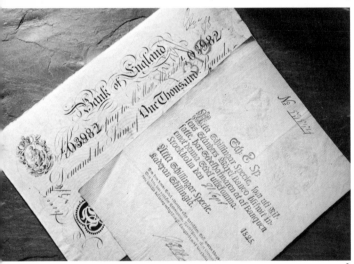

3 4

6   8

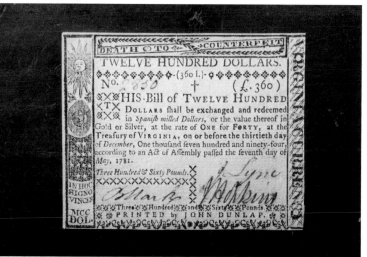

7   9

1. L to r: United States, 20 dollars, 1852; Australia, sovereign, 1852.

2. L to r: France, 5 francs, 1808; Italy, 5 lire, 1808; Westphalia,
5 frank, 1808.

3. Top to bottom: England, £1,000, 1846; Sweden, 8 skilling, 1825.

4. L to r: France, franc, 1867; Switzerland, franc, 1861; Italy, lira,
1867; Belgium, franc, 1867; Greece, drachma, 1868; Romania, leu, 1870.

5. Top to bottom: France, Banque de France, 50 francs, 1894; United
States legal tender note, dollar, 1880; Italy, biglietto di stato,
10 lire, 1888.

6. L to r: United States, Continental Currency, 8 dollars, 1775;
Maryland, 4 dollars, 1775; North Carolina, 10 dollars, 1778;
South Carolina, 90 dollars, 1779.

7. Virginia, $1,200, 1781.

8. L to r: France, sou, 1789; 12 deniers or sou, 1791; sou, 1793.

9. French assignats. L to r: 25 sols, 1792; 100 francs, 1794–1795.

Below. France, from Republic to Empire. L to r: 5 francs, 1802; 5 francs, 1803; 5 francs, 1804; 5 francs, 1809. Far r. Political upheaval in Spain. Illustrated are 8-real pieces struck in the names of Charles IV, 1808 (top), Joseph Bonaparte, 1809 (lower l), and Ferdinand VII, 1808 (lower r). Opposite, below: Old German print of a coinage workshop.

Above. Insurgent Latin American coinage. L to r: Colombia, 2 reales, 1813; Mexico, 2 reales, 1813; Mexico, 4 reales, 1814. Opposite, clockwise from l: Mexico, 8 reales, 1824; Bolivia, 8 soles, 1828; Chile, 8 escudos, 1838.

teenth centuries had two major effects on money's development. First, they vastly increased the amount of coins minted and circulated. More coins were needed to pay workers, increasingly grouped in large factories, in cities—places where barter would no longer suffice. More coins were required to invest in speculative enterprises, designed to make more money still.

But the second effect which the economic revolution had on money was even more important. During this period, paper money became the normal medium of exchange in many large business transactions and some small ones. This should come as no surprise. As we have seen, one of paper money's attractions was that it was easier to handle and safer to transport than was coinage. This attraction could only increase as the world economy grew, as payments had to be made over distances of several hundred or

even several thousand miles. There were still the old risks, of course. Public faith in the currency could decline, with disastrous results. The period was dotted with such instances, dating from the time of the American Revolution (1775–1783) through the French Revolution (1789–1799), on to widespread collapses of private, note-emitting banks in Britain in the 1820s and in the United States in the 1830s and 1850s. But still, when paper money worked (and it did most of the time), it was a tremendously attractive medium of exchange, one which could be instrumental in both private enterprise and state expansion. So its usage increased, despite the risks of periodic collapse.

Nor were its adherents overly concerned with the problem of counterfeiting. Paper money had always been falsified on a private level. By the late eighteenth century, it was also being counterfeited on an official

one, as governments found that they could manufacture dangerous replicas of each other's currency, thereby weakening enemy faith in paper money. This measure was adopted in the late 1770s by the British, who fought to regain control of their North American colonies, and by France, who used it against an Austrian enemy during the Napoleonic Wars.

To both private and governmental counterfeiting, the solution was a simple one—make new notes that were impossible to duplicate. As the nineteenth century wore on, fancy vignettes and involved designs became the norm on paper money, as did complicated watermarks, designs pressed into the paper upon which the notes were printed.

By around 1850, the old, simple, one-color (black) format was being abandoned in favor of multicolor bills. At first, only one additional color was added in a second printing, and it had little to do with the overall design. By the early 1860s, this was changing, and the world was beginning to become familiar with true multicolor paper money. The new bills were more beautiful than ever before, but esthetics were not the prime consideration here. The new notes were more difficult to counterfeit.

It should be emphasized that most early paper money was the product of private banks, which fairly accurately reflects the unregulated state of economic affairs in general during the period. This, in fact, was partially responsible for the periodic collapses of paper currency. In the absence of any national regulatory authority, honest banks would issue paper money in strict accordance with their cash reserves, while dishonest ones would print paper money far in excess of their redemption ability. In time of economic distress, these shaky note-issuing banks were among the first casualties, and the panic which their fall engendered often led to a domino effect, in which good and bad banks alike were forced to close their doors.

This was one reason for a prominent phenomenon of paper money in the late nineteenth century. More and more of it would be issued by a central, usually state-controlled, banking agency. In the United States of America, the Treasury Department took over the printing of paper money in the 1860s. In France, it was the Banque de France; in Germany, which finally became unified in 1871, it was the Reichsbank, and so on. The disappearance of privately issued currency in favor of national paper money did not occur everywhere at once, nor did it come about overnight. But it would be the way of the future. Today, every nation has some sort of central, state-run currency authority, and private bank notes are virtually nonexistent.

The shift from private to public currency was both a necessity and an advantage for the state. By being able to regulate the money supply, the new states of the late nineteenth century were in a position to regulate their national economies, to direct spending into certain channels—and, if they so desired, to present the public with patriotic designs and slogans on the currency, useful in building a deeper sense of nationality among their people. It is not entirely coincidental that the growth of national paper-money systems took place at the same time as did the growth of nationalism itself. We will discuss this nationalism later on, for it had a major role to play in money during the Age of Revolution.

Paper money was intended in part to make long-distance economic transactions easier, and another set of economic practices adopted during this period was intended to do the same thing. The late eighteenth and particularly the nineteenth centuries saw the world moving toward a concensus on international coinage standards. There was nothing new in this. Even in the days of ancient Greece, when commerce grew between a number of polei, it became apparent that if each city involved in trade struck coins on the same standard and of the same size, commercial transactions could be made easier. The Greeks in fact achieved some success in this field, and silver coinage on the Attic (Athenian) standard enjoyed widespread popularity for many years. Something similar could be said for the medieval penny and its later descendents, the grosso and the florin. The latter coins saw wide circulation outside Italy, and they were imitated all over Europe and well beyond. But the nineteenth century saw the birth of a much more determined attempt to set up a universal monetary system, in which the coins of one country would be instantly convertible into those of another. This was the Latin Monetary Union, and its origins may be traced to France in the days of Napoleon the Great.

Napoleon succeeded in temporarily establishing a multinational French Empire. At its height around 1810, this polity embraced France itself, most of Spain, Holland, Italy, and parts of Germany. Wherever Napoleon conquered he set up mints, striking gold and silver coins corresponding to the French monetary unit, a franc consisting of one hundred centimes. In his system, gold and silver coins identical to regular French issues, except for a mint mark, were struck in Utrecht, Rome, Geneva, and Turin, while coins with a different name (a lira, in Napoleon's kingdom of Italy, or a *frank* in Westphalia, ruled by his brother Jerome) but based on the French standard saw the light in other parts of the empire. Some of these monetary arrangements continued in force even after the fall of Napoleon. His nephew, Napoleon III, resurrected the idea of a universal standard with his Latin Monetary Union, which was formally organized late in 1865.

Napoleon III had a good deal to work with. By 1865, Switzerland, Italy, Belgium, and several other countries were already informally striking coins on the French standard. The Latin Monetary Union enshrined this practice in international law, as well as extending it to other parts of Europe and the world. Soon, many nations in the Americas were striking at least part of their coinage based on the standards of the Union. Russia had adopted the new system for some of her coinage, and several countries in southern and eastern Europe, notably Greece, Romania, and Bulgaria, were basing their monetary systems completely on the Latin standard (whether the coin was called a franc in France, a *drachma* in Greece, a *leu* in Romania, or a *leva* in Bulgaria, it was still the same coin). This international cooperation in coinage standards and denominations was a logical development in this Age of Revolution, which was businesslike and rational-minded as well as revolutionary. It did not long survive the end of the period, however. Fourteen years into the twentieth century, the First World War erupted, which, among other things, would tend to indicate that men were not as rational as they had commonly supposed. The war swept much away, including the Latin Monetary Union. This in turn heralded the lack of economic cooperation which would distinguish the later twentieth century, an international state of mind which often led to economic warfare, long after the military warfare had come to an end in 1918. The Latin Monetary Union and its coins nevertheless stand out as a notable attempt at monetary rationalization and standardization on a world scale.

The combination of technological and economic factors which distinguished the Age of Revolution had a major influence on the events of those years. Technology increased production and also brought people closer together. Technology and economics built the factories which made a few individuals rich and many others better off than they had ever been. But these aspects of the Age of Revolution had other effects too. The third facet of the period is a political one, in which "Age of Revolution" is meant in the literal sense of the term. Growing nationalism and increasing political and economic discontent contributed to making this century and a half one of the most turbulent eras in history. Technological and economic factors were at the bottom of much of the trouble, and the political upheavals which they helped to generate would also find expression in money.

The prime political ingredient of the Age of Revolution was nationalism. It was frequently accompanied by sentiments of republicanism, by yearnings for democracy, as in the case of the American and French revolutions, as well as in those at mid-century. This was not always the case, however. While the unifications of Germany and Italy were triumphs for the spirit of nationality, they did not herald the coming of liberal, republican regimes in either country. Of the two political aspects of the Age of Revolution, nationalism and liberalism, nationalism was the more important. Many of its roots are to be found in the technological and economic changes mentioned earlier, but others go back further.

For example, the nationalistic roots of the American Revolution went back to the beginnings of English colonization in North America. At first, the colonists considered themselves transplanted Englishmen, and they were very dependent upon the mother country for economic, military, and financial support. But as time went on, events took place which altered their views of themselves and England. A flourishing trade developed, much of it with England, but a good deal of it with other parts of the world, especially Spanish America. This trade was not exactly legal, for in theory the commercial network between England and her colonies was a closed one, and foreign trade did not have a place in it. The English did not ordinarily enforce their trading regulations, however, and business boomed.

As both legal and illegal trade grew, so did the differences between residents of England and those of her colonies. For the colonials had to face a set of problems unknown among their metropolitan counterparts—opening the land, pushing back Indian tribes, fighting against the encroachments of colonials of other nations. These differences eventually brought about a new feeling among the colonists. No longer were they thinking of themselves as Englishmen who happened to reside in Massachusetts or Virginia. They were becoming a new people, a distinct offshoot from the parent English stock. They began to consider themselves Americans, and any attempt by London to

make good Englishmen of them was likely to meet with stiff resistance.

The resistance began to go into effect after the end of the French and Indian War (1754–1763). English and American armies evicted the French from Canada. Faced with a large financial burden because of the war, the English now attempted to regulate colonial affairs more closely, to make the colonies a paying proposition. They even advanced the naïve idea of having their colonials pay for the upkeep of the English troops defending them. Colonial resistance went into effect. Americans were content to remain English subjects as long as the Crown required little or nothing of them, but when demands were made, the newly acquired sense of American nationality asserted itself. The inevitable flash-point occurred at Lexington in the spring of 1775. The Revolutionary War began, and it dragged on for the next eight years. It would engender a new nation, the United States of America.

Wars must be financed, and the Americans soon ran into problems in this area. Where would they find the money to arm and train troops, to purchase supplies, to do everything necessary to win their bid for independence? No deposits of gold or silver existed in the colonies. The American solution was an obvious one. They would print paper money to finance this war, just as they had paid for previous ones. Beginning in 1775, both the provisional national government, the Continental Congress, and the individual colonies (or states, as they began calling themselves) undertook the printing of paper, and they continued to do so through most of the war. National issues bore pious vignettes with Latin inscriptions, most of them suggested by Benjamin Franklin. They urged American unity, called for stiffened resistance to England, and promised that all would be well in the end. The state notes carried a stronger

message. A Maryland issue showed George III setting fire to an American city. North Carolina notes incorporated political commentaries and statements about the British, in English rather than in Latin. One South Carolina bill showed an American Hercules strangling a British lion. These notes are an early indication of the rediscovery of the use of money for propaganda, something we have not seen since Rome, but an element of growing importance in man's money from this time onward.

All of these slogans and vignettes could not forestall the collapse of the American paper-money system. In 1775 and 1776, the notes were circulating at par; by 1780, federal issues circulated at two-and-one-half cents on the dollar. Individual state issues fared even worse.

Obviously, American faith in paper currency had suffered a disastrous drop. Two considerations may account for this. First, in the case of earlier American paper printed to finance a war, there was always the promise of British redemption standing behind each note issued. Obviously, the British were not likely to redeem paper printed to fight *this* war. Second and more seriously, had the Revolutionary War been seen as of limited duration, with promises of a smashing American victory at the end of it, paper money would have circulated at or near par. Public optimism about the war's outcome would have been transferred to the money printed to pay for it.

But it soon became apparent that, unlike earlier colonial wars, this one would be different. It would go on year after year, with colonial success no better than a fifty percent possibility most of the time. It would involve the actual enemy occupation of many of the most productive portions of the new United States. A case in point: George Washington lost New York City in 1776; the Amer-

icans did not regain it until after the conclusion of peace, in 1783.

So public faith in the emergency currency progressively declined, and so did its value. By 1780, the whole system was in a shambles; fortunately, the Battle of Yorktown late in the following year decided the issue of independence in America's favor. The shooting phase of the Revolutionary War ground to a halt, and the American financial system was given time to revive and reform. When it did so, it would eschew the printing of paper currency by federal or state authorities. Americans had been hurt so badly by government-issued paper that it would not be reintroduced until the time of the Civil War, when an extraordinary crisis once again demanded an extraordinary fiscal response. American currency is abundant in the period from the 1780s to the 1860s, but it is private, not public.

The success of the American Revolution helped determine the tone of the rest of the eighteenth century and most of the nineteenth. It appealed to people on two levels. Here was a colonial people, wishing and choosing to join the family of free nations, and actually succeeding in doing so! Furthermore, this new nation had rejected the trappings and pretensions of monarchy; it was calling itself a republic and had a new Constitution to give substance to the name. This twin set of ideas was immensely attractive to people around the world, and many of them would soon be experimenting with independence, political liberalization, or both.

The first to do so were the French. The economic distress of inept Louis XVI led to his convening of the Estates Général, France's parliamentary body, in 1789. Louis' financial needs must have been great, for the last time the Estates Général had met was in 1614! Originally convened to vote additional tax revenues, the Estates Général, influenced by the new political ideas from America and the tremendous economic distress of France in the late 1780s, took matters into its own hands. Changing its name to the National Assembly, it effectively became the new government of France. Louis' position deteriorated, as his coins show. In 1789, he is still firmly on his throne, as the inscriptions on a *sou* of that year inform us. The titles—in Latin—make reference solely to Louis and his possessions. By 1791, Louis' titles are given in French, not Latin, perhaps an indication of a heightened French self-awareness proceeding from revolutionary events. And while Louis is still king, a reverse inscription on a sou refers to Nation, Law, and King—in that order. Within a year, the unfortunate sovereign would be dethroned and shortly decapitated, and new French coins would reflect these events, too. A 1793 sou of the new French Republic is filled with slogans referring to human rights and equality, and the regime considered the proclamation of the republic in September, 1792, so important that it used the event as the basis for a new dating system, which appeared everywhere, including on coinage. (On the piece depicted on page 181, L'AN II refers to the second year of the republic, which lasted from late 1793 to late 1794). All of this revolutionary exuberance led to a quick reaction from the monarchical powers of Europe. By late 1792, most of them were at war with France.

Quite naturally, the French government wished to defend the country. Equally logically, it wished to export the virtues of the new French social and governmental systems to the less enlightened countries surrounding Revolutionary France. All of this would require a large amount of money, of course, and in this latest financial crisis, the French government resorted to the expedient which the Americans had used so disastrously a dozen years before. It turned to paper money.

French governmental issues of this period are known as *assignats*. They were theoretically backed by lands expropriated from the Catholic Church (this anticlerical aspect of the French Revolution didn't sit particularly well with the conservative monarchies of Europe, either). Unfortunately, the French printed far more assignats than they could possibly redeem, and the value of this paper declined as precipitously as had its American predecessor. By 1796, it was virtually worthless, and late that year the government declared it so, repudiating the entire issue. The experiment with assignats would leave the French with a distrust of paper money similar to that of Americans, and paper would not resume an important place in the national monetary system until the late nineteenth century.

Despite the abandonment of its paper-currency system, the French Revolution was doing very well for itself in other areas. It had removed the foreign threat by this time, and it was beginning to export its precepts of nationalism and political liberalization to other countries. This exportation reached its height during the reign of Napoleon Bonaparte (1799–1814), one of the bright young men brought to fame during the early phases of the revolution. Bonaparte was one of the greatest generals in the history of the world; under his ministrations, the French Revolution spread all over Europe, supported by the bayonets of his Grande Armée. As it did so, however, much of the revolutionary, liberal impact of the French Revolution was lost. By 1810, other Europeans saw it as an expression of French national chauvinism and imperialism, not as a liberal movement at all. Though Napoleon started out as a military leader under the republic, he had overthrown the legal government late in 1799, and installed himself as First Consul (or dictator of France, if you prefer). Five years after that,

**Below. The British Empire. Clockwise from top: India, rupee, 1879;
India, rupee, 1879; Mombasa, rupee, 1888; half rupee, 1890;
Australia, pattern 6 pence, c. 1855; Canada, 50 cents, 1871.**

Below. Top row, l to r: Venice, 5 lire, 1848; Roman Republic, 40 baiocchi, 1849; Hungarian Insurrection, 3 kreuzer, 1848; center row, l & r: Germany, mark, 1873; center: Italy, 5 lire, 1862; bottom row, l to r: Serbia, 2 dinara, 1875; Romania, 10 bani, 1867; Bulgaria, 2 leva, 1882.

any pretense that France was still a republic was dropped, as Napoleon had himself crowned emperor of France.

His coins show the transition from republic to empire. On a five-franc piece minted late in 1802, no reference is made to Napoleon's one-man rule; the inscriptions and imagery refer to the republic, nothing more. By early 1803, however, Napoleon begins to appear on the coinage, with his title as First Consul. By 1804, he had proclaimed himself emperor, and the obverse of a five-franc coin minted that year shows the change. Curiously, the reverse still made a reference to the French Republic; perhaps the French were a bit uncertain as to their political status. It was not until 1809 that the reverse inscription would tally with the obverse. By this time, too, the French Revolutionary calendar was no longer used to date French coins. The transition from monarchy to republic and back to monarchy had been completed.

The French Revolution, at once a cause and an expression of heightened French nationality, led to two other upsurges of nationalism—one in Europe, the other in Latin America. The European one started out as a war of resistance on the part of Germany, Austria, Russia, and Spain against France. In the case of Germany and Russia, the established monarchs took a prominent role in this movement, and they soon realized that nationalism could be turned into a tool to defeat a revolution, just as it could be employed on its behalf. Calling for a national crusade against the invaders, the tsar of Russia and his counterparts farther west managed to gain greater popularity with their subjects, solidify their own regimes for the time being, and, incidentally, defeat Napoleon and the French in 1814–1815. As they did so, the tsar of Russia, the king of Prussia, and other prominent leaders did not find it necessary to make liberal concessions to their subjects; for the

latter, the defeat and eviction of the French was enough—temporarily. Pressures for liberal reform would soon spring up, however, in Germany, Austria, Russia, England, even in France itself. For people soon realized that, while the French Revolution had turned into an imperialistic bid for power, the original political ideas it had expressed were sound.

The second upsurge of nationalism took place in Spanish America, between 1810 and 1825. Most of this sprawling continent and a half was under Spanish rule, and by 1800 the examples of the American and French revolutions had struck a responsive chord in the minds of many of the intelligentsia of Mexico, Peru, and northern South America. They, too, would like to be free, but their road to independence was rendered more difficult by an important consideration. Most places in Spanish America were populated by a small, Creole minority of white or near-white stock. This group was the one dreaming of independence from Spain. Unfortunately, it was sitting atop a much larger group of Indians, Mestizos, and blacks. If the firm hand of Spain were removed, these people, the poor and the oppressed, might take the occasion of independence to inaugurate a race war, in which the Creoles would lose their positions—and quite possibly their lives and possessions as well. So any war for independence in Latin America must, from the Creole viewpoint, be a controlled revolution, whose paths of development were plotted by the Creoles themselves. Leaders of a Latin American war for independence might talk of the rights of man, for that was a good way of attracting adherents. But they were unlikely to do much beyond talk, once independence had been achieved.

Napoleon acted as the unwitting catalyst of Latin American independence. When his armies conquered Spain and captured its king in 1808, an important legal bond was

194

1

2

3

4

1

2

3

4

severed. In theory, the Americas were the personal realms of the king himself, not the Spanish nation. It could be (and was) argued that, once the king had been removed, any loyalty the Americas owed to Spain was null, and that the Americas were henceforth free to do as they pleased.

It would take a decade and a half before this point of view won out, however. Napoleon installed his brother Joseph on the Spanish throne, but Latin Americans refused to recognize him as their king and instead pledged their loyalty to Ferdinand VII, son of the former Spanish ruler. This was done not out of love for Ferdinand but rather to stall for time until the Latin Americans were in a strong enough position to declare their independence from everyone. What ensued was a chaotic, confusing period in which Creoles fought Spaniards, Indians fought both, and Mestizos fought for the highest bidder. After 1814, a newly liberated Spain was able to send over crack Spanish troops to fight the insurgents, but the latter, aided by unemployed soldiers from England and elsewhere (who had suddenly found themselves out of work with the end of the Napoleonic Wars), were achieving success by the beginning of the 1820s. By 1825, almost all of Spanish America had gained its freedom.

The insurgent period produced relatively little coinage. Most of the Spanish colonial mints remained in loyalist hands until fairly late, as did most of the mines producing precious metals. So what insurgent coinage there was was struck mainly in base metals. It was fairly crude in comparison to royal issues, for the men who struck it were soldiers, not coiners.

As independence was achieved, the new Latin American countries began striking coins of their own. Designs and slogans tended to be nationalistic in nature, the old Mexican emblem of an eagle on a cactus with a snake in its beak being a good example. National heroes, such as Simón Bolívar, after whom the new nation of Bolivia was named, appeared on some coinages; others made reference to Law and to the constitutions of the new republican regimes.

In terms of designs and inscriptions, the coins of the new Latin American states represented a distinct, nationalistic departure from the Spanish colonial past. In terms of their denominations and finenesses, however, there was virtually no departure at all. The old, heavy colonial coin, the Piece of Eight, was struck in silver slightly more than ninety percent pure. Its replacement in Mexico, Peru, and Guatemala was a coin of the same size, the same silver percentage—and the same denomination, eight reales. And so it went with other denominations and metals. This highlights an important aspect of the coinage of newly emerging nations: while they are likely to represent a departure in terms of design, they are generally based on a well-known, older coinage standard, ordinarily that of the former mother country. This holds true even for the first United States coinage. While it was decimal and was based on a new unit, the dollar, the dollar in turn was inspired by the Spanish-American Piece of Eight—which, after all, was what Americans had used in trade for a hundred years.

The American, French, and Latin American revolutions contributed to a climate of liberal nationalism which distinguished much of the nineteenth century. This was bolstered by a rising industrial discontent among the new factory workers in the cities. Radical new socioeconomic theories were devised and discussed—Socialism by the 1820s, Communism by 1848. These developments would lead to still further upheavals and changes in the world of the nineteenth century. Nationalism fared much better than did liberalism, both in terms of politics and

Opposite. European coinage on the outbreak of World War I, 1914.

of economics, for it was a stronger current at the time, widely shared by many elements in society, including a large percentage of the upper and middle classes. These classes were not likely to espouse widespread liberal reforms, for their own positions might thereby be weakened. They, too, wanted a controlled revolution.

So in the nineteenth century nationalism grew; middle and upper classes wanted it. Even in the cases of countries which were already free, heads of state would assiduously cultivate feelings of uniqueness among their people, for in so doing they were ensuring their own popularity as defenders and promoters of the national idea.

Nationalism swept nineteenth-century Europe in several currents. In a spate of activity centering on the year 1830, Greece became independent, as did Belgium. Poland tried, and failed. In France, a new, more nationally minded king, Louis Philippe, was installed on the throne after the reactionary Charles X, last of the Bourbon line, had been overthrown. This king and his successor would lead France off to new national adventures.

The second wave of nationalism occurred at mid-century, centering around the revolutions of 1848. It is probable that the national movements of this time were somewhat more radical than their counterparts of 1830; perhaps for that reason, they accomplished less in the short run. No new nations emerged, although the groundwork was laid for the birth of two new, strong national states in areas which had lacked unity since the Middle Ages. These were Italy and Germany. The French would act as midwives in the birth of both nations, deliberately in the case of Italy, when they aided Piedmont-Savoy in its struggles against other powers on the Italian peninsula; unwittingly in the case of Germany, when they lost a war (1870) to

Prussia, which thus gained the power and prestige necessary to proclaim and maintain a new, Prussian-based German Empire (1871).

These currents caused ripples of nationalism elsewhere. Romania became an independent principality in 1866. Its neighbors, Bulgaria and Serbia, began a long struggle for independence and unification which would eventually help touch off the First World War. Efforts by these new Balkan states were directed primarily against the Turkish Empire, as had been Greece's successful war of independence several decades previously. The Greeks, too, joined in the fray, in an attempt to liberate other Greek-speaking lands from the Turkish yoke.

By the late nineteenth century, nationalism was in full flower in Europe and well beyond. It must be stressed that nationalism had a very limited connection with liberalism by this time, especially as established rulers found that the spirit could be used to take people's minds off their problems at home.

Nationalism led directly to a final political development of this Age of Revolution—imperialism. If one's national identity, culture, and language were superior to those of other nations, was there not a sacred duty to export them to other, less enlightened parts of the world, places whose lands and peoples might (incidentally) have a certain economic value to the mother country, places which might constitute a risk to national security were they to fall under someone else's control?

This combination of pious claptrap and vulpine economic considerations was the stuff of which empires are built. While the roots of imperialism go far back into history (one can see them in the Roman mind), the later nineteenth century produced a peculiar set of circumstances which brought about the expansion and then the actual practice of the idea. By 1870, the Industrial Revolution had

produced a great manufacturing plant, one which required increasing amounts of raw materials if it were to function at maximum efficiency. It had also brought about the rise of a wealthy middle and upper class, with money to spend on colonial ventures, and an increasingly angry working class which might be placated by a showy foreign policy.

At the same time, a revolution in transportation had made it easier to get from place to place. This had been one factor in drawing people together into nationalism, and it also meant that virtually any spot in the world could now be reached, if there was a good enough reason for going there.

All of these things would come together, making imperialism inevitable. The English and French led the way. England had an empire, of course, long before imperialism became fashionable. She held Canada and India, but she proceeded to add a goodly portion of Africa to her domains at this time. She finished taming Australia and New Zealand, and she began penetrating the Far East, using Hong Kong as a base.

The French were not far behind. They had invaded Algeria as early as 1830. In 1838, Louis Philippe sought to give his regime an added luster by invading Mexico. His attack was a dismal failure, but it emboldened France's last monarch, Napoleon III (1852–1870), to try again, to emulate his glorious uncle, to bring the benefits of French culture to the distracted Mexicans. This second Mexican invasion lasted for five years (1862–1867) and ended in failure. It weakened France for her coming showdown with Germany, but did not blunt the French drive toward empire. In the 1880s and 1890s, France acquired huge tracts of land in northern and central Africa, and took Indochina.

Other nations soon joined the scramble. Tiny Belgium acquired the Congo, an area around eighty times the size of Belgium herself. The Russians concentrated on expanding into contiguous territories in Siberia and central Asia; they, too, were on the march. Two other European nations, Germany and Italy, also sought their places in the sun. National sentiment was strong in both countries, for German and Italian unification were both recent events. Neither achieved much success in acquiring foreign lands, however. By the time they arrived on the scene, the British and French had taken most of the best lands. Italy got a modest collection of rocks and sand on the Horn of Africa, and Germany received bits of land in Africa and the Pacific that no one else wanted.

Two other nations joined the race, and they came as something of a surprise. One was the United States, which was a republic and was therefore supposedly above such things. The other was Japan, which until fairly recently had been looked upon as a target for imperialism, not as one of the participants.

The Americans had spent several centuries expanding into next-door areas, just as the Russians were now doing. By around 1890, they had settled both coasts and everything in between. They were hopeful of exporting their brand of government elsewhere, as well as afraid of being thought of as of no account if they failed to join in the race to empire. Since the better lands were already in the possession of other colonial powers, the Americans built an empire by taking the colonies of one of the oldest colonial nations of all, Spain. In the brief but glorious Spanish-American War (1898), the United States acquired the Philippines, Guam, and Puerto Rico as outright possessions and a control over Cuba that would last in one form or another until 1934. The Americans had meanwhile bought Alaska from Russia in 1867, and they annexed Hawaii in 1898. By the turn of the century, the United States, too, was an imperial power, with far-flung political and economic interests.

Japan had similar inclinations. This chain of islands off the Asian mainland had been converted to Western ideas by the 1870s. A strong state and military force had been built up under the reforming emperor Meiji (1867–1912), and when Japanese thought added these elements to those of overpopulation and the heady idea of national expansion as a problem-solving device, the results were bound to lead to imperialism. Japan annexed several adjacent islands in the 1870s, fought a brief but successful war with China in the mid-1890s (by which she received Taiwan), and by 1900 she was moving into Korea and Manchuria, where she would shortly collide with Russia.

As the imperialist nations expanded, they brought their monetary concepts along. For the first time in human history, money of one particular type—in this case, a Western machine-struck type—came into general use all over the world. The British, Italians, Belgians, Germans, and French struck coins for their new colonies, or in a few cases had them struck in the colonies themselves. Other countries, such as Russia, Japan, and the United States, simply extended their own coinages to the places they acquired.

In many areas, money of the colonizing powers were the first coins ever seen by the native peoples. This was true in most of Africa and the Pacific islands. In these cases, there was an instantaneous jump of two thousand five hundred years, a direct move from a barter system to one using modern coins. In other areas, such as Indochina, parts of the Far East, and North Africa, native peoples had long possessed distinctive coinages of their own. In the new era, these, too, were replaced by money of the type current among the Western nations. As we have seen, Japan and China had adopted the new-style coinage as part of a general modernization program to strengthen themselves against European penetration. In other places, such as Indochina, the new coinage was imposed by outside authority, in this case, the French.

Why did the imperialist nations insist upon striking distinctive money for their colonies? One explanation may be found in the nature of coinage itself. It has always been regarded as one evidence of sovereignty, of a nation's independence or, in this case, of its hegemony over a colony. The new coins would serve notice on native and European alike that the lands in which they circulated were the possessions of a colonial power, whether French, British, Belgian, or Italian. This went along with the coins' designs and inscriptions, which usually made reference to the mother country and which frequently portrayed the ruling monarch on the obverse.

One final point in regard to the colonial coinage resulting from imperialism: while designs might be different for colony than for homeland, the coinage standards and denominations were usually identical, interchangeable. This was a sensible development. The colonies, after all, were intended as economic ventures in part, and a double standard would be bad for business. There were exceptions, such as Canada, whose coinage was linked to the United States dollar, not the British pound, but a franc was ordinarily the same coin in the Belgian Congo as it was in Belgium, the Italian lira was the same in Eritrea as it was in Italy, and so forth.

The scramble for Africa and other regions by the imperial powers increased friction between them. Imperial rivalries would be a factor in the outbreak of World War I in 1914. That war, and the ensuing peace, would be central events in the twentieth century. The world's money would faithfully reflect the pressures from these and other occurrences.

9

Preceding pages. Modern money reflects the chaos of modern times. Below. L to r: France. 100 francs, 1911; Italy, 100 lire, 1912; Austria-Hungary, 100 corona, 1908.

Bottom. Money of the Mexican revolution. L to r: Guerrero, 2 pesos, 1915; Oaxaca, 60 pesos, 1916; Durango, peso, 1914; background: Chihuahua, 20 pesos, 1915 (above), and Sonora, peso, 1913 (below).

Modern Money and the Modern State

Without question, the twentieth century has been the most turbulent period in the entire history of humankind. Changes and upheavals for both good and bad have been the order of the day. When we look back seventy-five years to the placid face of Europe and America, calm areas where everyone knew his place in society, when we consider Latin America, Asia, and Africa, whose millions were under the political or economic control of the Western nations—it all seems to have little to do with the world we know today. The events of those times might easily have taken place two thousand years ago, not seventy-five years. In terms of our identification with them, they could almost have occurred in another world.

Much of this strangeness, however, lies on the surface. The people of 1900 were not so different from their counterparts of the late twentieth century. They had needs, hopes, fears, desires of a nature similar to those we possess. And there were historical processes in place by 1900—the Industrial Revolution, economic and political discontent, nationalism—which would shape the important events of the new century and would make it "modern," in fact.

This underlying identity and continuity may be difficult to see because of the great number of far-reaching events which have distinguished the twentieth century. In a more-or-less chronological order, they are: the Mexican Revolution (1910–1920); World War I (1914–1918); the Russian Revolution (1917–1923); the rise of totalitarian, nationalistic dictatorships in Europe, Asia, and Latin America in the 1920s and 1930s; a world-wide economic depression in the 1930s; another world war (1939–1945); the rise of Communism in Europe and Asia and the ensuing Cold War, from the mid-1940s to the present; and, finally, the economic and political emergence of Africa and Latin America from the late 1950s to the present. It is to be noted that these are only the *major* events of the twentieth century. Were we to add those which influenced one country only, the list could be extended indefinitely.

The major events of the twentieth century have had a great importance for the numismatic record. They have influenced money directly, shaping it and changing it with time's passage. At the beginning of the century, most nations were on a gold standard, one which tended to cut across national boundaries. The coins of many places were tied together, either by colonial connections or by individual agreements among various countries. Thus, a Belgian franc equaled an Italian lira, and a lira from Eritrea and a franc from the Belgian Congo were equal to each other. And coinage, whether directly convertible or not, formed the backbone of the world's monetary systems. Coinage in gold and silver was plentiful; paper was used predominantly for large transactions.

By late in the century, all this had changed. Gold coinage had become a thing of the past, and silver coinage was fast disappearing. Paper money was being used for most large- and medium-sized transactions, and what coinage existed was subsidiary in nature, of low value, usually struck in copper, nickel, or aluminum. At the present time, credit cards and personal checks are taking the place of paper money; most of our business is conducted on paper, and the largest purchases we make do not commonly involve traditional forms of money at all.

In short, changes elsewhere in the twentieth century have had their reflection in the money of the period, on its form, its usage, and on its inscriptions and designs. Let us follow the chronological approach and see what the main themes of the twentieth century have done to its money.

Opposite. Emergency money of World War I.

The first event mentioned here was the Mexican Revolution. It is not as well known as many of the other items on the list, but perhaps it should be. For events in Mexico had wide repercussions in Latin America and elsewhere. The Mexican Revolution was in part an attempt to throw off foreign control, in this case, foreign economic control. As such, it would stand as an example to later insurgent colonial peoples.

It began as a purely political revolt against the continuation of the long dictatorship of Porfirio Díaz (1876–1911). The revolution broke out in late 1910, and its leader, Francisco Madero, overthrew the aged dictator in the spring of 1911, much to everyone's surprise. Madero and his moderate supporters had increasing trouble keeping order among the Mexican people, however. The latter saw the new, liberal political climate as a splendid opportunity to right the social, political, and economic wrongs which they had suffered over the centuries. They were impatient for reform; Madero's inability to satisfy them led to increased turbulence, and this in turn led to a political *coup* early in 1913, in which Madero was overthrown and murdered by General Victoriano Huerta, who then installed himself as head of a right-wing military dictatorship.

All Mexico rose against him. Politicians, military leaders, and out-and-out bandits, of every political shade from moderate to extreme left, took the field against Huerta. They overthrew him in 1914 and then they turned upon each other. For the next six years, Mexico was treated to a combination of social revolution, civil war, race war, and xenophobic outpouring which would leave several hundred thousand dead. It would also occasion an invasion by the United States on behalf of American interests (1916–1917)—and, incidentally, it would establish the right of the state to nationalize foreign-held property, which would be essential were Mexico to become the economic mistress of her own house.

As with any other war, this one needed to be financed. The Mexican Revolution gave the world a new kind of money, one with which it would become increasingly familiar in the years to come: emergency money. In Mexico it would largely take the form of paper currency, due in part to a lack of bullion, due also to the fact that it was far easier to produce than was coinage. All the same, some coins did see the light, including a huge sixty-peso gold coin from Oaxaca, located in southwestern Mexico.

It was one thing to print paper money to pay the bills; it was quite another to get it accepted at face value. Much of it was put into what is known as forced circulation, meaning that if you didn't accept it as money, those who printed it were likely to make you wish you had. Still, even forced circulation could not make this emergency paper money circulate at par with regular coinage. The money of the dozens of different insurgent authorities fluctuated in value with the success or failure of their causes, but none of it was worth face value. It was produced in tremendous quantities, and this again lowered the value. It has been estimated that Francisco Villa alone was responsible for more than a billion pesos' worth of paper money, and his notes are so common today that they are sometimes used as stage money in dramatic productions.

By 1917, Mexican affairs began quieting down. Carranza, the original leader of the anti-Huerta combination, was firmly enough in power so that a new constitution, incorporating some of the social and national gains achieved over the past seven years, could be written and ratified. It is still Mexico's basic law, and its provisions have influenced the constitutions of many

1   2

3   4

other emerging nations. Mexico's emergency money was replaced by orthodox, national issues. Reflecting the rise of national feeling in Mexico, the new money would eventually begin depicting Mexican heroes, including Carranza himself.

Events in Mexico were soon dwarfed by those in Europe. There, the First World War erupted in the summer of 1914. Before it had run its course, it would leave millions dead, millions more homeless. It would totally disrupt the world economy. It would alter the political balance of power. These were its short-term effects. Its long-term influences were even greater. The outcome of the war would bring about a pervading mood of cynicism and despair among the victors, and it would engender a burning desire for revenge among the losers. These attitudes would produce bitter fruit. Among other things, they ensured that there would be another world war.

The 1914–1918 conflict had several major effects on money. The Latin Monetary Union was an early casualty of the war, as were so many other hopeful experiments in international cooperation. The war also prompted the issue of a large amount of emergency money. (In German, this is called *notgeld*.) This makes good sense, for in a time of national emergency or unrest, people are afraid and hoard ordinary coinage because they desire to set aside something in the way of precious metal as a hedge against the future. Still, they must use something for daily transactions. And during the First World War, notgeld entered the picture to fill their needs.

Notgeld was issued by local cities and towns, or, less frequently, by businesses. The prestige and resources of whoever issued it were used as collateral. Most notgeld was manufactured in the form of paper money, although a large number of low-value tokens

also saw the light toward the end of the war. The term notgeld would suggest that it was essentially a German phenomenon, though it was not. The French made widespread use of this type of money, as did the Belgians, the Austrians, indeed, even the Americans (to a very limited degree). The issue of emergency money went on for several years after 1918 in France, Germany, and Austria, for conditions in those countries remained unsettled into the early 1920s.

But their issues of emergency paper money were dwarfed by those of Russia. From 1917 to 1923, Russia experienced a revolution and a civil war which probably created the greatest mass chaos in human history. Under Lenin, the Communists seized power in Petrograd (today Leningrad) and Moscow. This was late in 1917; for the next few years, they had to contend with counter-revolutionary armies, from democratic socialists to right-wing monarchists, oppressed minorities (the Ukrainians, Armenians, and others who saw the removal of the tsar as an opportunity to gain their independence), and various expeditionary forces sent in by the Allies and Germany to overthrow the new Communist state. By 1920, Lenin's supporters were winning on most fronts, but complete order would not be achieved until 1923.

This civil war occasioned the issue of astronomical quantities of emergency money by the contending factions, money used to purchase supplies, to pay troops, etc. This was inevitable. As in the case of Mexico a few years previously, most normal money had gone underground as soon as trouble had broken out.

Virtually all of this emergency money appeared in the form of paper currency, for reasons similar to those operating in Mexico. And virtually every contending faction issued it and tried to force its circulation—the Communists, or Reds; the anti-Communists, called Whites; the emerging national groups; and, for good measure, cities, towns, cooperatives, factories, and even individuals.

None of this paper had any particular backing behind it, and the public knew it. The result was a round of disastrous inflation, one in which the value of the *ruble* sank to virtually nothing. In 1921, the Communists, who were by this time winning the war, still found it necessary to issue a note in the denomination of one hundred thousand rubles. The fact that these bills are still fairly common today would indicate that the Soviets found it necessary to print a good many of them. The fact that the bills are often found in uncirculated condition would also indicate that they were not accepted by the people. This inflationary period lasted into 1924, by which time the new Soviet state was strong enough to reform its currency.

Inflation was a major problem for many nations in the early 1920s, and it was a direct legacy of the war. That conflict had cost an astronomical amount of money, more than anyone had dreamed of in 1914. More money was needed than ever before, to purchase tons of supplies, to train, equip, and send into battle millions of men, to care for their dependents. Inevitably, both sides resorted to the printing press to pay the bills. It seemed a sound idea at the time. After the war, each country imagined that it would exact heavy reparations from the losers and thus redeem outstanding currency. Unfortunately, it didn't work that way. It is obvious that not everybody can win a war. There has to be a loser, and that loser has to make reparations. In the case of the First World War, this would mean that the Central Powers (Germany, Austria-Hungary, and Turkey) would have to reimburse the Allies (Britain, France, and the United States). Realities ren-

dered this simple plan impossible, however. None of the defeated nations had the financial wherewithal to make the enormous reparations demanded by the Allies, and they would not be likely to do so even if they had the resources.

In short, the world money supply had become artificially inflated during the war, and it remained so after its end. Inflation drove prices up, made for economic and political discontent. It was kept within bounds by the Allied nations, who, after all, had won the war and were receiving some reparations from their defeated adversaries. But it was another matter for the losers of the war. Inflation was rampant in Austria, Hungary, and the other former Central Powers; one of them, Germany, saw the worst inflation in human history up to that time.

The German monetary unit was called a mark. In 1914, it took 4.2 of them to buy a dollar. Four years of unsupported currency emissions took their toll. By 1918, the value of the mark had dropped fifty percent. But that was minor as compared to what would shortly begin. In 1918, the German Empire was abolished, and a new, republican government took its place. This government bore the onus of having made peace with the Allies, and it was fairly weak, unable to maintain order in a defeated country. The German people distrusted the new government and its paper currency.

In 1921, the value of the new, republican mark began a precipitous downward slide. Larger- and larger-denomination notes were printed. In May, 1923, a five-hundred-thousand-mark bill made its appearance. By early 1924, the republic was printing notes theoretically worth one hundred *trillion* marks. The German monetary system was in ruins.

Large loans from the United States were secured later that year, and the Ger-

1. Germany. L: 5 mark, 1934; r: 5 mark, 1936.
2. Portugal. L: 20 centavos, 1916; r: 10 escudos, 1928. 3. Coinage of the Vargas dictatorship in Brasil. L to r: 300 reis, 1936; 1,000 reis, 1932; 400 reis, 1940. 4. Spain. L to r: 25 centimos, 1937, 5 pesetas, 1949; 50 ptas., 1958. 5. Above: Albania, Italian occupation, lke, 1939; lower l: German protectorate of Bohemia-Moravia, koruna, 1943; lower r: Manchukuo, fen, 1936. 6. Top: Belgium, 25

1

2 3   4

centimes, 1938 (1) and 1942 (r, German occupation); bottom: Poland, 20 groszy, 1923 (left) and German occupation coin of same denomination, dated 1923 but issued 1941–1944 (r). 7. L & r: France, francs, 1943; center: Norway, German occupation, 5 öre, 1943. 8. Japanese occupation paper money. Top to bottom: Indonesia, 10 cent; Burma, rupee; Philippines, peso; Malaya, 1,000 dollars. All 1942.

5

6

7

8

man mark was stabilized at its old, 1914 value. But irreparable damage had been done. The faith of a people in their government is directly illustrated by their faith in its money. And the hyperinflation showed that, in the case of the struggling German Republic, this faith was very slim indeed. Any hope which the German people might have had in their post-war government had evaporated. A pervading atmosphere of cynicism and contempt took its place, as more and more Germans, disgusted with a bumbling democracy which was unable to regain Germany's old position in the world order, began looking for a new leader who would be more efficient and make Germany a world power once again. The man they were looking for burst on the scene during the height of the inflationary period. His name was Adolf Hitler, and the world would soon be hearing a good deal about him.

Germany was not alone in its mood of cynicism and discontent. These feelings were common throughout much of the world at this time. The recent war had demanded great sacrifices, and states and their peoples had expected much from it. It would ensure the world-wide spread of democracy. It would end war forever. It would enrich those countries who won. When, as things turned out, the war accomplished none of this, a reaction born of disappointment was bound to take place. There was a world-wide retreat from the idealism of earlier days. This was manifested in two ways. In some nations, mainly those who had won the war, there was a strong desire for political leaders who would promise and deliver little, but who would leave the people alone, demanding no further sacrifices. Warren G. Harding, president of the United States from 1921 to 1923, typifies this new type of politician, but he had his counterparts in Britain, France, and elsewhere.

Other nations, mainly those who had lost the war or who felt betrayed by its outcome, searched for another kind of leader. They were looking for someone who would promise much and fulfill his promises, even if this meant that he scrapped democratic procedures in the process. They had had quite enough of foggy-minded idealists who failed to produce, enough of mediocre, democratic politicians who became ensnarled in the procedural red tape which is an inevitable by-product of the democratic process. They wanted men who would get results.

They found them. In Turkey, which had lost the war and most of its empire as a result, the caliph was overthrown in 1922 and a dynamic national leader appeared, Kemal Atatürk. He placed Turkey under a strongman rule which lasted until his death in 1938, a feverish sixteen-year period of wholesale reform of everything from the alphabet to the wearing of veils by Turkish women. Atatürk also reformed and modernized the Turkish monetary system. The star and crescent, symbol of the resurgent Turkish state, appeared on coins and paper money alike.

Below. Yugoslavia, 100 dinara, 1963.
Opposite. The decline of the lira. Top, l to r: 10
lire (gold), 1863; 10 lire (silver), 1936; bottom,
l to r: 10 lire (aluminum), 1946; 10 lire (aluminum)
1951.

This use of symbology would be seen in another totalitarian dictatorship which also made its debut in 1922, that of Benito Mussolini in Italy. Italy had fought on the winning side during the First World War, but when the spoils of that conflict were handed out, she was largely ignored. Frustrated nationalism, unemployment, and other social and economic problems, together with a bungling, unstable, and corrupt government coalesced into a desire for a strong national leader, one who would achieve Italian aims even if he had to be a dictator in order to do so. This was the background for the rise of Benito Mussolini and his fascist party. Mussolini established his dictatorship in 1922; it would last until 1943, at which time he was overthrown by irate Italians, who had had enough of fighting on the losing side in a war which Mussolini's nationalistic policies had helped to bring about.

In the dictatorships of the 1920s and 1930s, symbols counted for much. The hammer and sickle, emblem of the new Soviet state, appeared on all of its coinage and paper money. Atatürk used the star and-crescent device. For Mussolini's fascists, it was the *fasces*, a bundle of rods bound around an axe. This was an old Roman symbol of authority, and it appeared everywhere in Italy during Mussolini's dictatorship—on public buildings, posters, jewelry, and money.

The identification with ancient Rome, manifested in the choice of a Roman symbol for a modern political state, was an essential part of Mussolini's regime. For he promised modern-day Italians nothing less than the resurrection of the Roman Empire, along with the glory and wealth it had enjoyed. In his desire to persuade the people that he was the man who would bring about the reestablishment of ancient Rome's power and majesty, he constantly reminded them of their splendid Roman heritage and their equally glorious destiny under his leadership. One way of achieving a connection between Rome and himself in the public mind was to produce coinage which was highly reminiscent of ancient Roman issues. As he did so, Mussolini was resurrecting a Roman coinage tradition by using money for propaganda.

In this, he was not alone in the 1920s. The Russians and Turks were placing party emblems on their money, and a party badge is certainly a piece of propaganda. But Mussolini's coinage employed a sort of double-barreled approach. While the fasces usually appeared on his issues, the rest of their designs were copies of ancient Roman coins, adopted to convince people that Mussolini's new order was in effect the legitimate successor of the Roman Empire.

As a result, we find an odd juxtaposition of elements. An attractive five-lire piece of 1926 shows a Roman eagle perched on a fasces. A beautiful twenty-lire coin of the following year shows two figures, one standing, the other seated with a shield, a design directly inspired by Roman coins. But the standing figure leans on a fasces, and this element is modern.

Still, the thing which most impresses us about these coins is their great similarity to ancient ones. On the 1928 twenty-lire piece depicted on page 211, the head of Vittorio Emanuele III, nominal ruler of Italy, is rendered in a manner comparable to the best Roman coinage portraiture, and the inscriptions surrounding his head have a Roman style about them. The similarity between Roman coins and Mussolini's issues perhaps becomes most striking when we consider a twenty-lire issue of 1936. It is almost identical in design to an ancient denarius, struck more than two thousand years previously.

Mussolini's desire to recreate the Roman Empire came to an inglorious end. The Italians managed to conquer Ethiopia in 1935–1936, but by that time they were being overshadowed by a far more active, far more menacing dictator, Adolf Hitler. Some of the elements in Hitler's rise to power, such as German cynicism concerning republican in-stitutions and a thirst for revenge for the loss of the First World War, have already been mentioned. During the 1920s, however, these elements were not sufficient to bring down the republican form of government. A wide-reaching prosperity had come to the western world by the mid-1920s, and Germany shared in it. At the same time, her leaders began receiving greater cooperation and respect from her erstwhile enemies. Germany was being readmitted to the family of nations.

But the new prosperity in Germany and elsewhere rested on shaky foundations. While prices and industrial production increased worldwide during the 1920s, wages remained relatively stable. As a result, there would come a time when there were more goods available than there were people with the money necessary to buy them. This was beginning to be the case by the late 1920s. The inevitable panic and financial crash took place in 1929. The world moved into the depression years of the 1930s, and the new,

harsher state of affairs would propel Hitler to power.

Around the world, the business failures and high unemployment which characterized the economic collapse would leave an indelible mark on the story of money. For one thing, less money was now needed than before, and world wide, coinage and paper money production was lower in the early 1930s than it was in the late 1920s. The United States is a good example of this phenomenon. In 1933, the three United States mints (Philadelphia, Denver, and San Francisco) issued only one-cent pieces and half-dollars, and very limited amounts of each. The logic was simple. When millions were unemployed, unable to acquire the coins already in circulation, why bother to strike more?

In the United States, the Great Depression saw a resurgence of emergency currency. The entire national banking system collapsed early in 1933, which meant a temporary shortage of money. The lean economic times encouraged hoarding anyway, and this added to the problem. Local cities, towns, and businesses took matters into their own hands by issuing a special type of emergency currency, called *scrip*, whose value, like that of the earlier notgeld, was guaranteed by local authorities. This scrip saw service for several months, until the incoming Democratic administration had succeeded in reforming the American banking system. Confidence returned, money came out from under mattresses, and the scrip was retired. Much of it still exists today, a vivid reminder of a time of local decision-making in a national emergency.

If the United States was hard-hit by the depression, Germany fared even worse. Unemployment was terribly high, relief and welfare services woefully inadequate. To the cynicism and frustrated nationalism which Germans had shared during the 1920s was added a new element,

Opposite. Hungarian inflation. Center: 5 pengo, 1938; above: 10,000 pengo, 1945; below: 200 septillion pengo, 1946.

that of economic despair. And now the climate was right for the advent of Adolf Hitler. For Hitler was promising answers and solutions which no German could possibly ignore. To counter unemployment, Hitler proposed large public works projects and rearmament, which would provide jobs. Instead of the incompetent leaders of the republic, who had no idea of how to combat the economic woes of Germany, Hitler promised action—the action of the strong man who can cut through bureaucratic red tape. And in place of Germany's present role as a former big power, reduced to small-power status by its loss of the First World War, Hitler promised a new Germany, stronger than ever before, with a new empire, mistress of Europe and the lands beyond.

His appeals won out. He became chancellor of Germany in 1933; within a year and a half, he had turned the country into a one-party state, ruled by himself. And he delivered on his promises: things *did* get done, unemployment *did* decrease, Germans *did* gain a new sense of national self-respect. The price they—and the rest of the world—would be asked to pay would be fantastically high, of course, but no one had any way of knowing that at the time.

As did other total states of the period, Hitler's Germany coined money with a propaganda intent. As in Turkey, the symbol predominated—the *häkenkreuz*, or swastika, symbol of the Nazi party. At first, its use was limited. It is fairly small on a five-mark coin of 1934, celebrating the first anniversary of Nazi Germany. Within two years, it had achieved a much more prominent place in coinage design, as evidenced by a 1936 coin, also in the five-mark denomination. Henceforward, it would appear on virtually every German coin issued, down to the extinction of Hitler's Third Reich in the spring of 1945.

Dictatorships based on the Italian and German models appeared in many places during the 1920s and 1930s. In Portugal, Antonio Salazar took power in 1926 and held it for more than forty years. Portugal's coins reflect the change from a republic to a quasi-fascist dictatorship. Instead of a head of Liberty, which had been the main design on republican coinage, the coins of the Portuguese dictatorship celebrated events in the national past and paid homage to eminent Portuguese statesmen and explorers, in an attempt to extend to the new regime some of the glory of Portugal's golden age.

Much the same can be said of the coinage of one of Portugal's former colonies, Brasil. There, Getulio Vargas overthrew the republican regime in 1930, installing a fascist dictatorship in its stead, which he called *O Estado Novo* (the New State). Vargas headed the New State for fifteen years, after which he, and it, passed into oblivion. Brasilian coins of the period reflect the heightened nationalism which was one of the props of the regime. Like Portuguese coins, Brasilian issues honor national heroes, important events in the country's history, and so on. Infrequently, Vargas himself appears on his coins.

A third fascist dictatorship was installed in Spain after a three-year civil war, in which the Nationalists, led by Francisco Franco, enjoyed German and Italian assistance in overthrowing the Spanish Republic. This inaugurated thirty-six years of one-man rule, which ended only with Franco's death in 1975. His coins reflected the new state of affairs in Spain. Only one political party was allowed, the *Falange*, and its symbol, the Yoke and Arrows (chosen to express the idea of national unity), appears on a great many Spanish coins. So does a portrait of Franco himself. The latter is a fairly uncommon practice among fascist dictators, who are usually content to depict the symbol of their power

219

in the form of a political party badge.

The establishment of authoritarian, one-man rule in many places during the 1920s and 1930s may be taken as an indication that the peoples of a number of nations were in an angry mood, growing increasingly nationalistic, desiring a larger role for themselves and their countries than had previously been their lot. Unfortunately, this would lead to war, for nations could only grow at the expense of each other, and this would inevitably lead to an armed clash.

By the mid-1930s, the stage had been set. There were highly nationalistic dictatorships in Italy, Germany, and several other places, including Japan. These nations all set about building empires—the Italians in Africa, the Germans in adjacent countries, and the Japanese on the Asian mainland. Each nation was successful for a time. Italy took Ethiopia and Albania. Germany occupied the Rhineland, then Austria, and finally Czechoslovakia. The Japanese took Manchuria, which they set up as a puppet state, Manchukuo, and they were carving away bits of China itself by 1937. The success of these aggressor nations may be credited to the weakness of democratic forces in Western Europe and the United States. Britain, France, and the United States had all fought in the First World War. They had been disillusioned with the results, and they decided to avoid any actions which might propel them into a new war, one which most people felt would be even worse than the previous one. So they would mind their own business and congratulate themselves on the wisdom of their decision to do so.

Eventually, they were no longer able to maintain this hands-off policy. By 1939, British and French attitudes were hardening against the fascist dictators who wanted too much, they felt, and had to be stopped. This new, harder line was put to the test in the early fall of 1939, when Hitler invaded Poland, after having given solemn guarantees that he would not. Britain and France belatedly came to Poland's defense, and a second global war ensued.

This Second World War truly was a global conflict. It was fought in Europe, Africa, Asia, Oceania, and, at its height, virtually every inhabitant of every country in the world was involved to some degree. Unlike the previous war, where static, trench warfare had been the rule, this war would be one of movement, involving the occupation of entire enemy countries and their colonies. The coinage of these occupied areas is interesting, because it directly reflects the movement characteristic of this war.

When the Nazis overran most of Western Europe, they had coins made for use by their new subjects. This coinage was of base metal, most commonly zinc, of which German minor coinage was made. In some cases, in countries where the Germans did not bother to set up puppet regimes on the fascist model, the coins minted were often virtually identical to prewar issues, except for metallic content. Belgium and Poland are good examples of this practice. In other occupied areas, the Germans did set up puppet governments; here, the coinage was still of zinc or other nonessential metals, but it was likely to differ in design from earlier national types. German issues in Norway under the regime of Vidkun Quisling dropped the king's monogram, which had previously been an important design element. In its place was substituted a Norwegian lion on a shield, flanked by the symbols of the Norwegian fascist organization. In France, the old national types were retained for a year after the German occupation of that country, but the puppet regime of Marshal Petain soon adopted new types for its coinage. On the obverse, there is a double-bladed axe, symbol of the new fascist French State, and on the reverse, the new motto *"Travail, Famille, Patrie* (Work, Family, Fatherland),"* meant to replace the old republican slogan, "Liberty, Equality, Fraternity."

The Germans were the Axis power most active in providing money for occupied nations, although the Japanese were not far behind. As Japan took the Philippines, Burma, Malaya, and other parts of southeast Asia and Oceania, they produced copious amounts of paper money for their new acquisitions. These Japanese issues were tied in to the local, pre-war currency systems. Thus, denominations on notes for the Philippines were expressed in pesos, those for Oceania in shillings, etc. All the notes bore simple designs. On small-denomination issues, this usually consisted of the name of the issuing authority and the value, in Japanese and the language of the erstwhile colonial power. For larger bills, a vignette of a local scene was used. Philippine issues depict the monument to José Rizal, a national hero. Those for Burma portray a local temple; issues for Malaya show an ox cart with palm trees in the background. None of these notes is dated, but most seem to have originated in 1942, which represented the high-water mark of Japanese, and indeed of Axis, expansion.

As the tide of war began to turn against the Axis powers, new forms of occupation money made their appearance. The Philadelphia mint struck coins for liberated France and Belgium in 1944. Presumably, these coins were intended for use by those countries until they were able to resume their own coinages. The circulation of these made-in-America French and Belgian coins was a brief one, for the French began minting their own coins late in 1944, the Belgians shortly thereafter.

Paper money formed the backbone of the Allied occupation currency systems. In 1943, the Americans printed small occupation notes in denominations ranging from one to one thousand lire, for use in Italy. This system worked so well that its usage was extended to France in 1944 and, ultimately, to a defeated Germany and Japan as well. In the case of Germany, American printing plates were given to Russian authorities, and the Soviet Union printed occupation currency of its own, for use as its armies swept westward across the crumbling German Reich. The Russians devised and printed distinctive occupation notes of their own for other parts of central and eastern Europe, including Poland, Romania, Czechoslovakia, and Hungary. Interestingly, the place of printing for notes used in the liberated nations would fairly faithfully correspond to the future configuration of the two sides in the Cold War. Eastern Europe ended up in the Russian orbit, Western Europe in the American—and Germany was divided between the two.

The Second World War and its aftermath brought an old problem to the world's attention, that of inflation. Learning from their experiences during the first global conflict, the warring states of the 1940s initiated stringent rationing systems. As a result, by the end of the Second World War, citizens of the Allied powers had fairly large amounts of money saved up which they had been unable to spend during the war years. And with much of the world devastated, with national industrial plants still geared to war production, there was tremendous competition among consumers for the few civilian goods available. Inevitably, prices shot up.

As this was taking place, the value of money itself was decreasing. As with World War I, so with World War II: a conflict of this scale had necessitated the production of astronomical amounts of money to pay expenses. As a result, the values of the monetary units of many countries sank. This was reflected in a widespread phenomenon—the disappearance of precious metals, gold and silver, as coinage mediums, and their replacement by base metals.

The English shilling had been made of silver since the days of Henry VIII. The last silver shilling was minted in 1946. In the following year, a new shilling was introduced, with designs identical to previous ones, but made of copper-nickel. This held true for every other erstwhile silver British coin; all of them switched to copper-nickel in 1947. This approach to inflation and the price of silver would be followed by several other countries, including Canada and the United States. While designs would remain unchanged, metallic content would shift from precious metals to base ones.

Elsewhere, coinage changed in design and metallic content alike. The Italian ten-lire coin tells an interesting story. Early issues were struck in gold. By the time of Mussolini's dictatorship, ten-lire pieces were being made of silver. Obviously, their value had decreased, but they were still attractive coins with a considerable intrinsic worth. After the end of the Second World War, the designs for the ten-lire coin were changed—and so was its metallic content. It was now made of aluminum, not silver. And in 1951, the Italian government added insult to injury by reducing the size of the aluminum coin! Silver was reintroduced for coinage in Italy, but only for issues of high denomination, five hundred- and one-thousand-lire pieces. Gold disappeared entirely as a coinage medium. The Italian experience has been shared by most nations around the world. At present, gold is not struck for circulation anywhere, and silver is only employed for coins of high denomination, if at all. It is unlikely that gold and silver coinages will be resurrected in the fu-

ture. A two-thousand-five-hundred-year-old monetary tradition is coming to an end.

But a new one has taken its place. As precious-metal coinage began disappearing, the medium of paper currency began taking its place. Providing the government which issues it enjoys the support and respect of its people, paper can function perfectly well as a monetary form, even achieving a relative stability through time. For example, the Yugoslav hundred-dinara note illustrated on page 216 is a fairly high-denomination bill, but the note is readily accepted and circulates freely, due to the faith of the people in their government and their belief that the government can redeem the bill if necessary. When this faith is shaky or nonexistent, however, paper becomes a most unstable medium of exchange, and it may have deleterious effects on the political and economic fortunes of a nation.

We have discussed examples of rampant inflation at work, from the American and French revolutions onward. Inflation was a by-product of the First World War. But runaway monetary depreciation also appeared in several nations during and after World War II. One of these countries, Hungary, has the dubious distinction of having suffered the worst inflation in all of human history, with important economic, social, and political repercussions.

The basic Hungarian unit of exchange was called a *pengo*. In 1938, it took about five of them to buy a dollar, and, in fact, a large silver coin of a five-pengo denomination enjoyed widespread circulation. Then came the Second World War. Hungary entered the conflict on the Axis side, having been promised large awards of territory by Hitler. As it turned out, the Hungarians were defeated along with the other Axis powers. In common with other countries, Hungary experienced some inflation during the war

1

2

3

4

1

2   3   4

1. **Coin: India, 10 rupees, 1969; background: detail from a 100-peso note, Mexico, 1974.**
2. **L to r: Guinea, 25 francs, 1962; Malawi, shilling, 1964.**
3. **Ghana. L to r: 2 shillings, 1958; penny, 1958.**
4. **L to r: Egypt, piastre, 1968; Mali, 100 francs, 1975.**

years. The five-pengo silver coin metamorphosed into a piece of paper money, then back into a coin made of aluminum. So the pengo had lost a good deal of its value during the war.

But this was minor in comparison to what took place after the war. Hungary's first postwar government enjoyed little support among the Hungarian people. It began printing high-denomination notes in great quantities, which everyone knew it could not possibly redeem, given the state of the Hungarian economy, which lay in ruins.

By the summer of 1945, inflation was out of control, and it remained so for about a year. A ten-thousand pengo note made its appearance in July, one for ten million in November. But this was modest inflation in comparison with events during the first few months of 1946. By the end of May, a note purporting to be worth two hundred *septillion* pengo (a figure expressed as a two followed by 26 zeroes) entered circulation. By that time, money had become completely worthless, and Hungarians had reverted to barter.

Faced with the collapse of its entire currency system, the Hungarian government obtained massive aid from the United States and the Soviet Union, scrapped the old monetary arrangement, and erected a new one in its place with a new unit, called a *forint*. Hungary's hyperinflation came to an end. But the damage had been done. As in Germany in the 1920s, rampant inflation produced cynicism toward and alienation from the government, which was shortly replaced by a new political organ, a Communist state on the Russian model.

By now, Communist governments were beginning to appear throughout Eastern Europe. The Cold War, a period of almost constant confrontation between East and West, had begun. It had a major effect on money throughout the world. In Eastern Europe, home of the new Russian satellite states, coinage became a good deal simpler. Obverses commonly bore the arms of the Socialist Republic, the reverses the denomination and the date. The contrast between old and new is graphically seen on two Albanian coins, both of the half-*lek* denomination, one made in 1926, at which time Albania was a kingdom, the other minted in 1947 by the new Communist state. These rather prosaic postwar Communist-bloc coinages were augmented from time to time by large, well-designed commemorative issues, intended in part as propaganda pieces. A Czech hundred-*korun* coin of 1949 paid homage to the seventieth birthday of J.V. Stalin, leader of the Communist world. Eastern European paper money followed a route somewhat similar to that of coinage. Designs became less florid, more starkly utilitarian, and there were often representations of peasants or workers on the notes.

Far to the east, China, holding a quarter of the total population of the world, had also become a Communist state by late 1949. This had come about as the result of a long civil war, which had gone on since the late 1920s. By the early 1930s, the forces of Mao Tse-tung had carved out an enclave for themselves in a remote corner of China, and they began issuing coins and paper money to pay the expenses of insurgent war. Their issues were crude, as one might expect. Coinage in copper and silver was inexpertly struck, and some "paper" money was actually printed on cloth, presumably for greater durability. Chinese Communist coins and currency abounded in Soviet slogans and symbols; a hammer and sickle superimposed on an outline map of China expressed hopes for the future.

The Japanese invasion of the Chinese mainland slowed the advance of the

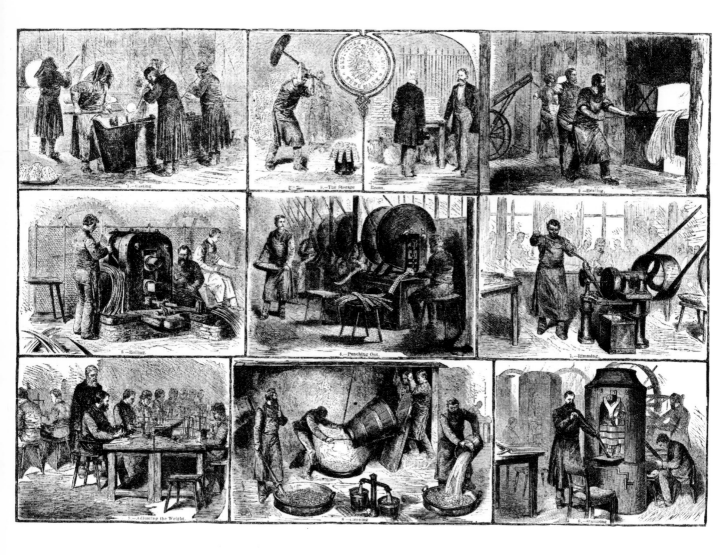

Communist movement. Mao and his followers entered into an uneasy alliance with the forces of Chiang Kai-shek, leader of the Republic of China, to defeat the common enemy. That was achieved in 1945, and civil war then resumed. In slightly more than four years, the Communists would take all of China except for Taiwan, an offshore island to which Chiang and his followers fled. This relatively rapid Communist advance may be ascribed to the fact that the Communists had used the war years to build a broad base of support among the Chinese people, while Chiang's forces had neglected this opportunity. Post-1949 Chinese notes and coins have followed Communist practice elsewhere, in terms of the austere simplicity of their designs.

The Communization of Eastern Europe and Mainland China prompted a reaction by the Western powers, especially the United States. The numismatic record is relatively silent concerning the fears of the West over the advances of the East, but we get a rather interesting indication of the Western state of mind in the form of a United States commemorative, issued between 1951 and 1954.

This coin, the Washington-Carver half-dollar, purported to render homage to two great leaders of Black America, Booker T. Washington and George Washington Carver. In common with other American commemorative coins, the Washington-Carver piece was to be sold at a profit, the difference between its value and its price of purchase going to a worthy cause. But now the psychology of the Cold War entered the picture. Money obtained from the sale of this commemorative was to be used, in the words of the United States government, "to oppose the spread of communism among Negroes in the interest of national defense." The design elements bore out this idea, particularly the reverse, with its appeal to "Americanism," one of the favorite catchwords of Joseph McCarthy and his supporters during these years.

The concern of the United States government about Communism spreading among Black Americans was groundless, although it does indicate that the government realized that minorities were not receiving their fair share under free enterprise, and might therefore be tempted by an economic system which promised them more.

As the Cold War continued, a new, awakening nationalism on the part of peoples in Asia, Africa, and Latin America entered the picture. The West tended to ascribe the movements for national liberation to Communist infiltration, and it was true that some of the leaders of the independence movements were aided and even trained by the Communist bloc. On the other hand, even if Communist influence existed, to whom could the insurgents of, say, French Algeria turn for support? They certainly couldn't expect it from France, and France, as a central element of the anti-Communist alliance, could exert enough pressure on her allies so that they, too, would keep hands off. That left the Communists as a possible source of outside help. Once this assistance was received and independence achieved, the nation might enter the Communist orbit, as did Vietnam and Cuba. But most likely, it would follow a middle path, playing off one side against the other. This policy has a perfectly legitimate background. Americans

found it of use during the Revolutionary War and well beyond, when they played Englishmen and Frenchmen off against each other.

By the middle 1950s, the old colonial arrangements, political in Africa and southeast Asia, economic in Latin America, were beginning to crumble. The Vietnamese drove out the French in 1954. In 1957, Ghana became the first British African colony to gain its freedom, and it was soon joined by other British colonies, as well as those of the French and Belgians. In 1959, Cuba, which had theoretically been free since 1902, but which in fact had had strong economic and political ties to the United States, came under the dictatorship of Fidel Castro, who would free the island from American influence (although he brought it under Soviet influence in the process—Castro, like the Algerians, had no one else to turn to). By the opening of the 1960s, nationalism was moving forward on all fronts. By 1975, it might be fairly said that the old colonial system, a legacy of the nineteenth century, had come to an end.

The heads of these new nations, who were often the leaders of the independence movements, faced onerous problems. They had to create viable economic states. Oftentimes, they had to build an industrial base from the ground up, for the former colonial powers had usually neglected to do so. They had to educate their people in the rights and duties of citizenship. They had to build schools and hospitals, establish monetary and banking systems—in short, they had to give new nations all of the trappings of the older, established countries, and they had very little time in which to do so.

But above all else, the new leaders had to build a sense of national identity among their peoples. In the case of the new Africa, many nations were composed of a con-

227

glomeration of tribal units, who had little in common except a dislike of colonialism. How could these peoples be made to think of themselves as members of a single nation, united behind a single leader, working together to build a modern state? One answer was to constantly repeat these ideals—in the press, on radio, in great mass-meetings. And money could be employed to communicate ideas, too. The money adopted by the new nations would be used to carry propaganda messages to the people.

There was a certain inevitability about this. Since a government has a monopoly on monetary production and distribution, it can obviously place anything it chooses on a coin or a bill, in the certainty that its people will see it. The people have no choice in the matter; they must use what governments provide for daily transactions. Furthermore, since coins and paper money have value, they tend to be eagerly sought and are widely used in trade. They will pass from hand to hand from one end of a country to the other. A maximum number of people will see that money, observe its messages and designs. This is of great importance in a newly emerging nation, which will often lack more orthodox means of communication. In short, the modern national states of Africa, Asia, and Latin America rediscovered the advantages of using money to influence public opinion and to bolster support for a regime and its policies.

Virtually every emerging nation has used money for these purposes over the past twenty years. Some of them, such as India and Mexico, use their coins and bank notes to honor deceased national heroes, as in the cases of an Indian *rupee* of 1969 and a Mexican hundred-peso note of 1974. Many more new nations portray their current leaders, as in the case of Guinea and Malawi, two former African colonies of the French and British, respectively.

Still other nations concentrate on the achievements of the independent regimes and their hopes and proposals for the future. An Egyptian *piastre* of 1968 commemorates the electrification program of the Nasser government, while a hundred-franc coin from Mali urges its citizens to produce more food.

In brief, the coinage of new nations is being employed to give their peoples a sense of collective identity, to emphasize the fact that there has been a break with the colonial past. However, in one aspect of the money of the emerging nations, there does remain a notable area of continuity. This is in the choice of monetary names and standards used by the new states. They are largely the direct descendants of the old colonial systems.

This continuation has been deliberate. If people are accustomed to a coin of a certain size with a certain name, a new state is likely to strike coins very much like it, if not identical, in the hopes that people will accept the new national issues as readily as they did the old colonial ones. Thus, while a Zambian shilling may have a design differing from that of its colonial predecessor, Rhodesia and Nyasaland, its weight and metallic content remain the same, and it is still called a shilling. Someone may eventually rename the Zambian shilling (it becomes ten *ngwee* in 1968), but the size and metallic content will still remain tied to the original colonial standard. With variations, this sort of monetary development has been the rule among the emerging nations of the world. In this, we see one final indication of the relationship between history and money. There are very few, perhaps no, hard-and-fast breaks between one historical event and another. For time is a river that flows in a continuous stream, changing as it does so, but abandoning its antecedents only with great reluctance. And the same can be said of money.

Epilogue: Money's Future

We have traced the story of man and his money through twenty-five centuries, from the days of the ancient Greeks to modern times. During those years, money changed and evolved: it was round; it was shaped like a spade; it was made of gold or silver; it was not made of metal at all, but paper; it employed propaganda in slogans and designs; it merely said where it was from and what it was worth. All of this belongs in the past and present. What might money's future hold in store for us?

We are not likely to see the disappearance of coinage, at least coinage of low denomination. Despite a global economy which relies increasingly on credit and paper money, coinage is too useful to be abandoned. Coins are more durable than any other form of money yet devised—as witnessed by the large number of ancient coins still in existence. Moreover, governments have found coinage useful as a propaganda vehicle in the past; they are likely to continue to find it so in the years to come. Finally, states and their peoples are likely to retain some form of coinage for minor transactions, since that is the easiest way of handling small sums of money. A personal check for ten cents causes far more paperwork for a bank than the check is worth. A ten-cent coin makes much more sense for all parties concerned.

So coinage will probably be with us for many years to come. All the same, its intent and form may very well change. It is likely to find increasing employment for presenting governmental points of view. As precious metals grow more scarce, they will tend to disappear from circulating coinage altogether. The coins themselves may become smaller. And they may not be made from metal at all.

The first point is almost inevitable. Developing and advanced nations alike have rediscovered the benefits to be reaped from using coinage to bring messages to the people. In an age of increasing nationalism, they are not likely to abandon the practice. They will use minor coinage for this purpose; in addition, they may strike high-denomination coins in gold or silver for sale to collectors, coins which are also intended to celebrate national heroes and anniversaries, to exhort the people, etc. Indeed, many governments have been engaged in this practice over the past twenty years. It is to be understood that such precious-metal coinage is not intended for circulation, but for sale, at a profit, usually to foreign collectors. And for this reason, such coinage will probably gradually disappear over the next few decades. The people for whom (ostensibly) it is struck do not use it for trade and therefore do not see the messages it carries. And the foreigners who collect it are unlikely to be concerned with its propaganda content. Added to this is the fact that so many countries have issued such coinage over the past two decades that it is becoming something of a glut on the numismatic market. So the showy gold and silver coins of high denomination, muted reminders of the days when precious metals formed the backbone of monetary commerce, will go out of favor and out of existence.

As far as "real" coins of gold or silver are concerned, gold has disappeared already, and silver is near extinction too. Neither is likely to be resurrected, for other, more easily employed forms of money now hold the field. From the vantage point of the average citizen, a bank note is far less cumbersome to use than a heavy gold or silver coin. From the viewpoint of his government, paper money has added advantages—it is far easier, quicker, and cheaper to produce than precious-metal coinage.

Coins of the future will be of low denomination. The metals used for their production will be copper, bronze, copper-nickel,

Opposite. Coins and coin dies.

brass, and aluminum. They will carry governmental slogans and propaganda designs somewhat more consistently than at present. And it is quite possible that, while denominations will remain what they are today, the size of the coins may change. They may become smaller.

We have already seen one such example in the case of the Italian ten-lire piece, which shifted from gold to silver to aluminum, and then to a smaller aluminum format. Other countries may be moving in the same direction. A Canadian proposal to reduce the size of the 1978 cent was tabled, due to private and public outrage at the idea, but it is likely to surface again in the future. And Canada has been making smaller one-dollar coins since 1968. Coinage in a reduced size is a very likely development in years to come, and it highlights a serious problem for the future of coinage itself. Even nonprecious metals are rising in value, approaching a point where, if present dimensions are retained, a coin could be intrinsically worth more than its face value. In the United States, the bronze cent seemed headed for extinction in the mid-1970s, as the price of copper skyrocketed. It was proposed that the cent's design and size be retained, but that it be struck from aluminum, a cheaper metal. The vending-machine industry protested, and the plan was dropped, but it does remain an option for the future.

There is also a possibility that metal will be removed from coinage altogether, replaced by with a manmade, cheaper substitute. The problems are onerous. How do you devise something hard enough to stand the rigors of circulation but soft enough to be struck from coin dies? In fact, will people accept such a metallic substitute even if one can be perfected? Historic precedent indicates that they will. In the closing months of World War II, the Japanese government experi-

mented with a nonmetallic coinage for Manchukuo and it apparently succeeded in gaining public acceptance for the new coins. At about the same time, the United States government was testing a nonmetallic one-cent piece, for copper was a critical war material. The Allied victory of 1945 brought an end to these pioneering attempts to make coinage from something other than metal. But as the value of metal—any metal—rises, we are likely to see similar, perhaps permanent moves in this direction. Such an innovation would be somewhat easier now than it was in the 1940s, for people are using paper money more, and coinage less, than they did at that time. Moreover, the technology of the late twentieth century has come up with a number of durable synthetic materials that would be quite workable for coinage.

The future will bring changes in paper money as well as in coinage. Paper currency has lagged somewhat behind coinage as a propaganda vehicle, but it is likely to make up for lost time very rapidly, especially as large coins, ideal tools for conveying governmental sentiments, have all but disappeared from use. As far as the appearance of paper money is concerned, the clean, crisp, multicolor formats adopted by Mexico, the Netherlands, and several other countries will probably grow in popularity, while the florid, somewhat old-fashioned scrollwork designs seen on the currency of the United States and several Latin American nations are likely to go out of favor. A prime argument for the retention of such outmoded designs—that they are especially difficult to counterfeit—no longer has validity, if indeed it ever did. With new sophisticated techniques of paper manufacture and multicolor printing, we have now reached a point where governments can produce modern, beautiful notes which cannot be convincingly counterfeited.

One final possibility in paper money's future is this: as the value of the dollar and several other currencies declines, low-denomination paper money may be replaced by coinage. At first glance, this seems illogical, running counter to earlier monetary experience, but it becomes more sensible when we consider one fact. A government will produce money in the easiest way available to it (always providing, of course, that its citizens can be persuaded to accept its product). Thus, there is now discussion in the United States about replacing the one-dollar note, which is fairly difficult to produce (and which does not stand up to circulation for more than a few months anyway) with a new, small, one-dollar *coin*, probably of copper-nickel, possibly multisided so that the public will not confuse it with other American coins of similar size. Other countries are moving in this direction, too. Mexico's five-peso paper note has been replaced by a new, multisided coin, and the ten-peso bill will probably suffer the same fate in the near future.

The future is likely to hold great changes in store for both coinage and currency. But these may be overshadowed by developments in other media of exchange, such as personal checks and credit cards. And the future may witness the arrival of totally new forms of money altogether. Let us speculate a bit.

In the case of personal checks, it is probable that no new, major developments will occur. Personal checks are a boon to commerce and consumer alike, but they are perilously easy to falsify or counterfeit. In terms of its sophistication, the personal check is about where paper money was in the year 1725. Checks are printed, not engraved, which makes them fairly easy to duplicate. The paper used in printing checks is also relatively simple to fabricate. And the values and the signatures—these, too, invite forgery. In brief, the personal check is a dangerous medium of exchange, and while some sort of personal money is likely to be with us for the forseeable future, it will probably adopt a different form from that of a check.

One possibility is the credit card. Credit cards have seen increasing popularity over the last fifteen years, with good reason. They are easy to use. They are durable. They are elastic—that is, one can use the same piece of money to pay for items costing different amounts, in transactions widely separated by time and space. Finally, credit cards are fairly difficult to forge, and, were some of the techniques learned in printing paper money applied to producing credit cards, the latter could be rendered virtually impossible to duplicate. Indeed, there have been movements in this direction since the very inception of this monetary form, and these improvements will most certainly continue.

Checks and credit cards are personal money of a private nature—that is, they are the products of business firms or banks, for utilization by private citizens. But what would happen if a government were to enter this field of money? A completely new form of money would emerge, one which might well be the dominant medium of exchange in the future.

At the present time, each American citizen receives a Social Security number when he or she begins work. The citizen has sole use of this number, which is retained until death. The number appears on governmental documents relating to that person, and it is the basis for pension payments upon retirement.

Now, let us suppose that a similar practice were extended to money. Upon birth, each person would receive an individual credit number and accompanying card, as an account with the corresponding number came into existence. As the individual secured employment, his wages would automatically be

credited to his account. As he made purchases, funds would automatically be withdrawn. In the case of a house, automobile, or other items costing a large amount of money, a set sum could be automatically subtracted from his personal account on a regular basis, until the debt was paid.

A few years ago, such a system would have been unthinkable, due to the incredible amounts of paperwork it would have necessitated. But with the advent of sophisticated computer technology, most of these objections no longer have force. In terms of current technological expertise, the system could be installed tomorrow.

Its advantages would lie in the fact that money could now be handled automatically, with a minimum of risk. Business would become easier for merchant and consumer alike. Such a system could cause a revolution in finance akin to that occasioned by the invention of the bill of exchange and later forms of paper money. And the results would probably be similar. Devise an easier way to transport and store wealth, and you are likely to stimulate commerce.

Such a monetary arrangement would have to have a government at its cen-

ter, for reasons similar to those which got polities into the business of minting coins. The agency assigning a credit number, issuing a credit card—or striking a coin—must be *neutral*. People must see it as having no particular axe to grind, as employing the system for the benefit of all, not merely the advantage of some. And for better or worse, governments tend to have such a reputation among their citizens; large private businesses do not.

So a government-issued, personal credit card may come to represent a common form of money in the future, and we may even move away from coins and currency entirely, employing the card for all transactions. If we do so, however, we will have changed the form of money, but not its intent. Coinage was invented to facilitate commerce, to make buying and selling easier. Paper money was eventually devised for the same purpose. Today, it bids fair to supersede most or all coinage. Tomorrow, a governmental credit system may replace *it*. But if it does so, indeed, whatever form money takes in the future, it will still be geared to the same objective as it was twenty-five centuries ago. And the relationship between man and his money will continue to be as close, as indissoluble, as ever.

Bibliography

Album, Stephen. **Marsden's Numismata Orientalia Illustrata.**
New York: Attic Books, Ltd., 1977.
(A guide to Islamic and Oriental coins with values -RGD)

Angus, Ian. **Paper Money.** New York: St. Martin's Press, 1974.

Bachtell, Lee M. **World Dollars, 1477–1877: Pictorial Guide.**
Jesup, Georgia: Sentinel Press, 1974.

Becker, Thomas W. **The Coin Makers.** Garden City, New York:
Doubleday & Company, Inc., 1969.

Bellinger, Alfred R., and Grierson, Philip, eds.
**Catalogue of the Byzantine Coins in the Dumbarton Oaks
Collection and in the Whittemore Collection.** 3 vols.
Washington, D.C.: Dumbarton Oaks Center
for Byzantine Studies, 1966–.

Carson, R. A. G. **Coins, Ancient, Mediaeval & Modern.**
London: Hutchinson, 1962.

Catalogue of Greek Coins in the British Museum. 29 vols.
Reprinted Bologna, Italy: Arnaldo Forni, Editore, 1963–.

Charlton, J. E. **Standard Catalogue of Canadian Coins,
Tokens & Paper Money.** 26th ed. Toronto, Ontario:
Charlton International Publishing Inc., 1978.

Clain-Stefanelli, Elvira. **Select Numismatic Bibliography.**
New York: Stack's, 1965.

Coole, Arthur Braddan. **Coins in China's History.**
4th ed. Mission, Kansas: Inter-Collegiate Press, Inc., 1965.

Craig, William D. **Coins of the World, 1750–1850.**
Ed. Holland Wallace. 3d ed.
Racine, Wisconsin: Western Publishing Co., Inc., 1976

Doty, Richard G. **Coins of the World.**
New York: The Ridge Press/Bantam Books, 1976.

——. **Paper Money of the World.**
New York: The Ridge Press/Bantam Books, 1977.

Furber, E. A., ed. **The Coinages of Latin America
and the Caribbean.** Lawrence, Massachusetts:
Quarterman Publications, Inc., 1974.

Grierson, Philip. **Monnaies du Moyen Age.**
Fribourg, Switzerland: Office du Livre, 1976. (An English
translation is expected soon,
and the book is very good -RGD)

——. **Numismatics.** London:
Oxford University Press, 1975.

Hessler, Gene. **The Comprehensive Catalog of U.S.
Paper Money.** Rev. ed. Chicago: Henry Regnery Company, 1977.

Hobson, Burton, and Obojski, Robert.
Illustrated Encyclopedia of World Coins. Garden City,
New York: Doubleday & Company, Inc., 1970.

Jacobs, N., and Vermeule, C. C. **Japanese Coinage.**
New York: Numismatic Review, 1972.

Jenkins, G. K. **Ancient Greek Coins.**
New York: G. P. Putnam's Sons, 1972.

Klawans, Zander H. **Reading and Dating Roman Imperial Coins.**
4th ed. Racine, Wisconsin:
Western Publishing Co., Inc., 1977.

Kraay, C. M. **Archaic and Classical Greek Coins.**
London: Berkely, 1976.

Krause, Chester L., and Mishler, Clifford.
Standard Catalog of World Coins. 4th ed. Iola, Wisconsin:
Krause Publications, 1977.

Mattingly, Harold. **Roman Coins from the Earliest
Times to the Fall of the Western Empire.** 2d ed.
London: Methuen & Co., Ltd., 1960.

Mattingly, Harold, Sydenham, M. A., and others.
The Roman Imperial Coinage. 9 vols.
London: Spink & son, Ltd., 1923–.

Newman, Eric P. **The Early Paper Money of America.**
Bicentennial edition. Racine, Wisconsin:
Western Publishing Co., Inc., 1976.

Newman, Eric P., and Doty, Richard G.
Studies on Money in Early America. New York:
The American Numismatic Society, 1976.

Pick, Albert. **Standard Catalog of World Paper Money.**
2d ed. Iola, Wisconsin: Krause Publications, 1977.

Plant, Richard J. **Arabic Coins and How to Read Them.**
London: B. A. Seaby, Ltd., 1973.

Porteous, John. **Coins in History.**
New York: G. P. Putnam's Sons, 1969.

Remick, Jerome, and others.
**The Guide Book and Catalogue of British Commonwealth
Coins, 1649–1971.** 3d ed. Winnipeg, Manitoba:
Regency Coin and Stamp Co., Ltd., 1971.

Schjöth, Fredrik. **Chinese Currency.**
Rev. and ed. Virgil Hancock.
Iola, Wisconsin: Krause Publications, 1965.

Seaby, H. A. **Greek Coins and Their Values.**
2d ed., rev. London: Seaby, 1975.

Sear, David R. **Byzantine Coins & Their Values.**
London: Seaby, 1974.

——. **Roman Coins & Their Values.**
2d ed., rev. London: Seaby, 1974.

Sutherland, C. H. V. **English Coinage, 600–1900.**
London: B. T. Batsford Ltd., 1973.

——. **Roman Coins.**
New York: G. P. Putnam's Sons, 1974.

(Taxay, Don). **The Comprehensive Catalogue and
Encyclopedia of United States Coins.** 2d ed., rev. and ed.
Joseph H. Rose and Howard Hazelcorn.
New York: Scott Publishing Co., 1976.

Taxay, Don. **The U.S. Mint and Coinage.**
New York: Arco Publishing Co., Inc., 1966.

Whitting, P. D. **Byzantine Coins**
New York: G. P. Putnam's Sons, 1973.

Wroth, Warwick. **Imperial Byzantine Coins
in the British Museum.** 2 vols in one.
Chicago: Argonaut, Inc., 1966.

——. **Western & Provincial Byzantine Coins of the
Vandals, Ostrogoths and Lombards.**
Chicago: Argonaut, Inc., 1966.

Yeoman, R. S. **A Guide Book of United States Coins.**
31st ed. Racine, Wisconsin:
Western Publishing Company, Inc., 1977.

Index

A

Actium (31 B.C.), 81
Aes grave (Roman coin), 74
Africa, 200, 227–28
Agrigentum Greek coinage, 24
Alamanni, 91
Alaska, 200
Albania, 225
Alexander the Great, 33–37, 42
Alexander Severus (Emperor of Rome), 90, 91
Algeria, 200
Aluminum coinage, 205, 230–32
American Revolution (1775–83), 185, 188–90
Anastasius (Byzantine Emperor), 108, 113
Ancestors on coinage, Roman, 73, 75, 82, 88
Animals on coins, 13
  Greek, 24
  Hellenistic, 41
  Lydian, 14
Anonymous Bronzes, 120–23
Antiochus I (King of Syria), 37
Antoninianus (Roman coin), 90–91
Antoninus Pius (Emperor of Rome), 88
Antony, Mark, 81, 82–83
Arcadius (Emperor of Rome), 100
Ardashir (Sassanian King), 49
Arsaces I (King of Parthia), 43–44
Artabanus III (King of Parthia), 44, 49
Ascendi (Montalcino coinage), 153
Asses (Roman coinage), 74, 75
Assignats, 191
Atäturk, Kemal, 214
Athenian coinage, 20–23
Augustale (Brindisi coin), 149
Augustus (Emperor of Rome), 83, 85
Aurelian (Emperor of Rome), 94
Aureus (Roman coin), 82, 87, 94–97
Australia, 178, 200
Austria-Hungary, 210
Austrian coinage, 138
Aztecs, 160

B

Bactria, 42, 43
Banking, 134, 160, 166, 170, 177
  paper money and, 186
Bank of England, 166
Banque de France, 186
Banque Générale, 166, 169
Barter, 57, 101
Basil II (Byzantine Emperor), 123
Belgium, 198, 200

Bill of exchange, 137, 166
Bimetallic currency, 14
Bohemian coinage, 134, 138
Bolivar, Simón, 197
Bolivia, 160, 197
Boulton, Matthew, 178
Boxer Rebellion (1900), 61
Bramante, Donato, 158
Brasil, 103, 219
Brass coinage, 230–32
  Chinese, 54–57
  Roman, 87, 98–99
Britannia, 88
Bronze coinage, 230–32
  Chinese, 53, 54–57
  Islamic, 128
  Japanese, 63, 66
  Korean, 69
  Roman, 73, 91
  Sassanian, 49
Bronze dies, 14
Brutus, 82
Bulgaria, 198
Bullion, 63, 178
Byzantine Empire, 100
  coinage of, 105–106, 112–25

C

Cabral, Pedro Alvares, 163
Caesar, Gaius Julius, 78–81, 82, 83
Caesaropapism, 116
California, 178
Caligula (Emperor of Rome), 85–87
Canada, 163, 188, 200
Capitalism, 169–70, 177, 178–85
Caracalla (Emperor of Rome), 90
Carranza, Venustiano, 206
Carthage, 74–75, 78, 126
Casting of coins, 14, 53, 63
  Roman, 74
Castro, Fidel, 227
Charlemagne (King of the Franks), 105, 110
Charles I (King of Spain), 153, 172
Charles II (King of England), 166
Charles VI (King of France), 145
Checks, 205, 233
Chiang Kai-shek, 226
Ch'ien (Chinese coin), 57
Chinese coinage, 13, 53–61, 137, 178, 225
Ch'ing dynasty, 60–61
Chi-Rho (cross motif), 98, 99
Chosroes (Sassanian Emperor), 128
Chogin (Japanese ingot), 63
Christian motifs on coinage
  in Middle Ages, 105, 113,

  116, 120
  of Rome, 97–101
Claudius (Emperor of Rome), 87
Claudius II (Emperor of Rome), 94
Clipping, 49, 58, 158
Cold War, 205, 225–27
Cologne, 145
Columbus, Christopher, 157, 158
Commemorative coins, 22, 226, 230
  Roman, 82
Commodus (Emperor of Rome), 88, 90
Communism, 170, 197–98
  spread of, 225–27
Constantine the Great
  (Emperor of Rome), 97–98
Constantinople, 100, 101
Constantius II (Emperor of Rome), 97–98, 100, 120
Consul, 81, 82
Copper coinage, 178, 205, 230–32
  Byzantine, 113, 115, 116, 120
  Chinese, 53, 54–57
  Islamic, 126–28
  Korean, 69
  Roman, 83, 87, 90–91
  Sassanian, 49
Copper-nickel coinage, 221
Counterfeiting, 158, 169, 185, 232
Cowrie shell coinage, 13, 57
Crassus, 78
Credit cards, 205, 233–34
Creoles, 194–97
Croat (Spanish coin), 138
Croesus (King of Lydia), 14
Cross on coinage, 29, 98, 101, 137, 173
  in Middle Ages, 106, 109–10, 113, 120
  Renaissance British, 141, 143
Croton Greek coinage, 27
Crusades, 134, 137
Cuba, 200, 227
Cup-shaped Byzantine coinage, 123, 125

D

da Vinci, Leonardo, 157
Daric (Persian coin), 43
Darius III (King of Persia), 33–34, 43
Dated coinage
  Byzantine, 113, 115
  Chinese, 60
  Parthian, 44
  Renaissance, 145
  thaler, 138
Decadrachms (Greek coin), 20, 22, 23

Denarius (penny), 110, 137
Denarius (Roman coin), 75–78, 83, 90–91
Depression, 205, 217–20
Díaz, Porfirio, 206
Didius Julianus (Emperor of Rome), 90
Didrachms (Roman coin), 74
Dies, 14, 133
  in Middle Ages, 112
  restraining collar for, 157–58
  of Sassanian silver drachm, 49
Dinars (Islamic coin), 128
Diocletian (Emperor of Rome), 94–97
Diodotus I (King of Bactria), 42
Dirhem (Islamic coin), 128
Dobla (Spanish coin), 145, 147
Dollar, 138, 197
Drachm (Sassanian coin), 49, 128
Ducat (Venetian gold coin), 138–40
Dupondius (Roman coin), 87

E
Economics of the Industrial Revolution, 178–86
Ecu d'or (French coin), 140, 145
Edward II (King of England), 138
Edward III (King of England), 141
Egypt, 33–34, 38–39, 41–42, 228
Electrum, 13, 14
Elizabeth I (Queen of England), 158
England, 110, 177–78
  American Revolution and, 188–90
  imperialism and, 200
  rise of nation-state, 133
  New World coinage of, 164–66, 170–72
  Renaissance coinage of, 138, 140
Engravers, 18–20, 24
Ethiopia, 217
Etruscans, 73

F
Fairs, medieval, 134
Fals (Islamic coin), 128
Fasces, 216
Faustulus, 75
Ferrara coinage, 153
Filing, 58
Fleurs-de-lis, 143, 145
Florence (Italy), 138
Florin (Italian coin), 138–40, 186
Foederati, 100
Follis (Roman-Byzantine coin), 94–97, 113, 120
  Islamic, 126
Forint (Hungarian currency), 225

Franc (French coin), 138, 187, 194
France, 110, 178, 194, 198
  coinage of, 138, 147
  imperialism and, 200
  Louis XIV coinage, 173
  New World coinage of, 163, 170–72
  rise of nation-state, 133
Franco, Francisco, 219
Frank, 91, 105, 113
French and Indian War (1754–63), 188
French Revolution (1789–99), 185, 190–91

G
Gallienus (Emperor of Rome), 91
Gama, Vasco da, 163
Gaul, 78, 91, 101
Gela Greek coinage, 24
Genovino (Genoa coin), 140
George II (King of England), 173
Germany and German coinage, 134, 138, 188, 194, 198
  Hitler's rise in, 217–20, 220–21
  imperialism and, 200
  inflation and, 210–14, 217
Ghana, 227
Gods and goddesses on coins
  Egyptian, 41–42
  Greek, 20, 21–22, 29, 42
  Macedonian, 41
  Roman, 74, 75, 82, 90, 91–94, 97, 99–100
Gold coinage, 137, 178, 205, 222, 230
  British, 110, 140, 141–43
  Byzantine, 115, 120, 123
  French Renaissance, 140
  Islamic, 126–28
  Italian, 138
  Japanese, 63–66
  Lydian, 13–14
  Macedonian, 33
  Mexican, 206
  New World exploration and, 158–61
  Persian, 43
  Roman, 82, 97, 100, 101
  Sassanian, 49
Gold standard, 205
Goths, 91
Granada (Spain), 157
Greece, 198
Greek coinage, 13
  art and technique of, 18–29
Greek Orthodox Church, 112–13, 116
Groat (English coin), 138, 149
Groschen (German coin), 138
Grosso (Venetian coin), 137, 186

Gros tournois (French coin), 137–38
Guam, 200
Guatemala, 197
Guinea, 228

H
Hadrian (Emperor of Rome), 88
Halos, 116
Hannibal, 75
Harding, Warren G., 214
Hawaii, 200
Hegira, 125
Hellenistic coinage, 33–49
  Parthian, 43–44
  Persian, 42–43
  Sassasian, 44–49
Henry II (King of England), 145–47
Henry III (King of England), 140, 147
Henry VII (King of England), 149
Heraclius (Byzantine Emperor), 116
Hexagram (Byzantine coin), 120
Hitler, Adolf, 214, 217–20
Holed coinage, 53–54
Honorius (Emperor of Rome), 100
Huerta, Victoriano, 206
Humanism, 133
Hundred Years War (1337–1453), 143, 149
Hungary, 222–25

I
Ichibu gin (Japanese coin), 63–66
Iconoclasts, 120
Imperialism, 177, 198–201
Imperium, 81
Incas, 160
India, 163, 200, 228
Indochina, 200
Industrial Revolution coinage, 177–201
  economics and, 178–86
  politics and, 186–201
  technology and, 177–78
Inflation, 8, 123, 169
  between the World Wars, 210–18
  Hungarian, 222–25
  Roman, 78, 90–91
Ingots, 57
Inscriptions on coinage
  Byzantine, 115, 120
  Chinese, 53–54, 58–61
  of French Revolution, 191
  Hellenistic, 37
  Islamic, 126–28
  Japanese, 63
  Middle Age Western Empire, 108, 109

Parthian, 44
Renaissance, 143, 153
Roman, 74, 82–101
International coinage standards,
    186–87
Ionian Greek coinage, 13
I pi ch'ien (Chinese ant-nose money), 58
Iron dies, 14
Islamic coinage, 105–106, 125–28
Italy and Italian coinage, 188,
    198, 222
  gold, 138
  imperialism and, 200
  Mussolini and, 216–17
  profile and portraiture on, 153

J

Japan and Japanese coinage, 61–69,
    178, 226
  imperialism and, 201
  World War II and, 220, 221
Jerusalem, 126, 134
Joachimsthaler (Austrian coin), 138
John (King of England), 147
Julian (Emperor of Rome), 98–99
Justin II (Byzantine Emperor), 116
Justinian I (Byzantine Emperor),
    113, 115
Justinian II (Byzantine Emperor),
    120

K

Kao Tsu (Emperor of China), 58–60
Kavad I (Sassanian King), 49
Kings and rulers on coinage
  British, 173
  Byzantine, 113, 115
  Hellenistic, 37–42
  Louis XIV, 173
  Middle Age Western Empire, 108,
    109
  in pennies, 110
  Persian, Parthian, Sassanian,
    42–49
  Renaissance, 143, 145–47
  Roman, 81–101
Knife coinage, Chinese, 57–58
Kobans (Japanese coins), 63
Koran, 125, 128
Korea and Korean coinage, 69, 201
Korun (Czech coin), 225

L

Latin Monetary Union, 186–87, 209
Law, John, 166, 169
Lek (Albanian coin), 225
Lenin, V. I., 209

Leo II (Byzantine Emperor), 120
Lepidus, 81
Liberalism, 188, 191, 194, 197
Lira (Venetian coin), 153
Livia (Empress of Rome), 85
Lombards, 116
Louis IX (King of France), 137
Louis XIV (King of France), 163, 173
Louis XVI (King of France), 190–91
Louis Philippe (King of the French),
    198, 200
Lydian coinage, 13–14
  minting process of, 14
Lysimachus of Thrace, 42

M

Macedonian Empire, 21, 29, 33–37
  early coinage of, 33
Madero, Francisco, 206
Magnentius (Emperor of Rome), 98
Malawi, 228
Mali, 228
Mame gin (Japanese coin), 63–66
Manchuria, 201, 220
Manoel I (King of Portugal), 163
Manufacturing, 177
Mao Tse-tung, 225
Marcus Aurelius (Emperor of Rome),
    88–90, 105
Marius, 78
Maronea Greek coinage, 27
Martel, Charles, 126
Massachusetts colony coinage, 164–67
Maximian (Emperor of Rome), 94, 97
Meditations (Marcus Aurelius), 105
Meiji (Emperor of Japan), 69, 201
Mercenaries, 172
Merchant class, 134
Merovingian Franks, 110
Mestizos, 194–97
Metapuntum Greek coinage, 24–27
Mexican Revolution (1910–20), 205,
    206–209
Mexico, 160, 194, 200, 228
Mexico City mint (1536), 161
Middle Ages coinage, 105–28
  Byzantine Empire, 105–106, 112–25
  Islamic, 105–106, 125–28
  late, 133–53
  Western Empire, 105–112
Milan coinage, 145, 153
Mining, 178
Minting of coins, 14
  by machine, 157–58
  in Middle Ages, 112
  in New World, 161–66
  steam powered, 178

Mithridates I (King of Parthia),
    43–44
Mithridates III (King of Parthia), 42
Modern coinage, 205–28
Mohammed, 106, 125
Monasteries, 106
Moneyers, 75, 83
Mongol coinage, 60
Multicolor paper money, 186, 232
Musa (King of Parthia), 44
Mussolini, Benito, 216–17

N

Nami sen (Japanese coin), 66
Napoleon Bonaparte (Emperor of the
    French), 187, 191–94
Napoleon III (Emperor of the French),
    187, 200
National liberation wars, 227
Nationalism, 143–45, 149, 177, 227
  in Industrial Revolution, 177,
    186–201
Nationalization of property, 206
Nation-states, 133, 143–45
Nero (Emperor of Rome), 87
Nerva (Emperor of Rome), 88
Netherlands, 169–70, 172
New World coinage, 161–66
Nicephurus II (Byzantine Emperor),
    123
Nickel coinage, 205, 230–32
Nimbate figures, 116
Noble (English coin), 141–43
North Africa, 106
Notgeld, 209
Nummi (Byzantine coin), 113

O

Obans (Japanese coin), 63
Obverse coinage, 14
Octavian, 81, 82–83
Odovacar (King of Italy), 101
Official coinage, 8
Origin of coinage, 13–14
Ostrogoths, 108, 109
Ottoman Empire, 123, 198

P

Pangaeum mines, 33
Pan liang (Chinese coin), 58
Paper money, 60, 137, 166–69, 222,
    232–33
  of American Revolution, 188–90
  of French Revolution, 191
  in the Industrial Revolution,
    184–86
  Mexican, 206

in modern times, 205
notgeld, 209–10
in World War II, 221
Parliamentary state growth, 172–73
Parthia, 42–43
Parthian War (161–66 A.D.), 88–90
Patricians, 73–74, 78
Pedro I (King of Spain), 145, 147
Pelopennesian War (431–404 B.C.), 22–23
Pengo (Hungarian currency), 222–25
Penny, 110–12
   in Renaissance, 133, 134, 140
   of steam-powered press, 178
Pergamum, 34, 37
Persian Empire, 22, 33–34, 39, 116
   coinage of, 42–43
Peru, 160, 194
Peso (Mexican coin), 206
Petit royal assis (French coin), 140
Philetaerus (King of Pergamum), 37
Philip I (Emperor of Rome), 94
Philip II (King of Macedonia), 33
Philippines, 200, 221
"Pieces of Eight," 161–63, 197
Planchet, 14, 22, 120, 157–58
   of Sassanian silver drachm, 49
Plants on Greek coins, 24–27
Plating of coins, 23, 90–91
Plebians, 73–74, 78
Poland and Polish coinage, 134, 138, 198
Polis, 18, 23, 24
Politics of Industrial Revolution, 186–201
Pompey, 78, 82
Pontifex Maximus, 82, 83
Portugal, 163, 170–72, 219
Portraiture on coinage, 18, 20, 219
   Chinese lack of, 53
   English, 138, 173
   Greek, 20, 24, 27–29
   of Hellenistic period, 34–49
   Islamic lack of, 128
   Italian, 217
   Middle Ages, 112, 115, 120, 123
   Ostrogoth, 109
   Renaissance, 145–53
   Roman, 75, 81–91, 94–97, 101
Postumus (Gallic Emperor), 91
Probus (Emperor of Rome), 94
Propaganda, coinage and, 228, 230
   Roman, 75, 85, 100–101
Ptolemy (Kings of Egypt), 37, 38–39
   coinage of, 41–42

Pu (Chinese weight coinage), 57
Puerto Rico, 200
Punic Wars, 74–75, 78

R
Railroads, 177
Reales (Spanish coins), 161, 197
Reconquista, La, 134
Reduction in coin size, 232
Reichsbank, 186
Renaissance coinage, 133–53
Republicanism, 187
Restraining die collar, 158
Reverse coinage, 14
Revolutions of 1848, 198
Rhodes Greek coinage, 27
Richard I (King of England), 147
Riel (German coin), 145
Rizal, José, 221
Rolling press, 157–58
Roman Empire coinage, 29, 73–101
Romania, 198
Romanus IV (Byzantine Emperor), 123
Russia and Russian coinage, 134, 194, 200, 221
   spread of Communism and, 225–27
Russian Revolution (1917–23), 205, 209–10

S
Salamis (480 B.C.), 22
Salazar, Antonio, 219
Sassanian Empire, 43–49, 91, 116, 126
Saxons, 113
Scandinavian coinage, 134
Sceattas (Frankish coin), 110
Screw press, 158
Scrip, 218
Scythians, 44
Seljuk Turks, 123
Senate of Rome, 78, 83
Septimus Severus (Emperor of Rome), 90
Serbia, 198
Serfdom, 97
Sestertius (Roman coin), 87, 88
Sextus Pompeius Fostlus, 75
Sextus Pompey, 82
Shih Huang-ti (Emperor of China), 58
Shilling (English coin), 138, 158, 222
Sicily, 74
Siglos (Persian coin), 43
Siliqua (Roman coin), 100
Silver and silver coinage, 134, 178, 205, 222, 230

Byzantine, 113, 120
Frankish, 110
French, 137–38
Greek, 23
groat, 138
Islamic, 126–28
Japanese, 63–66
Korean, 69
Lydian 13–14
New World exploration and, 158–61
Persian, 43
reales, 161–63
Roman, 74, 75, 78, 90–91, 94, 97, 100
Sassanian, 49
shilling, 138
thaler, 138
Venetian, 137
Social War of Rome, 78, 81–82
Socialism, 170, 197–98
Solidus (Roman coin), 97, 99–100, 101
   Byzantine, 108, 110, 113, 120, 123
   Islamic, 126
Sol Invictus, 90, 94, 97
Sou (French coin), 191
South America, 160, 194–97
   Mexican Revolution, 206–209
South Africa, 178
Sovereign (British coin), 147
Spade coinage, Chinese, 57–58
Spain and Spanish coinage, 74–75, 106, 108, 126, 133, 194, 219
   New World exploration and, 158–61, 169–72
   Renaissance, 138, 145
   South American independence and, 191–94
   wars against Islam in, 134, 157
Spanish-American War (1890), 200
Spanish Succession War (1701–13), 172
Square coinage, 42
Standardization of coinage
   Latin Monetary Union, 186–87, 209
   Macedonian, 37, 39–41
Staters
   Lydian, 14
   Macedonian, 33, 41
Steam engine, 177
Steamships, 177
Stockholms Banco, 166
Striking of coins, 14, 112, 157
Sulla, 78, 82
Swastika on coins, 219
Sycee (Chinese coin), 57
Syracusan decadrachm, 23

Syria, 34, 37, 42, 126

T

Tael (Chinese measurement), 57
Tai (Emperor of Korea), 69
Tai Ping rebellion (1850–64), 60–61
T'ang dynasty, 137
Tarenton Greek coinage, 24
Technology of the Industrial
    Revolution, 177–78
Telegraph, 172
Tenochtitlán, 13
Testoon (English coin), 138
Testone (Italian coin), 153
Tetarteron (Byzantine coin), 123
Tetradrachm
    Athenian, 20, 22, 23
    Egyptian, 42
    Macedonian, 34–37, 41
    Parthian, 44
Tetrarchy, 97
Thaler (Austrian coin), 138
Theodahad (Ostrogoth king), 109
Theoderic (Ostrogoth king), 108
Theodosius (Emperor of Rome),
    100–101
Tiberius (Emperor of Rome), 83–85

Tigranes (King of Armenia), 42
Tokens, 178
Tokugawa shogunate, 63
Tours (732), 126
Trajan (Emperor of Rome), 88
Trajan Decius (Roman Emperor), 94
Treasury Department, 186
Tremissis (Byzantine coin), 108,
    109, 110
Tribune, 81
Triumvirate, 78–81, 82
Turkey, 210, 214

U

United States, 178
    American Revolution, 185, 188–90
    depression, 217–18
    imperialism of, 200

V

Valentinian I (Emperor of Rome),
    99–100
Valentinian II (Emperor of Rome),
    100, 108
Vargas, Getulio, 219
Venice, 125, 137, 138–40
Vespasian (Emperor of Rome), 88

Vietnam, 227
Villa, Francisco, 206
Visigoths, 100, 108, 109
Vittorio Emanuelle III
    (King of Italy), 217

W

Wa do kaiho (Japanese coin), 63
Wang Mang (Emperor of China), 58
Washington-Carver half dollar,
    226–27
Watermarks, 185
Watt, James, 177, 178
Western Roman Empire, 100–101,
    105–12
World War I (1914–18), 205, 209
World War II (1939–45), 205, 220–22
Wu shu (Chinese coin), 58
Wu Ti (Chinese Emperor), 58

Y

Yezdigird (Sassanian Emperor), 128
Yuan (Chinese dollar), 61
Yugoslav hundred-dinara note, 222

Z

Zinc coinage, 220